R. R. Griffiths

SURVIVAL SKILLS FOR MANAGERS

by

Marlene Wilson

Published by
Volunteer Management Associates
279 South Cedar Brook Road
Boulder, Colorado 80302

Printed by
Johnson Publishing Company
Boulder, Colorado

Preface

This book is a statement about people and what happens to them in today's technocratic, hierarchical organizations.

Far too often, the workplace has become a battleground. The war that is being waged is subtle, undeclared, and deadly. It is, in fact, a war for survival for individuals across this country.

The writing of this book has been a three-year personal journey for me. It is the result of my own experience in an organization like the one I describe. It is my search for understanding regarding not only what occurred, but why . . . and further, what had I needed to know that no one had taught me.

I began the project convinced that it must be possible for creative managers (and employees) to survive and even flourish in today's workplace. Now *I am certain we can do both* if we deal with the survival skills described in this book. There are no simple solutions here, but there are tools presented to help you find your own answers.

This book is first of all a philosophical one, dealing with both the responsibility and incredible opportunity of being entrusted with leadership in today's organizations. The definition of a manager is "someone who works with and through others to accomplish organizational goals," so it follows that how we view people will determine everything about how we manage them. This in turn will be the critical determinant of whether those led will die, survive, or flourish as individuals in the workplace.

3

In my opinion, too much of the management literature today concentrates almost exclusively on the programmatic competencies required to manage well (i.e., planning, organizing, staffing, directing, controlling). These are essential if we are to acquire the strengths that come from competency. However, we must not stop there, for it is often within "well-managed, efficient" programs that people are hurting most. The skills that set exceptional managers apart are those that help them free up others to be their best. Then the organization becomes a good place to be, because people become as important as the product or the program . . . and they know it.

Although I began this book seeking answers to my own personal questions, I have been encouraged, prodded, and applauded in the effort by scores of other managers I have met in my extensive travels as a consultant and trainer. They have assured me that my questions are their questions—and all too often, my experience has been theirs as well. My interaction with them has been the impetus I needed to stay with the writing and research.

A word about the choice of content. I begin with a chapter on *creativity*. I am personally convinced that if we do not understand and nourish creativity in ourselves, others, and our organizations, none of us will be able to respond to the great changes we are facing as we move into the next century. Our personal, organizational, and national survival hinges on it!

But to encourage innovation and creativity without seriously examining the realities of resistance to change and new ideas is irresponsible. So we move on to an in-depth study of *creative problem-solving, power*, and *negotiations*. Why seek to have ideas if we do not know how to move others to accept and act on them? (One definition of power is the ability to cause or prevent change— so creativity without power is often futile.)

The final three chapters deal with *conflict, stress*, and *time problems*. These are almost inherent in the job of being a manager today. It is therefore essential that we learn to manage ourselves in respect to each of them. These are the skills that help us survive as emotionally and physically healthy individuals.

Each chapter can stand alone, so I would advise browsing through the book first to find the topic that speaks most clearly to your needs at this time. (I do believe they are all essential if you are to gain a full understanding of the problem, though. It is the difference between having only the appetizer or the whole feast.)

I also urge you to live your own personal experience throughout the book. I have been cautious about sharing too much of my experience so you might have room to illustrate the concepts with your own. My hope is that these pages will guide you on your own journey of understanding and discovery.

My growing conviction is that our nation and our communities can no longer afford good people and good programs that fail. Nor can we tolerate the continued loss of creative, dedicated people who are chewed up by the system. We *must* deal with the problem openly and intentionally. How can we nurture creative pragmatists who can and will make our organizations more humane? That is the question before us.

I would suggest that the options we have in dealing with the ever-changing world of today's manager can be likened to the options I have seen people choose in dealing with the tides of the ocean:

There are the *victims*—those who walk out into the waves; get knocked down; turn around and walk back into the waves; get knocked down; and on and on. They never seem to learn from their experiences (and they do not seem to have much fun either).

Then there are the *floaters* who decide being knocked down by the waves does not make much sense, so they get an inflatable air mattress which supports them above the waves. The turmoil of the waves goes on around them, but they float on unconcerned. The only problem is—they never go very far.

The *snorklers* are usually those who become curious about what is going on beneath the waves. So they obtain snorkling equipment and get totally absorbed in looking at the coral, rocks, and fish. They become detached observers.

And finally, there are the *surfers*. These are the venturesome ones who have very likely been victims, floaters, and snorklers at some point. But then they become convinced that there is more to dealing with the ocean than first meets the eye. So they take surfing lessons from someone who knows how. Some other traits I admire about surfers are that they are not afraid of risks, so they go out further than anyone else, and they are also apt to fall off their boards a lot while learning, but they keep getting back on. The skill the successful surfer eventually learns is to discern which waves to just let go by and do nothing about and which waves will take them all the way into shore, exactly where they want to go!

I would suggest that organizations today need a great many surfers. My hope is that this book may help equip you to become one.

Marlene Wilson
Boulder, Colorado
September 1980

Acknowledgements

There are so many people I am indebted to for openly sharing their experiences and ideas with me that it is difficult to know where to begin in acknowledgements. Perhaps the best I can do is to set apart those who have seen me through the entire process. My deepest gratitude goes to Dr. Ivan Scheier, Sue Vineyard, Gay Beatty, and Ruth Hattendorf for their invaluable assistance in critiquing each chapter. Miriam and Armando Gingras and Vicki Groninger shared their considerable expertise in editing and typing the manuscript and have earned my respect and thanks in the process.

And a very special word of gratitude to my dear family, Harvey, Rich, and Lisa, who not only encouraged me to take this journey, but also supported and sustained me every step along the way. It is to them that I lovingly dedicate this book.

Contents

Preface 3

Acknowledgements 7

Chapter I   *CREATIVITY: MAKING PEOPLE AND PROGRAMS COME ALIVE* 13

     This chapter examines the critical lack of attention most organizations have directed toward developing, encouraging, or rewarding creativity and innovation. The creative process is defined in light of new understandings about the brain itself. Blocks to creativity are explored and strategies suggested to help today's managers become more creative in spite of living and working in a highly technocratic society.

Chapter II   *PROBLEM SOLVING: GENERATING CREATIVE ALTERNATIVES FOR ACTION* 55

     The common managerial dilemma of solving symptoms of problems rather than problems themselves is dealt with in this chapter.

Trends that will greatly impact employees at all levels in the decade ahead are examined. Creative and practical "how to's" are suggested that make problem solving fun as well as more productive in a rapidly changing world.

Chapter III *POWER AND NEGOTIATIONS: HOW TO MAKE IDEAS HAPPEN* 95

To make good ideas happen in organizations requires influencing others. Power is not a four-letter word. It is essential to the vital process of change. Concepts in defining and understanding the various kinds and levels of power within organizations are explored in depth. The process of negotiating is examined as one involving strategizing to persuade others to say yes to needed change.

Chapter IV *CONFLICT MANAGEMENT: MANAGING IT INSTEAD OF IT MANAGING YOU* 131

The complex dynamics of conflict in interpersonal relationships and between groups in organizations are dealt with realistically. Unhealthy competition (as opposed to collaboration) destroys many groups and persons within them. This chapter presents practical tools to help today's managers understand and "do conflict" more effectively.

Chapter V *STRESS MANAGEMENT: TAMING THE QUIET KILLER* 189

The ravages of stress cost organizations billions of dollars annually and create great anguish in people. Heart disease, high blood pressure, ulcers, alcoholism, absenteeism, turnover, and suicide are just some of the possible outcomes. The fact is, in the fast-paced, ever-changing world we live in, stress can and does kill! This chapter examines the causes and results of stress and suggests concrete strategies to cope with it.

Chapter VI   *TIME MANAGEMENT: ORGANIZING FOR ACTION* 229

The vital ingredient needed to accomplish all of the other survival skills discussed in this book is time. Therefore, time traps and time wasters are critically examined. The necessity for planning daily activities in light of personal "life goals" is emphasized. Practical "how to's" are suggested to help determine what the best use of your time is—right now!

CHAPTER I

Creativity: Making People and Programs Come Alive

*Everyone looking for answers to problems is engaged in creative work
. . . whether the end result is a painting, a report, or a reorganization
plan. Creativity occurs when there is successful communication between
a person and his work.*

Desey Sofan-Girard

*The creative person may be at once more naive and knowledgeable . . .
more primitive and more cultured . . . more destructive and more
constructive . . . occasionally crazier and yet adamantly saner than the
average person.*

F. Barron

There is nothing that frees up our natural spontaneity and creativity more than someone giving us permission to be the best that we
can be in the work that we do. The reality is that very few organizations or agencies even attempt to grant that permission in today's
complex technocratic society. In fact, *it is almost never even an
issue with most of them.*

I would like to share this allegory with you:

Once upon a time there was a land where the whole community lived under one big glass dome. For generations the families had been born, lived, and died under the glass dome. And the story that passed down from generation to generation was if you ever DID step outside of the glass dome, you would surely die. So no one had ever dared to step outside the glass dome.

In fact, the community had decided that there was one crime so dastardly that the punishment for anyone who committed that crime would be to banish him outside the dome, which would be certain death for him.

No one–but no one–had ever committed that crime. Then one day, to the community's horror, a man DID commit such a crime.

The punishment was swift. The whole community escorted the man to the edge of the glass dome and pushed him out into the world beyond. Then they all pressed their noses to the wall of the glass dome to watch the man die.

At first the man laid on the ground, face down, shivering in his fear of how death would come to him. His muscles were all clenched up as he braced himself for what would certainly happen.

But nothing happened. After a bit, he rolled over and looked around, and seeing nothing threatening in sight, he ventured to sit up and look around. As the people in the glass dome watched intently, the man slowly stood up and looked all around him. And then, to their amazement, the man began to dance softly in the green, green grass–moving this way and that way, trying out his arms and legs that seemed to work perfectly well.

And then he began to jump up and down, and to shout joyously, and to beckon to the people under the glass dome to COME ON OUT AND DANCE WITH ME!! The people were filled with confusion and bewilderment to see this happy dancing man when they had expected to see him die a horrible death. The confusion and stress grew so great within them that they finally had to take action. They got buckets of black paint and large paintbrushes. They started at the bottom of the walls and painted the walls solid black, up just as high as they could reach and as high as necessary so they could no longer see the dancing man. Then they all breathed a sigh of relief and went back to just the way things had been before that day.

And what was the crime the man had committed . . . he was an INNOVATOR.

Wallace Ford

Each time I read this allegory, I find myself reacting in a very real and personal sense. It is so reminiscent of situations I have both experienced and witnessed in organizations. It vividly illustrates a phenomenon that I feel contributes heavily to turnover in organizations. I call this phenomenon *turnout* (not to be confused with a much more frequently discussed cause of turnover, *burnout*).

By *turnout* I mean the rejection by organizations of some of the very people they need the most—the innovators. This is done in several ways:

—by rejecting them at the time of employee selection;

—by underutilizing them during the course of employment, either by keeping them from decision-making positions or withholding promotions; or

—by terminating them as troublemakers.

Perhaps it is important to clarify terms, for the words "innovative" and "creative" have been used so frequently in recent years their meaning may have become lost.

To create: to evolve from one's own thought or imagination

To innovate: to bring in something new for the first time; to make changes in anything established; to introduce new things or methods

Another, more poignant definition of what we are discussing was used to describe Robert Kennedy by his brother Ted: "Most people see things as they are and ask why. He saw things as they might be and asked why not?"

As we carefully examine these definitions, it becomes more obvious why an innovator is often regarded as a thorn in the side of an organization. In the book *Management and Machiavelli*, Antony Jay discusses a few of these reasons.[1]

1. *Creative or innovative people often question the status quo.* They have an annoying way of questioning policies and decisions, even those that have nothing to do with them personally. This is because they tend to see the organization as a whole. (They think in a holistic, rather than fragmented fashion.)

    If you have ever tried this, you have no doubt found that in some organizations it is considered bad taste to raise questions such as "Why?" or "Why not?" The automatic response is all too frequently:

    —"But it isn't in your job description";

    —"We *always* (or never) do things that way here"; or

15

—"Don't be concerned about that—just do your job and we'll take care of ours."

2. *They are not likely to be obedient, at least not all of the time.* It is difficult, sometimes impossible, for these people to comply with orders or decisions which they believe are wrong.

3. *Their primary loyalties are fequently downward (on the organizational chart) rather than upward.* This, according to Jay, relates to a central and very strange dilemma in organizational life. "In a mid-management position there is only a certain amount of credit and goodwill a person can get; the more he gets from below, the less he gets from above."

   It is characteristic of creative leaders that their loyalties are:

   —first to their own ideas; and

   —second to the people whom they believe will help them carry out these ideas (frequently subordinates).

   Both of these take a higher priority than loyalty to supervisors. (Their naiveté is apparent here, for it is the people in positions of power who can say "yes" or "no" to their ideas.)

4. *Creative persons tend to be "bad courtiers" or organizational game players.* Jay describes the *courtier* as one who constantly tries to be identified with all the successful projects in the organization and none of the unsuccessful ones. They become ingenious at hedging their bets with statements like "other things being equal, this should work out well—so long as we can be sure that other things will stay equal." This allows them to maneuver their position into seeming to have been right whether the idea fails or succeeds.

   The creative person, on the other hand, will probably take a strong stand for or against the idea from the start and "if it succeeds he will be one of many to share the credit; if it fails, he will be the only one left with the blame."

5. *They do not assume their supervisors in the organization will always make the right decisions on questions referred to them.* They weigh the boss's track record and expertise. They occasionally have the annoying habit of making decisions on their own initiative or managing not to see memos giving them instructions that they do not agree with or believe in.

Jay summarizes:

For all of these reasons, there is a danger that the few potential

16

creative leaders may not rise like cream but be kept down like vinegar—which indeed they resemble more closely. It is only too possible that their immediate superiors will dislike and resent them, report adversely on them, and promote the docile, obedient, easy young executive instead.

(Robert Frost acknowledged this danger as well when he observed that "Some people want to homogenize society everywhere. I'm against the homogenizers in art, in politics, in every walk of life. I want the cream to rise." Oh, for more Frosts!)

Although Jay's book relates primarily to industry, I must ask: do we see anything resembling this happening in human services agencies as well? If we do, does it help to explain why we do not seem to be getting very far in dealing with human and community problems?

It would seem that if Jay is correct in his analysis, then the last thing the up-and-coming organization person would want is to develop a desire and ability to be innovative. It sounds like "the kiss of death."

Why then do I devote a chapter—in fact, the first chapter—in a book concerned with managerial survival to the topic of creativity? It is because I feel that it is central to the survival of individuals, organizations, and society. Let us examine this premise further.

In the book *The Organization Trap*, Samuel Culbert relates a touching story about an outgoing deputy director of a public agency.[2]

As he stepped forward to speak, tears began streaming down his face. To the audience's surprise, he did not try to cover up. There were no platitudes about his sorrow in leaving. Instead, he frankly admitted his tears were of pain and disappointment for allowing himself to be chewed up by the system. In the speech he stated he had compromised himself, accomplished little, gone along with outmoded methods, stopped taking stands on what needed to be changed, and generally had become a mediocre, ineffective leader. Needless to say, the cost to him as a person was tremendous—but he realized it too late.

There is a sense of urgency in dealing with this dilemma from a larger perspective as well. Bob Samples states that we live in a culture "that stands on the knife-edge between catastrophe and transformation." Rollo May elaborates further by stating, "We are living at a time when one age is dying and the new age is not yet born . . . we are called upon to do something new, to confront a no-man's land, to push into a forest where there are no well-worn paths . . . to leap into the unknown." He then brings the challenge directly home to us as individuals. "*If you do not express your own original ideas, if you do not listen to your own being, you will have betrayed yourself. Also you will have betrayed our community in failing to make your contribution to the whole."*[3]

And yet, at this very moment of great need and possibility, we do not seem to be training people to be creative. Quite the contrary. Henri Nouwen observes, "If there is any culture that has succeeded in killing the natural, spontaneous curiosity of people and dulling the human desire to know, it is our technocratic society."[4]

It seems to me that it is crucial for us to find ways to rekindle our own creative energies and then consciously strategize to see that this creativity of persons begins to impact institutions. That is why I link the topics of power and problem solving with creativity. To illustrate, let us return to our story of the glass dome. I keep wishing I could simply rejoice with the man in his new-found personal freedom and vicariously enjoy his blissful dancing. But I continue to be haunted by the fact that *he did not change anything in the glass dome*—"they all breathed a sigh of relief and went back to just the way things had been before that day."

The question before us then would seem to be: How can we encourage and develop creativity in ourselves and those who work with us, and then understand and utilize power effectively so that we do, in fact, impact organizations, and their services, without getting "turned out" in the process?

It is an awesome undertaking. It is essential that we approach it with great courage and vigor. We are suggesting nothing short of each of us being willing to prepare for and undertake "the hard and high-risk task of building better institutions in an imperfect world."[5]

DEFINING CREATIVITY

Let's look a bit more closely at the concept of creativity—what it is and is not; how it is nurtured; what organizational climate helps it to flourish or die.

Beyond the definitions given earlier ("to evolve from one's own thought or imagination . . . to bring in something new . . . make changes"), here are some other observations about creativity.

Rollo May, in his excellent book *The Courage to Create*, defines creativity as[6] "The encounter of the intensively conscious person with his or her world." The key words here are *encounter* and *intensively conscious*. May believes it occurs almost exclusively in those areas in which a person has worked hard and to which he feels a strong sense of dedication. He later refers to the need for "passion." This is a vivid portrayal of a person far removed from the weekend dabbler in art, music, or crafts; the armchair philosopher; the passive observer/critic; or the "head trip genius." May states that today we have plenty of talent but we lack passion.

James Austin also comments on the "passionate tensions that free creative expression."[7] He observes that "the best creative work represents passion fulfilled, whereas a neurosis may be thought of as passion thwarted." He goes on to say, "Enthusiasm is the elixir that pervades creativity, inspires it, frees it so that anything seems possible, and enlists others in the cause."

Perhaps our societal preoccupation with "hanging loose" and "staying cool" may be contributing to the lack of creativity we have discussed.

Some further observations May has on the subject are:

- The creative person is forever dissatisfied with the mundane, apathetic or conventional, and is therefore constantly threatening the status quo by seeing and then pushing on to new worlds (much as Jay described in his book);

- Creativity requires an intensity of emotion and heightened vitality . . . sometimes rage! It is important therefore not to eliminate all conflict, as it can be creative; and

- Creativity is first an act of destruction, for the birth of something new comes out of the death of what already is . . . and again, that is bound to be a threat.[8]

Let's see what some other highly creative people have said:

Love of something sparks creativity . . . it's more than just being different–that's not necessarily being original . . . what you have to do is know where you're coming from, be able to do what's gone before, but go on from there in your own way. Making the simple complicated is commonplace; making the complicated simple, awesomely simple–that's creativity.

Charles Mingus (jazz musician)

We can almost view some creative persons as missionaries on both an external and internal quest. Their well-rationalized quest may appear to be for an elegant answer, one that will throw a new light of understanding into a dark corner of the impersonal cosmos. But their internal quest is for a highly personalized, idealized interpretation–one that brings order and meaning to their OWN universe . . . the five most important

19

traits of a creative person are curiosity, imagination, enthusiasm, discrimination, and persistence. [9]

James Austin (neurologist)

The master word . . . directly responsible for all advances in medicine during the past 25 centuries is . . . work.

Sir William Osler (scientist)

Let's see if we can summarize the ingredients mentioned that seem to be significant as we try to understand creativity: knowledge of one's subject . . . hard work . . . curiosity . . . love . . . consuming interest . . . dedication . . . conscious encounter with the task . . . hard work . . . high emotion/passion/rage . . . courage . . . vitality . . . enthusiasm . . . time . . . hard work.

Yes, I am aware that I listed hard work three times. This was done both because the other resources emphasized it repeatedly and also because I am convinced that unless we understand this and decide the cause is worth the immense time, energy, and effort, it will not happen. It will be another good intention or exciting idea that aborted.

In management, for example, we have all encountered the instant expert who joins an organization and three months later has answers for everyone's problems in all departments. These people often exert little or no energy trying to understand "how things are" but rather concentrate only on "how things should be." They rarely invest the effort needed to thoroughly conquer the skills and knowledge required to do the job as it is presently constituted. They want to change things before they even understand what they are attempting to change. As a consequence, they have little credibility with either peers or superiors.

I strongly advocate in all of my management training that it is only after a person becomes skilled and effective in basic program management that he should begin to innovate. That takes time, training, and seasoning. But once you attain that level of competence, it is essential to look beyond the typical management literature or training to acquire the "survival skills" dealt with in this book if you are to succeed in being creative without getting chewed up by the system.

UNDERSTANDING CREATIVITY

One way to try to understand creativity more fully is to understand "From whence it comes" . . . the brain itself.

Although this "inkish-gray, mushy membrane is slightly larger than a grapefruit and weighs less than three pounds, a computer capable of handling a single brain's output would cover the entire earth. The brain sorts one hundred million bits of data from the eyes, ears, nose, and other sensory outposts each second." So says James M. Randall who also claims that the door to the mind is ajar at last and science stands poised on its threshold.[10]

He observes that "the brain is like an enchanted forest, incredibly dense, with many different kinds of foliage that constantly grow, wear out, and are replaced—all the while whispering in a complex cellular language that controls each of our mental and physical functions."

One of the most promising discoveries about the brain made thus far that is becoming increasingly accepted by the scientific world is often labeled split-brain psychology. This theory contends that the brain is split into two distinct hemispheres, and that each hemisphere controls very different mental functions. In fact, split-brain psychology was the hottest fad going in psychology in the '70s according to Rom Zemke in *Training* (January 1978). Since 1970, articles relating to it have appeared in such prestigious magazines as *Psychology Today*, *Harvard Business Review*, *American Psychologist*, *Human Behavior*, and *Saturday Review*, and well over a dozen books have been written on the topic.

My intent is to simply summarize this literature as it relates specifically to creativity. The most helpful resource I discoverd was a book entitled *The Metaphoric Mind: A Celebration of Creative Consciousness*, by Bob Samples.[11]

Samples explains the difference between the functions of the right and left hemispheres of the brain as follows:

Left Hemisphere	*Right Hemisphere*
Intellectual/language skills	Inventive/creative
Logic	Intuitive
Organization	Metaphoric-"world that cannot be measured"
Conforming/rational	Challenges conformity
Fragmented perceptions	Holistic perceptions—"all inputs are simply fragments of reality looking for a whole to relate to"
When damaged, affects:	*When damaged, affects:*
Language, writing, analytical thinking, logic	Drawing, music, depth perception, relationship to whole

(Einstein called the left brain a "faithful servant" and the right brain a "sacred gift.")

In *Science News* of April 3, 1976, the following table appeared which delineates the differences still further:[12]

Left Hemisphere	Right Hemisphere
(Controls right side of body)	(Controls left side of body)
Speech/Verbal	Spatial/musical
Logical, mathematical	Holistic
Linear, detailed	Artistic, symbolic
Sequential	Simultaneous
Controlled	Emotional
Intellectual	Intuitive, creative
Dominant	Minor (quiet)
Worldly	Spiritual
Active	Receptive
Analytic	Synthetic, Gestalt
Reading, writing, naming	Facial recognition
Sequential ordering	Simultaneous comprehension
Perception of significant order	Perception of abstract patterns
Complex motor sequences	Recognition of complex figures

The important insight that this information brings is that *we all normally have the capability to be creative because the ingredients for creativity reside in our right brain.* What has happened, according to Samples, is that we have overindulged the left side of the brain at the expense of the right in our culture and society . . . this has caused "mental myopia." In other words, we have allowed creativity to be conditioned out of us!

He urges us to recognize that the right hemisphere is a veritable "geyser of pent-up energy" waiting to be tapped.

> *It is enriched by an infinity of knowings and it ceaselessly repatterns these to be a compound infinity of possibilities as it wanders across the face of the world. It creates poems, equations, cities and universes where none has existed before. In all its knowing, it seems only to lack one thing,* the knowing that something is impossible.[13]

The best way to grasp the difference between right and left brain behavior is by observing the differences between children and adults. Children usually approach every situation or problem as though it had never happened before, so they must figure out what to do about it. There is an attitude of freshness and spontaneity and a lack of stock answers. As adults, on the other hand, we come with a "rich repertoire of cultural experience" which tends to encourage us to stick to the known, tried, and true answers rather than experiment and risk. (That is where the answers like "We *always* do it this way" or "We *never* do that here" originated.)

Abraham Maslow once said an adult is one who, when he has a hammer, treats the whole world like a nail, whereas a child might take the same hammer and dig with it; sculpt with it; weigh down papers with leaves pressed between; or knock down apples with it![14]

This may be why a teacher commented recently that the real

challenge of teaching should not be to make adults of children but rather children of adults.

So, we have two very important hemispheres of our brains and most experts seem to say that one is no more important than the other. *The crux of true creativity is to develop and utilize them both to the fullest extent possible.* Jonas Salk observed that wisdom arises from both parts of the brain. What we need to consciously strive for is a better balance between the two. *Creativity (right) without order (left) is chaos. Order without creativity is stagnation.* "A runaway right brain never proves anything or makes much happen. A lone wolf left brain never finds new facts to process."[15]

And it is for that very reason that we have begun this exploration of creativity with left-brain information and will end it with right brain application. Both cognitive and affective learning are important—we must step back and forth between them if real learning is to occur. We should alternate between:

Imagining and investigating,
Categorizing and creating,
Selecting and summarizing,
Reasoning and relating,
Experiencing and evaluating,
Communicating and celebrating.
Jeanette Fagerberg

It is important, for example, that we go beyond just reading the tables presented on page 21 relating to right and left brain functions. It will not become anything more than semi-interesting information until we process it internally. I suggest that you go through the lists and check those traits that you feel most closely describe your present style of thinking and working. Are you utilizing primarily your right or left brain?

If you seriously want to become more creative, you must consciously practice right brain behaviors—even though they may seem foreign to you at first. I have found it necessary to discipline myself to rein in my practical, logical, systematic tendencies and to allow more intuition, playfulness, and nonconformity to surface. I have discovered the value of having fun while I work, of thinking in pictures instead of only words, and of giving my imagination permission to speak and be heard. One of the most significant experiences I had which helped me learn to exercise a relatively inactive right brain was to take a creative writing course at a local community college.

23

The point is, know your own style and determine if you are satisfied with it. The following Creative Leader/Manager Exercise is an excellent tool to help you with this. I suggest you take time to fill it out now.

ARE YOU—OR CAN YOU BE— A CREATIVE LEADER/MANAGER?

A study of creative executives identified 25 traits they held in common. If you are interested in becoming creative leaders/managers, you would do well to evaluate yourself against this yardstick of characteristics to see: 1) Are you satisfied with the extent to which you have developed each trait? Or, 2) If not, do you want to work to develop this trait?

If you want to work to develop a trait, what are some concrete steps you might take? Creativity does not just happen without effort and intentionality!

Choose 2 or 3 action steps you WILL TAKE, beginning tomorrow, to start moving along towards becoming a more creative leader.

A CREATIVITY CHECK LIST

	Yes	No	Want to Develop
1. Have I maintained a youthful curiosity about most things?			
2. Am I able to remain relatively open to new, unusual or venturesome ideas?			
3. Am I sensitive to problems and eager to find fresh approaches to solving them?			
4. Do I dare to transcend accepted patterns of thinking and stick to convictions in the face of possible discouragement or censure?			
5. Am I willing to give up immediate gain, comfort or success to reach long-range goals?			
6. Do I have a greater than average amount of energy?			
7. Do I have many hobbies, skills, and interests?			
8. Am I comfortable toying with ideas vs. needing to find quick solutions?			
9. Can I tolerate ambiguity and juggle many possibilities simultaneously (even though they may seem conflicting or even contradictory)?			
10. Am I able to choose the more fundamental and reject the superfluous?			
11. Do I possess a "creative memory" which rearranges, prunes, discards, relates, and refines data and ideas?			
12. Do I allow incubation time for ideas so I can contemplate, reflect and let them "gel"?			
13. Am I conscious of my own personal rhythm of out-			

24

put? (Am I creative in the morning, late night, outside, sitting at a desk?)

14. Do I persevere in spite of obstacles and opposition?

15. Can I evaluate my own ideas objectively *after* I have elaborated them?

16. Do I feel I (and those who work with me) have untapped potential?

17. Do I have a lot of initiative?

18. Do I eagerly ask questions?

19. Do I compete with myself rather than others?

20. Am I willing to listen to every suggestion but judge situations for myself?

21. Am I open and direct with people, respecting their rights?

22. Am I often irritated by the status quo and do I refuse to be bound by habit or norms?

23. Do I like ventures involving calculated risks?

24. Do I avoid making excuses for my mistakes and keep from blaming others?

25. Am I willing to stand alone when integrity demands it?

Action steps I will take, beginning tomorrow, to develop some of the traits of a more creative leader:

1. _____

2. _____

3. _____

Developed by Marlene Wilson from an article, "Are You A Creative Executive," which appeared in *Management Review* (February 1978).[16] Copyright Volunteer Management Associates, 1980.

I have used this exercise with many training groups. After all participants complete the form, I have them discuss it in dyads. Their discussions center on those traits they each want to develop. Lively interchange results when they begin sharing their personal "how to's." I recommend you try it with a friend or small group.

If you feel you are utilizing only a part of your capabilities, this right and left brain information could be truly significant. Creativity can be developed!

THE CREATIVE PROCESS

Hopefully by now you have a better intellectual understanding of creativity. It is therefore time to move on to determine how you can use a practical, workable process to become more creative. And once again, remember that we are speaking about creativity in problem-solving, planning, and all aspects of the work you do, as well as in the more commonly defined arenas of art, writing, music, etc.

Two of the most concise and useful references I have found in dealing with the "how's" are James H. Austin's book *Chase, Chance and Creativity*,[17] and Desy Sofan-Girard's article in *Psychology Today* (January 1978) entitled "How to Unblock."[18] I would like to summarize them here.

Austin identifies the logical sequence of the creative process as:

> Interest
> Preparation
> Incubation
> Illumination
> Verification
> Exploitation

Sofan-Girard calls them:

> Perception
> Elaboration
> Expression
> Evaluation

Let's examine them briefly.

INTEREST

It is vitally important to seek out those topics or projects in which you have a deep personal interest or "need to know." Such a personal interest will not only generate the energy and enthusiasm you need, but it will ensure your persistence in seeing it through to completion. Be sure it turns *YOU* on!

Then seek out some lively, vital people who share your interest to serve as mentors, questioners, and models for you.

Austin warns, "Select guides, not drivers, bright persons you can respect, mentors wise enough to help you find your own way, secure enough to keep your own best interests in mind, mature enough to let go at the right time."

PREPARATION/PERCEPTION

Both authors emphasize strongly that you must work hard to

become well grounded in your field. Understand the information, data, and techniques available until they become second nature to you. *Practice solving problems of steadily increasing complexity.* Stretch yourself! Then find that particular need or problem with your name on it . . . the one you find yourself getting more and more intrigued with and excited about pursuing. This is when you must listen to your own questions. What do you wake up thinking about? What keeps coming back to haunt you? If you choose the right questions to pursue and are bold enough to tackle them, Austin says you will grow to meet the challenge, so don't be timid.

I personally find this step of "listening to my own questions" the key. It tells me what I am ready to learn more about and the resulting work becomes an adventure of discovery, because I want to know.

INCUBATION/ELABORATION

If you have chosen the right problem to work on, you will often become almost obsessed with it. Now you must create solid, undistracted blocks of time to work on it.

Perhaps we are now beginning to understand one reason it is so difficult to be creative in many jobs. Finding unbroken blocks of time (other than between midnight and 6:00 a.m.) is a definite problem for most managers. Try sitting in your office just thinking for an hour. Your co-workers will probably frown at your unproductiveness and you will undoubtedly feel guilty. This is why creating group norms that value quiet thinking and planning time for managers is so important.

Another problem at this stage is that you will hit the inevitable blocks where your thoughts seem stale and you lose your enthusiasm. Relax and "free the problem to go underground." It needs time to incubate or get into your subconscious, so back off and do something completely unrelated. This is a terribly critical stage, so do not overlook or short-change it.

Martin Buber, the noted theologian, probably unwittingly coined the term "pregnant idea" when he wrote:

When a man grows aware of a new way in which to serve God, he should carry it around with him secretly, and without uttering it, for nine months, as though he were pregnant with it, and let others know of it only at the end of that time as though it were a birth.

27

I have personally experienced this phenomenon repeatedly while writing. It is an almost physical sensation of "suspended animation." It begins when I consciously decide to delay writing until I have done all the necessary reading and research. Then comes the moment when I put all the resources away and begin to write. At times I hit blocks and feel agitation. When I feel it, I know it is time to walk away from my work (or the problem) for a while—to let it perk in my subconscious. I go for a drive, take a walk, go visit friends . . . anything but try to keep on writing. There are connections with buried data that are struggling to be made, or new insights just around the corner *if* I discipline myself to refrain from pressing on, no matter what. Since I am by nature very goal-oriented, this has been a difficult relearning for me, but it has paid handsome dividends in the quality of my work. (Austin observed, "Completing the manuscript is like giving birth to a cactus that has bloomed long before.")

If you are unwilling to tolerate ambiguity and uneasiness you tend to shorten this crucial stage. You must allow ideas and feelings to sort themselves out. It is how you make a "deeper connection with your work." This is so important in problem solving of all kinds if you really want to stop the tendency to find "an answer" and search for "the best answer."

ILLUMINATION/EXPRESSION

At this stage you simply allow your own uniqueness to influence your work. "Each time a person creates something, he projects part of himself into it."

That is why it is so critical to allow the information and data to filter through your own person—so that it truly becomes yours and you can add your own interpretation, insights, and viewpoint to the work. Otherwise you are simply a reporter of what others say or think, or a copier of original art. *You* are the ingredient that must be added to make the work truly creative.

The poet Goethe once said, "I have never tried to pretend my poetry. I never put into verse or expressed otherwise things I do not live, things that do not make me feel hot under the collar, or that did not keep me awake nights. I wrote love poems only when I was in love." This to me is another eloquent way of saying what May did regarding creativity—it is "the encounter of the intensively conscious person with his or her world."

As I mentioned in the Preface, this book has grown out of my experiences on the organizational battleground. I have felt the frustration and indignation of being an excellent program manager who was considered insubordinate and troublesome; I have experienced "turnout"; I have witnessed the incredible waste of under-utilized, over-controlled human resources; and I have met scores of creative people who have nearly been destroyed by organizations. After six years as a manager in industry and seven years as an executive director of a human service agency (that was part of a metro-wide hierarchy) this topic of survival in today's organizations is indeed one that "keeps me awake nights."

One danger we face at this stage of expressing our own uniqueness is our internal critic telling us things like "it's a dumb idea," "it will never work," "whoever heard of a flower that looks like that," and so on and on. In Transactional Analysis terms, watch out for the "critical parent," as we would tend to respond like chastened children rather than self-confident adults. After all, we are still not too sure it makes sense either. Once we have added our own unique imprint on the effort, it becomes more scary. For if it is rejected, it can seem like a personal rejection rather than a purely intellectual disagreement. The point is, we need to evaluate our work, but *after* expression, not during it.

Austin reminds us that a well-rested, healthy mind and body are more apt to be alert to the flashes of insight or intuition that come to us. "Major insights can be unforgettable, but they are rare. Most other flashes of insight are of lesser intensity, and they can vanish quickly unless you immediately write them down." Someone once said that a hunch is creativity trying to tell you something.

VERIFICATION/EVALUATION

This is when we activate the left brain and take an objective, honest, critical look at what we have done. Creativity requires both freedom and containment, and much of bad art, bad problem solving, or bad writing is an exercise in self-indulgence. Sofan-Girard calls this stage *evaluation* and says this about it:

> When the work is done, the creative person must be able to disrupt his oneness with the work, to stand back and assess coolly what has happened. Few people associate the joys of creativity with these self-confrontations, but they are a vital part of creation. . . . While involvement in what we do is essential to creativity, we must also be detached enough to assess whether what we have done is fitting. The inability to let go of irrelevancies and excesses marks the amateur in any field.

Austin agrees and challenges the creator to ask the hard "so what" questions at this point. We must try not only to verify what we have come to believe, but also to prove ourselves wrong. Others will question us, so we might as well anticipate their doubts and work through them to our own satisfaction. And believe me, this is difficult to do.

Here I would also suggest the value of utilizing others whose judgement you trust to critique your work or ideas. I have found this painful at times, but absolutely invaluable in helping me spot the irrelevancies and excesses that need to be eliminated, but which I have not been able to see because I was too close to the work or had too much invested in the problem-solving idea.

I shall never forget the experience of asking my husband to critique the first chapter of my first book. I asked for his honest opinion and suggestions, but what I really wanted was his unqualified endorsement (due to my own insecurity at that point). When he handed it back to me with penciled additions and phrases struck out or rewritten, I believe we had one of our most significant confrontations in eighteen years of marriage! He saw my injured pride and then asked me to clarify for him what I had really wanted from him. I had to work through the emotions and realize I really *did* want his honest opinion because I respect his judgement tremendously. Once we had that settled, he became and still is my most valued critic. (Do we ever do that to subordinates when we ask their opinions or evaluation of a project and then feel hurt if they give us negative feedback?)

Just one word of caution. Rollo May acknowledges that he has a tremendous impulse to destroy his creations at this stage. I have experienced this urge as well, and I am sure it comes from doubt and insecurity. Be very careful not to be so critical that you destroy ideas that deserve to live!

EXPLOITATION/IMPLEMENTATION

Austin urges that we concentrate our creative energies on those ideas and theories that can lead to action—*that can actually cause change.* That means that we cannot stop here . . . not if we are going to make a difference. We must follow through to see the idea into reality. That is not someone else's problem—it is ours. And this is exactly where so many truly creative ideas abort. *The creator shuns the responsibility of implementation.*

That is precisely why I have linked the subject of creativity with that of problem solving, power, negotiating change, conflict management, stress management, and time management. These are, in my opinion, the missing tools to help us move ideas into action. The answer to becoming and remaining creative managers in today's technocratic, organizational world may exist in acquiring these "survival skills."

STUMBLING BLOCKS TO CREATIVITY

After defining creativity and looking at the process, it does not seem all that hard. Why, then, don't we just close the book and begin being creative instead of *thinking* about it? Unfortunately, what will probably keep us thinking instead of doing is one or more of the following blocks the experts have identified, most of which are cultural or emotional in nature. Let's see if we can examine a few of the most common ones and then suggest some ways to climb over, around, or under them.

1. Fear of failure or of the unknown
2. Reluctance to play
3. Resource myopia
4. Frustration avoidance
5. Tradition and conformity
6. Impoverished fantasy life and sensory dullness
7. Reluctance to exert power or influence
8. Failure to see things in a holistic fashion

FEAR OF FAILURE OR OF THE UNKNOWN

What does this look like? An excessive concern with success often keeps us from experimenting or risking. We prefer to live with an unsatisfactory "known" rather than risk the unknown.

As Elizabeth O'Connor describes it, "When we do not allow ourselves the possibility of failure . . . we are controlled by perfectionist strivings that inhibit the mysterious meshing of divergent lives within us. Spontaneity dies and the emergence of the unexpected ceases to be a possibility. We are literally tied and bound."[19]

Someone once said: True success is overcoming the fear of being unsuccessful.

What can be done about it? It sometimes helps to attach words and images to the vague concerns and anxieties we feel about the new or unknown.

We frequently do not realistically assess the probable consequences of a creative act. We either blithely ignore any consequences or our general fear of failure causes us to attach excessive importance to any mistake. One way this can be dealt with is to take a guided fantasy to explore the situation in your mind.

That might go something like this. First of all, complete the following statements:

a) Some goals of my program/project are: _____

b) If we were really doing our job well right now, we would be (list something you feel strongly should be happening that is not): _____

c) My frustration/concern about this unrealized goal is:_____

d) What I'm wishing for is: _____

e) Therefore, my goal is (list a creative act): _____

f) One of the things I would be afraid to try in an attempt to reach that goal is: _____

Now, relax completely, close your eyes, and imagine you just tried what you listed in (f) and what you feared would happen does happen. How does that *feel*? Picture yourself coping with the situation. How does that *look*? Is it succeeding or failing? If it seems like failing, fantasize *through* the failure to see how that *feels* and deal with "what is the worst that can happen—and is that so bad?"

James Adams suggests another simple exercise to help you decide if a risky, creative idea is worth pursuing. Write a one or two page "catastrophic expectations" report in which you list as precisely as possible what would happen if everything that could go wrong went wrong IF you pushed your idea. "By making such information explicit and facing it, you swap your analytical capability for your fear of failure—a good trade."[20]

It is important that we learn to accept failure as opportunity for growth and not avoid it at all costs. Accept some failures as proof that you are growing, risking, and searching. No failures might just indicate that you have "retired without leaving." The important thing is to realistically assess the possible outcomes of an idea.

Norman Vincent Peale once observed, "In any worthwhile endeavor there is an element of risk, you may run into opposition, you may be laughed at. *But you have to be willing to be vulnerable*—to be, if necessary, a fool for God, knowing that the rewards of righting a wrong, or improving your world, far outweigh the possible risks or hazards." A wise teacher once advised "Behold the turtle—he makes progress only when he sticks his neck out!"

RELUCTANCE TO PLAY

What does this look like? An overly dominant left brain causes us to view problem solving as serious business. We therefore view humor or fantasy as out of place. After all, playing is for children and we have put away childish things. The tendency here is to fear sounding or looking silly or foolish. We often short-circuit the creative process due to our internal parent not allowing us to chew our mental cud long enough.

What can be done about it? First of all, set aside time in which you give yourself permission to daydream, fantasize, and laugh. Arthur Koestler, one of the world's foremost authorities on creativity, lists humor as one of the most essential ingredients of creativity. In an essay, "The Three Domains of Creativity," he identifies these domains as *artistic originality* (which he calls the "Ah!" reaction), *scientific discovery* (the "A-Ha!" reaction), and *comic inspiration* (the "Ha-Ha!" reaction).

In *Conceptual Blockbusting* James Adams states,

> *Creative groups with which I have been associated have been funny. So are creative people I have known. Humor is present in all manner of ways. I am not suggesting that creative activity is all fun, since it is fraught with frustration, detail work, and plain effort. However, humor is an essential ingredient of healthy conceptualization.* [21]

Robert Farrar Capon once observed," Necessity is the mother only of clichés. It takes playfulness to make poetry."

As an example, I was recently a part of the planning committee for a national conference. It was one of the most productive and satisfying experiences I have had recently. Not only did we design an exciting pilot program that has never before been attempted by such a group, but we laughed a lot. The "creative juices" were allowed to flow freely. One of the most creative members of our team of six was the chairman (a quiet, organized, seemingly left-brained fellow). He lovingly shepherded us through important structural necessities such as agendas and deadlines but never in a way that inhibited the creative flow of ideas. The product is one we are all proud of, and our group members all grew in the process. Why can't more planning and problem-solving sessions look and feel like that?

Here is where you may need to change group norms regarding how you problem solve—to make it fun! Try some of the suggestions listed in Chapter II on creative problem solving. The most frequently used method to get a group's creative juices flowing is "brainstorming." This is the free flow of ideas around a clearly defined problem. The rules of brainstorming are:

a) No evaluation of ideas presented;

b) Everyone is encouraged to think of the wildest, most creative ideas possible;

c) *Quantity* of ideas is important (evaluation and quality come later); and

d) Everyone is encouraged to build on or modify the ideas of the others. You also need a recorder so no gems are lost.

Let me share a specific example where I utilized brainstorming in a training event to help a group begin to deal in a new way with a very old problem—volunteer recruitment.

I was working with the staff of a national health organization for two days and they were attempting to blame most of their financial and staffing problems on the lack of volunteers. They also wanted to try to convince themselves (and me) that this lack was because people did not care as much anymore—and also that the traditional female volunteers had all gone to work for pay.

To try to point out to them that they had used very traditional, unimaginative recruiting techniques, I split the group of thirty into two teams, chose a recorder for each group, and put the teams at opposite ends of the room. We then had a brainstorming contest. The assignment was—in ten minutes—come up with as many ideas as possible about where and how to recruit volunteers for this organization. The pace, excitement, noise level, and laughter increased steadily as ideas poured out on the flip charts. They were competing and having great fun.

At the end of ten minutes, one team had listed 67 ideas; the other, 94. They now had enough embryonic ideas to work on for a year—and they could hardly wait to begin.

These methods and others tend to kindle enthusiasm and playfulness. One person's idea sparks someone else and defenses come

34

down. Playing with ideas and concepts is great exercise for the right side of the brain.

As for your personal creative journey: Make believe; go on fantasy trips; look for at least one comical thing each day (at work, home, subway) and tell another person about it. Also watch children. A mother once said, "I brought this two-year-old into the world; the least I can do is let her show it to me."

The point is, so often we find what we look for. Try looking for the humor in situations and the fun in problem solving.

RESOURCE MYOPIA

What does this look like? A common tendency is to overlook our own strengths and those of others. We fail to see the potentialities and possibilities of people—and situations. We become too pragmatic, basing our judgments on "what is or has been" instead of being imaginative in thinking "what might be."

What can be done about it? Peter Drucker, in his excellent book *The Effective Executive*, states that one of the most consistent and important traits of successful executives is that they build on the strengths (as opposed to the weaknesses) of themselves and their superiors, colleagues, and subordinates. They acknowledge and accept their own strengths and weaknesses and *are able to accept the best in others without being threatened.* They also recognize their opportunity and responsibility to help others grow. "They feed opportunities and starve problems."[22]

This may sound simple, but we so seldom consider people valuable resources to be as carefully and consciously tended as funds, equipment, buildings, and products. In my opinion, *a good manager must be as concerned with the people led as with the program or product produced.* If goals are accomplished, but the people accomplishing them are diminished in the process, the program is a failure in the long run.

Elizabeth O'Connor, in her insightful book *Eighth Day of Creation*, reminds us why discovery of potentialities (ours and other people's) is so crucial. "Because our gifts carry us out into the world and make us participate in life, the uncovering of them is one of the most important tasks confronting any one of us."[23]

She also relates the legend about Michelangelo pushing a huge rock down a street. When asked by a curious neighbor why he was working so hard over an old piece of stone, Michelangelo reportedly said, "Because there is an angel in that rock that wants to come out."

But how do you find out about these gifts, or hidden capabilities? For yourself, once again I would suggest making lists—both of your strengths and weaknesses. Don't be self-conscious or embarrassed about either. We have to feel good about ourselves before we are free to fully accept the strengths and weaknesses of others, otherwise threat becomes too much of an issue. You may want to extend the list to include "suspected or untapped strengths"—where you consciously assess your potential skills and strengths that are waiting to have a chance to surface. The question might be: "If given the chance, I think I might be good at _____." (Try completing the following questionnaire to help in your self-examination.)

DISCOVERING MY GIFTS

Answer the following questions from the standpoint of those areas of your life that you are currently most excited about (job, home, family, school, church, social life, leisure time, hobbies, etc.).

1. Some things I believe I do well are:
2. Some things I think I'm not very good at are:
3. If given the chance, I think I MIGHT be good at:
4. One NEW thing I have tried recently and that went pretty well was:
5. Who encouraged me to try #4? What made him/her think I could do that? Does he/she often encourage me to try a new thing?
6. Who are the "mentors" (the wise, loyal advisers) in my life?

(Nancy Root, 1979)

Next, try to set aside preconceived notions about all who work with and for you and pretend that you are an outsider objectively assessing them. Have each one of them make their own lists or complete the questionnaire. Sit down with them individually to get to know each one more fully. This would be a great opportunity for both evaluation and future goal setting. I challenge you, the manager, to also show your lists and to welcome feedback from others regarding their perceptions of you as compared to your own. (How open and secure are you? Maybe it is a goal to work toward gradually.)

Two assessment tools that are constantly available to managers in getting to know people (their strengths, weaknesses, behavior, likes and dislikes) are: *To ask them and to observe them.*

We often overlook the fact that when people begin to chafe at assignments, begin to miss or become a problem, it is often a clue

36

that they are bored . . . that they no longer feel challenged as persons. That is when we should follow up and see if there can be enrichment or enlargement of the job, or if a transfer is in order. Herzberg, in his studies of motivation in industry, clearly found *growth and development* to be the strongest motivators in work situations.

Walt Disney, one of the most creative and productive leaders of this century, also had some very interesting ideas about the job of leadership. He compared the job of an effective leader/manager to that of a superlative mother. In his estimation, they both spend *all* of their time training. One-half of their time is spent in nurturing their people (employees or children) through these four levels of learning (starting with Level IV):

I.   *Unconscious Competence:* Knowing how to do something so well it becomes second-nature and no longer requires conscious thought.

                 ▲

II.   *Conscious Competence:* Learning to do it well, but needing to concentrate.

                 ▲

III.   *Conscious Incompetence:* Knowing what you don't know.

                 ▲

IV.   *Unconscious Incompetence:* Being dumb without knowing it.

He suggested that a leader must spend the time needed to bring people through all four steps so they all know what they are doing and do it well. The other half of a manager's time should be spent on "recycling people"—by giving them new challenges and assignments so they can start through all four steps again. That is one of the best ways to avoid "burnout" and keep growing. When did you last recycle yourself?

Another part of this block of resource myopia is our own reluctance to let go: we keep being the doer of too much instead of learning to delegate to others. Delegation is one of the most poorly used, but in my estimation, critical aspects of good management. If used well, it helps you find the time you need to recycle. It gives those working with you an opportunity to grow more efficiently and effectively because you are maximizing the strengths and minimizing the weaknesses of the whole work group. And surprisingly,

37

when done well, delegation tends to increase instead of diminish a leader's power and influence with the group. It also leaves behind a well-trained, strong group to carry on the project when you leave or move up in the organization.

One other comment about resources. When you assess the physical resources (funds, equipment, space, etc.) that you really need and compare that with what you have to work with , the results are often extremely depressing, especially in many human services agencies. It is very easy to wring your hands and while away your energies dreaming of "if only's." Why not exercise the creative energies of your group and brainstorm where the resources are that you need, how you can get them, and who is the best one to do it. Let me share with you the results of just such brainstorming that we did at a voluntary action center I directed. Our first year's United Way allocation was $4,400, which was for space, equipment, and staff.

Problem	Outcome
Space	Obtained a deserted free county office. Volunteers painted, refurbished, and cleaned. Service clubs were involved.
Funds	Doubled the budget the second year through efforts of a Board task force on funding.
Equipment	Desks, file cabinets, chairs, lamps all given by large local industry.
Brochures and Posters	Graphics expert from a local industry volunteered. (He created a poster that won him an international graphics award.)

These are just a sample of the results. The primary benefit was that the center quickly became known by many segments of the community and they all felt some ownership because they had invested something (time, money, equipment) in our future. There were no general, community-wide panic appeals—just a step-by-step planned campaign for getting what was needed in a positive, even exciting way. And it set the tone for true participative management later in getting our program goals met as well.

FRUSTRATION AVOIDANCE

How does this look? An unwillingness to tolerate ambiguity and uncertainty makes us give up too soon. We cannot stand being in limbo. The tendency is to always strive for balance and order as opposed to confusion or disorder (left vs. right brain).

What can be done about it? First of all, it is important to realize that most of us do not like problems or conflict. When faced with them we have a natural tendency to grab the first solution that comes along. Doing *something* seems better than doing *nothing*! So we must use self-discipline to get past this block.

We must try to develop more trust in our instincts and those of others. Hold back on solutions until all alternatives have been explored; walk away from ideas that seem frozen in a half-formed state; hold up judgement on the ideas of others until you have heard them out and then let them incubate a while before deciding. (We will explore this in depth in Chapter II.)

Nicholas Murray Butler once said, "Time was invented by Almighty God in order to give ideas a chance."

There are physical things we can do to help alleviate the tension created by ambiguity. Get in the car and drive, have a chocolate sundae, read a novel, work on a totally different project, jog, lie in the sun, go for a hike, or have a lively conversation on an unrelated topic with coworkers, family or friends. The trick is to STOP consciously struggling to make the idea happen—to get your conscious mind to let go long enough for your subconscious to take over . . . to rest your left brain and crank up your right. You know best what relaxes and diverts you, so when the tension mounts, go do that!

TRADITION AND CONFORMITY

What does this look like? Tradition and conformity confine our thinking to stock answers—tried and true methods. We have an undue reverence for the past, and feel "what was, is, and ever more shall be."

What can be done about it? The easiest way to begin is to dust off and begin to use three very important words, "why?" and "why not?" We have been discouraged from using them over the years and for all of the reasons discussed earlier in this chapter.

What we need to develop is what Koberg and Bagnall call "constructive discontent":

> *Arrival at the age of 16 is usually all that is required for achieving half of this important attribute of creativity. It is unusual to find a "contented" young person; discontent goes with that time of life. To the young, everything needs improvement. . . . As we age, our discontent wanes; we learn from our society that "fault-finders" disturb the status quo of the normal, average "others." Squelch tactics are introduced. It becomes "good" not to "make waves" or "rock the boat" and to "let sleeping dogs lie" and "be seen but not heard." It is "bad" to be a problem maker.*

And so everything is upside-down for creativity and its development. Thus, constructive attitudes are necessary for a dynamic condition; discontent is prerequisite to problem solving. Combined, they define a primary quality of the creative problem solver; a constantly developing Constructive Discontent.[24]

In other words we must begin to view a constructively questioning attitude (in ourselves and others) as a plus, not a minus. We must straighten out our own attitudes first and then we can consciously begin testing out assumptions—about people, situations, norms, styles of work. (How do we know Christine would *never* be good at . . .; or that conflict is always bad . . .; that always starting at 8:00 is appropriate . . .; or that volunteers love to do . . . ?)

A poster many of you have probably seen at some time or another also helps illustrate the frustration of failing to check out assumptions:

I know you believe you understood what you think I said, but I am not sure you realize that what you heard is not what I meant.

One of the most frequent assumptions we make is that there are perimeters or boundaries that may not exist at all. (We sometimes create our own limitations and restrictions by never checking out our assumptions about them. Anyone who has raised children understands about this important testing process. The problem is, we have forgotten how to do this as adults.) To test this, try the following exercise:

Puzzle: Draw four straight lines (without lifting the pencil from the paper) which will cross through all nine dots.[25]

One answer is as follows:

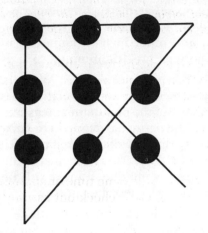

The constraint of staying within the boundary of the dots is in the mind of the problem solver, not in the definition of the problem. One far-out solution is:

IMPOVERISHED FANTASY LIFE AND SENSORY DULLNESS

What does this look like? We find ourselves distrusting emotions, imagination, and spontaneity in favor of logic and objectivity. We feel a reluctance to trust intuition and inner images (fantasies) in ourselves and others. Intense emotions are frightening, so it is much safer to keep cool and detached.

In various articles on creativity, the authors claim that in our American society, at the age of five, 90% of the population measures "high creativity"; by the age of seven, the figure has dropped to 10%; and adults with high creativity make up only 2% of the adult population. But if Freud was right when he said "Nothing is ever lost to the unconscious," then the creativity of early childhood must still be present in all of us—latent, repressed, crippled, but present!

What can be done about it? Try bombarding your senses with new sights, sounds, smells and tastes—different music, unusual foods, travel to a new neighborhood. Then record the reactions you have. Be aware of the impact on your senses. Try to describe the sensations as clearly and completely as possible.

Take classes to sharpen up these senses. Art, writing, literature, music, photography, or drama classes all exercise the senses in new ways and help combat the "sensory dullness" problem. (I recommend the book *Drawing With the Right Side of the Brain* by Betty Edwards for anyone who thinks creativity cannot be learned.)

Keep a daily journal in which you jot down not only events but much more importantly *your feelings about them.* This is your private journey in search of your own feelings and emotions, so get in touch and stay in touch with what you DO feel and not what you think you SHOULD feel.

I have also found it helpful to use several "mental languages" to express myself. Some situations or problems lend themselves to *mathematical thinking* (graphs, charts, numbers, statistics), others to *verbal thinking* (brainstorming, discussion, written reports), and still others can best be tackled with *visual thinking* (images, slides, scribblings, fantasies, pictures).

Since the last method is the one most frequently overlooked, may I give you two examples of how I have used it in my training to help interpret theoretical concepts. I have often done training sessions on planning. Two real-life incidents which help me create "word pictures" for my students are:

Example 1

As an aide in a mental hospital I worked with a patient who loved to knit. She would sit and knit happily all day. When I asked her what she was knitting, she confidently replied, "A dress, of course." After a day or two I noticed the knitting looked more like a scarf than a dress, so I helpfully offered to take her to a knitting class that was available. She indignantly refused. So she continued knitting contentedly until Saturday, which was the day of the big dance for patients. She wanted to wear her new knit dress and my job was to help her put it on. (By that time it was a very long, skinny, black scarf.) I will never forget the dismayed look on her face as she said, "What happened to my dress?" What happened was she had no pattern or plan for her project, so she was knitting a non-dress all the time and didn't know it! (Application: Do we ever "knit non-programs" for the same reason?)

Example 2:

It was after I had taken a vigorous mountain hike one vacation that another "picture" came to mind to help me interpret long- and short-range planning. Our daughter Lisa and I wanted to go on a hike. The guide pointed out our destination, which was a deserted mine about three-quarters of the way up a very steep mountain. I immediately wanted to give up the venture and turn back, for I was sure I was not in physical condition to be able to make it. He reassured me that I could, because there were switchbacks (short zig-zagging trails) all the way. Two hours later I stood triumphantly by the mine looking down on our small village shouting, "I did it! I did it!" (Application: If we provide good, achievable short-range plans or objectives (switch-backs), we are much more apt to eventually arrive at our long-range goals without burning out or feeling defeated.)

This tool of thinking in pictures has been the greatest help to me in creative efforts of anything else I have tried. And it's fun!

RELUCTANCE TO EXERT INFLUENCE OR POWER

What does this look like? This stems from a generally held negative view of power. It feels easier and somehow more acceptable to be a "victim." There is a reluctance to seem too aggressive or "pushy" and an over-concern with being a nice person, loved by all.

What can be done about it? Hopefully, by seriously studying

Chapter III of this book and pursuing some of the many references relating to power, your negative attitudes toward power and influence may be altered. The reality is, no matter how creative you are or may become, very likely some person or some group must be influenced to allow your creative ideas to happen. Without dealing with that fact, it remains simply wishful thinking. The problems we face today need and deserve more than that.

I would especially recommend the use of the Influence/Achievement Exercise on page 118. My husband, Harvey, devised this instrument and has used it on numerous critical problems with great success. Several of our students from University of Colorado Volunteer Management Seminars have also utilized it with very encouraging outcomes (and for the most part, they all began the course resisting the concept of power quite openly).

Try it on some small, but important influence problem first to get a feel for the process. We will deal with this in more detail in the chapter on Power and Negotiations.

FAILURE TO SEE THINGS IN A HOLISTIC FASHION

What does this look like? There is a tendency to polarize things as right *or* wrong, this *or* that, dark *or* light, instead of integrating and synthesizing. The either/or syndrome comes into play here. The problem is—being too overly influenced by segments of a problem or situation and losing sight of the whole.

What can be done about it? Peter Drucker again has a word of advice for effective leaders. He states, "They look up from their work and outward toward goals." In other words, it is important for us to be able to live and work in two time dimensions (present and future) for we "not only have to prepare for crossing distant bridges but we have to build them long before we get there."

This phenomenon also comes into play when we struggle with the need to integrate rather than choose between two things. An example might be the material in this chapter relating to right and left brain characteristics. The intent has not been to convince the reader of the value of developing right brain behaviors at the expense of the left brain. The key to creativity is the integration and balance of both—the development and utilization of both to the fullest extent possible.

Again, regarding the contents of this book, the goal is to break down the fragmented thinking that allows us to view ourselves as *either* a program (creative) person *or* a power (influence) person. We need to develop both qualities to be truly effective managers. Let me share a simple illustration of this with you that I have borrowed from another consultant, Michael Murray of Texas.

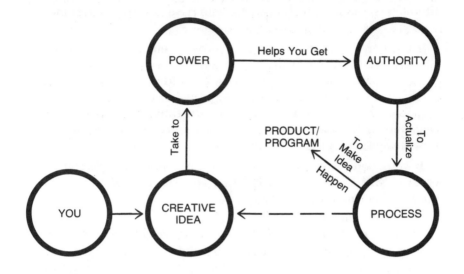

Interestingly enough, once we grasp the larger picture, it is frequently not only helpful but necessary to fractionalize the problem in order to get it resolved. The goal is to try to see the whole *before* concentrating too specifically on the parts. What we want to strive for is synergism—the concept that the whole is greater than any of its parts.

One simple but powerful strategy to help you remain open to other's ideas and keep them open to yours is to use the "Yes, *and* " rather than "Yes, *but* . . ." approach. For example, when someone states a counter idea or suggestion to yours, if you state your response as "Yes, but" the lines of battle are often drawn, as it appears to be an either/or situation. On the other hand, a "Yes, and " response indicates a willingness to hear the other person and collaborate with him, to build on the strengths of both ideas.

Another professional field that is paying a great deal of attention to this holistic approach is medicine. In many cities across the country, holistic clinics are springing up. The thrust of these clinics is to treat the whole person and not just a toe here, a headache there, and depression somewhere else.

45

The patient is interviewed by a staff consisting of a medical doctor, a psychiatrist or psychologist and a clergyman. The intent is to assess the patient's physical, emotional, and spiritual needs and devise a treatment plan that treats the whole person. The results are quite impressive. (An old medical joke speaks to this: "A general practitioner is someone who treats what you have; a specialist is someone who sees that you have what he treats!")

This opens another avenue as far as overcoming creative blocks is concerned. Creativity usually involves the whole person—mind, body, emotions, and spirit. Perhaps it would be well to try to assess if one or the other of these areas in your life needs attention. For example, if your mind is apathetic or unstimulated, taking time to read and think may be vital, for the thoughts of others can trigger new insights if you give them a chance.

If your body is tired and overtaxed, the energy required to be creative will likely not be available; so rest, recreation, exercise, yoga, or diet may do the trick.

It is the realm of the spiritual that I personally have found to be the most crucial. It is as though when my own spiritual well is dry I have nothing to draw on. It is then I am reminded anew that all creativity is indeed a gift from the *Creator* and I must stay close to that source. Retreats, quiet time, books on theology and philosophy, and meditation alone or with like minds soon replenish the well. (A wise friend once shared this bit of wisdom: You can't anymore give what you ain't got than you can come back from where you ain't been!)

So, no matter what the block might be, you can probably work through it . . . if you just care enough. I suppose one question each of us must ask at one time or another is: Does all of this really matter? Can the creative actions of one person or a small group of people make a difference when the problems are so vast and seemingly endless?

Obviously, I firmly believe so, and rather than ask you to take my word for it, I'll ask you to consider the success stories in Appendices B and C.

In his book *The Supper of the Lamb*, Robert Farrar Capon made this observation about people who have a "total lack of the playful spirit which helps us relish the elegant superfluity, the unnecessary variety of the world":

A curse on them all! May an endless variety of worms feed sweetly on their thrifty little efficiencies. Hell is the only place fit for such dismal crampings of the style of our being. Earth must not be entrusted to such people. Their touch is death to all that is counter, original, strange and spare about us. In their hands, the joy of our randomness and oddness is crushed under the millstone of monotonous consistency.[26]

REFERENCES

1. Jay, Anthony, *Management and Machiavelli*, Holt, Rinehart and Winston, Inc., 1967, p. 172-176.

2. Culbert, Samuel A., *The Organization Trap and How to Get Out of It*, Basic Books, Inc., 1974, p. 3.

3. May, Rollo, *The Courage to Create*, W. W. Norton, 1975, pp. 11, 12.

4. Excerpt from *Reaching Out* by Henri J.M.Nouwen. Copyright © 1975 by Henri J.M. Nouwen. Reprinted by permission of Doubleday & Company, Inc., p. 59.

5. Greenleaf, Robert, *The Servant as Leader*, Center for Applied Studies, Windy Row Press, 43 Grove St., Peterborough, NH 03458, 1972, p. 35.

6. May, p. 54.

7. Austin, James H., *Chase, Chance, and Creativity*, Columbia University Press, 1978, pp. 123, 145.

8. May, p. 32.

9. Austin, p. 112.

10. Randall, James, "The Magical Kingdom of the Brain,' *Mainliner Magazine*, March 1978, pp. 43, 44.

11. Samples, Bob, *The Metaphoric Mind: A Celebration of Creative Consciousness*, Addison-Wesley, 1976, pp. 14, 15.

12. *Science News*, April 3, 1976.

13. Samples, p. 62.

14. Ibid, p. 84.

15. Zemke, Ron, *Training*, January 1978.

16. Roudsepp, Eugene, "Are You a Creative Executive," *Management Review*, Feb. 1978.

17. Austin, p. 186.

18. Sofan-Girard, Desy, "How to Unblock," *Psychology Today*, Jan. 1978.

19. O'Connor, Elizabeth, *Eighth Day of Creation*, World Books, 1972, p. 48.

20. Adams, James L. *Conceptual Blockbusting: A Guide to Better Ideas*, W.H. Freeman & Co., 1974, p. 55.

21. Ibid, p. 36.

22. Drucker, Peter, *The Effective Executive*, Harper & Row, 1966, p. 23.

23. O'Connor, pp. 13, 14.

24. Koberg, Don, and Bagnall, Jim, *The Universal Traveler. A Soft-Systems Guidebook to: Creativity, Problem-Solving, and the Process of Design*, Wm,. Kaufmann, Inc., 1974.

25. Adams, pp. 16, 17.

26. Capon, Robert Farrar, *The Supper of the Lamb*, Doubleday & Co., 1969, p. 39.

"NO ORDINARY BIRD"

A Corporation Bid for a Jonathan
By Bill Stroud
First National Bank of Memphis, Tennessee

After reading Richard Bach's *Jonathan Livingston Seagull*, my mental furniture became crowded with images of soaring wings extended with mathematical precision, conforming to the law of aerodynamics. For days my own activities appeared feather-filtered. I almost became defensive, fearing that the next challenge presented to me in the Marketing Division would surely receive the dramatic response of flapping my arms. Well, why not? Who wants to be an ordinary bird?

After a modicum of naval gazing I then found myself viewing every associate in the bank as a Fletcher meandering through the office with beaks hungry for fishheads and pinions laden with tradition. Then after the initial impact of that symbolic, exhilarating story of Jonathan's adventure in self-fulfillment, I coolly decided that Bach had actually crystallized in dramatic form the Herzbergian, Maslovian and McGregorian dream of a self-actuated organizational man.

Ask any personnel director to characterize the "promising young executive type" which somewhere must be hidden within or behind—all those psychological profile sheets cluttering his desk. I am sure that when he concludes his apostrophe, you will be convinced that he is looking for the man who has the intellect of an Einstein, the industriousness of a Glenn Turner, and the soul of a Billy Graham.

But in reality what we are looking for—and hope to become ourselves—is a Jonathan. What a bird! What a flight!

Now Jonathan "was no ordinary bird." But he lived in an ordinary flock. (He was a Kierkegaardian individual moving Zarathustrian-like from a Nietzchean-hated herd.) He thought in terms of "doing what was never done." This gull had the gall to even fly in the dark. And to make matters worse, he was audacious to the point of "violating the dignity and tradition of the Gull Family."

Well, how would you like to be manager of a bird like that? He comes in late and has been out breaking all records. He short-circuits the procedure, joins controversial social groups, and openly proclaims that what has been first in traditional policy is barely second. That is no ordinary bird. And he requires no ordinary manager.

Jonathan couldn't define his life by something he was: being intent on becoming what he could be. He couldn't respond to "know thyself" because he wasn't finished yet. He didn't know where he was going, but was convinced he would enjoy the journey. He did understand one inner compulsion: "I just want to know what I can do in the air and what I can't, that's all, I just want to know," declared Jonathan.

Most organizational birds know too much. With organizational charts as a guide, they stare like owls, flutter around parroting the correct sounds, and live the life of mockingbirds. They see themselves transported F.O.B. to the next echelon in the department. They forget that their wings must flap faster at higher altitudes. They believe, like ordinary gulls, that "it is not flying that matters, but eating." But for Jonathan, "it was not eating that mattered, but flight."

Flight to Jonathan was not his task, it was his challenge. His energy was spent *not on sustaining but attaining*. He never depreciated the need for sustenance, but a fish-head existence was inadequate for his hungering spirit. And ironically, he discoverd that the freedom gained through riding the "high winds" offered him new opportunities to dine on delicacies. From here he saw sunsets never viewed by ordinary gulls; he experienced aesthetic moments: "the speed was power, and the speed was joy, and the speed was pure beauty." Only in these moments was there full realization of the worth of his labor.

49

Now Jonathan never pretended to be the Great White Gull. In fact, he had more tailspins than others. He accepted his limitations, bone and feathers. Yet he never whined about what he was; he was just determined to become what he wasn't. And Jonathan believed that what he wasn't was to be more of what he was: one with "the freedom to be yourself, your true self, here and now."

Jonathan didn't even feel he was special. He labored hard to soar high. *He didn't just dream about flying; he flew about dreaming. And though he asked strange questions he never questioned asking. That darn bird was strange!*

Like most achievers, organizational Jonathans try our patience and confound our plans. Their spirits stimulate us only a little more than they threaten us. Those independent souls who take such risks above traditional clouds make us dizzy. But each of us secretly admires them, for they somehow stimulate the Jonathan Livingston Seagull in us.

APPENDIX B
EXAMPLES OF PROJECTS SPEARHEADED BY
CREATIVE INDIVIDUALS OR GROUPS

Veronica Maz, Ph.D.
Washington, D.C.

After a few months of cooking hot meals for destitute men on the streets of Washington, D.C., Veronica Maz quit her job as a professor of sociology to devote all of her time to feeding the poor. She soon learned that while there were ten shelters for men in the city, there were none for women who wandered the streets, carrying their possessions in shopping bags and sleeping in bus terminals and doorways.

Determined to help those women, Dr. Maz raised money from the private sector and friends to rent an old house in a run-down section of the city where she could provide food and shelter. Since its opening in 1976, the House of Ruth has housed 2,500 women for a day, week, or month at a time. In return for food and a bed, the women help clean and cook. Besides the operation of the house, they are involved in the beginning of their own return to self-sufficiency. Eighty percent of the women who are taken in find jobs, housing, and medical or public assistance. Whenever possible, they are reconnected with their families.

To assist residents with their transition from the House of Ruth to the community, Dr. Maz rented a nearby building of apartments. Women who choose to move there are given help in finding jobs in return for a nominal rent. In addition, Dr. Maz has opened a separate shelter for battered wives. To support both houses, she solicits the community for donations and volunteer support. In 1977 two thrift shops operated by the House of Ruth and staffed by volunteers raised $250,000.

Herman Meyersburg, M.D.
Montgomery County, Maryland

Dr. Herman Meyersburg has been providing free or low cost medical services to the poor in one of the nation's richest counties for several years. The idea for the program came during his tenure as a volunteer tutor for children of low-income families. Concerned about the lack of adequate health care for them, he and a colleague founded Mobile Medical Care, a clinic in a van. Operating with no official or financial support from local health agencies, the van delivered medical care on a weekly basis. Within a short time, several other doctors learned of the project through word of mouth and volunteered their services. Their help, along with positive community response, made it possible to open three more mobile clinics in different parts of the county.

By 1977, Montgomery County, United Way, and Medicare/Medicaid programs had begun to support the program financially, providing for needed equipment and a small staff. Mobile Medical Care clinics are run by 120 volunteers recruited and trained by Dr. Meyersburg and other veterans of the organization. They include physicians from nearby governmental agencies, military bases, and medical facilities, as well as physicians from private practice and hospitals. There are also crews of nurses, lab technicians, and medical transcribers. In one year, some 2,500 patient visits were handled by the four clinics. Many patients now regard the volunteers as their family doctors.

Georgia Morikawa
Honolulu, Hawaii

Georgia Morikawa has been deaf from birth, but for the past 30 years she has served as an advocate for Hawaii's 56,000 hearing-impaired residents. In 1950 she founded the Hawaii Club for Deaf for recreation, interaction, and mutual support. In the '60s she became active in athletic programs for the deaf, managing a volleyball team and raising half of the $12,000 needed for national and international competition. (She cosigned loans to cover the remainder.) The popularity and success of these games gave impetus to the creation of the Hawaii World Games for the Deaf, a formal program now operating in conjunction with the YMCA.

More recently, Morikawa successfully lobbied the State Division of Vocational Rehabilitation to hire a counselor to make employment training programs accessible to the deaf. She also promoted the formation of a private sector advocacy organization—the Hawaii Council for the Hearing Impaired—which secured federal funds to establish an information and referral center for the deaf. The center monitors government and community-based services to bring them to the attention of the deaf. Through the council, the state increasingly has been made aware of the needs of its deaf constituency.

After enlisting the support of the government and private sector, Morikawa began a newsletter listing and explaining new opportunities for the deaf. As a result, the local Social Security office reported that for the first time they were inundated by requests from the deaf for benefits they had not known they were entitled to. And in 1977 a Deaf Awareness Week was proclaimed in Hawaii for the first time.

Project CARE (Concerned
Adolescents for Retired Elderly)
Buffalo, New York

Project CARE, a nondenominational effort sponsored by the Youth Department of the Catholic Diocese of Buffalo, involves 700 young people in a visiting and outreach program that reaches more than 300 senior citizens and shut-ins. Teenagers involved in Project CARE first must attend a training program. Then they are assigned in pairs to visit weekly with the person to whom they have been matched, running errands, doing household chores, or just talking. Each volunteer team is matched to an individual who lives within walking distance of their homes, so visits are convenient and do not depend on parents for transportation. In this way, the elderly feel more willing to call on the volunteers for help with special projects or with occasional tasks which might be dangerous for them.

Through Project CARE the elderly not only receive practical and necessary assistance but also experience relief from loneliness and isolation. For the teenagers, the program provides exposure to new experiences, insights into the aging process, a heightened sense of responsibility and potential for service, and a new respect for a population they may know nothing about. Many who were asked to make a six-month commitment have averaged a two-year involvement in Project CARE.

EXAMPLES OF INDIVIDUALS WHO HAVE OVERCOME APPARENT
OBSTACLES TO ACHIEVE PERSONAL GOALS

• An article about General William C. Westmoreland included a letter about him from a high school friend: "Westmoreland excelled in almost everything he attempted. There was one exception; he couldn't spell—and his English work was often marked down for faulty spelling. He showed, however, that ingenuity can overcome handicaps. He desperately wanted a good grade on a certain composition. He got it. His paper took the form of an exchange of letters between two people—poorly educated mountaineers, neither of whom could spell!"

● W. Somerset Maugham used to maintain that, if he hadn't stammered, he would probably have gone to Cambridge like his brothers. In such case, he would likely have become a don and published an occasional dreary book about French literature. Instead, thanks to his stammer, he avoided Cambridge and became a world-famous novelist.

● Albert was so slow to learn to talk that his parents thought him abnormal. His teachers called him a misfit and classmates avoided him. He failed his first college entrance exam. Fortunately his last name was Einstein and he turned out to be the most famous scientist in the world.

EXAMPLES OF CREATIVE IDEAS THAT PAID OFF FINANCIALLY

● Just released from the Army after World War II, young DeWitt Wallace told his father he had an idea. He wanted to start a new magazine. It would include articles and stories republished in "digest" form. His father expressed some doubts. The venture could cost at least $10,000, he said. Chances of success seemed minimal; nothing like it had been tried before. Besides, his son's college English grades had not been outstanding. Young DeWitt went ahead anyway. The result was the Reader's Digest, the world's most widely read magazine with a circulation of thirty million copies a month in thirteen languages.

● Back in 1914, a young Minnesota Swede named Carl Eric Wickman opened an agency for the Hupmobile auto. When he didn't sell a single car, friends suggested he had better return to mining. Instead the stubborn Swede started using one of his Hupmobiles as a taxi for miners between the small towns of Hibbing and Alice. For a four-mile jaunt over unpaved roads he charged 15 cents. Wickman's "jitney bus" proved popular and was rebuilt to include extra seats, with additional passengers clinging to the running boards and fenders. A few years later, with new partners, he was driving cars between Hibbing and Duluth. One innkeeper said the grey, dusty cars reminded him of so many greyhounds. Perhaps you guessed it. Wickman's jitney service eventually became the Greyhound Bus Company, the world's largest inter-city passenger carrier.

APPENDIX C
QUOTATIONS RELATING TO CREATIVITY

"Democracy, like love, can survive any attack—save neglect and indifference."
Paul Sweeney

"The capacity of our people to believe stubbornly and irrepressibly that this is a world worth saving and that intelligence and energy and goodwill might save it is one of the most endearing and bracing of American traits."
John Gardner
Self Renewal

"The answer to helplessness is not so very complicated. A man can do something for peace without having to jump into politics. Each man has inside him a basic decency and goodness. If he listens to it and acts on it, he is giving a great deal of what the world needs most. It's not complicated but it takes courage. It takes courage for a man to listen to his own goodness and act on it. Do we dare to be ourselves? This is the question that counts."
Pablo Casals
quoted by Norman Cousins
in *Present Tense*

"All the forces in the world are not so powerful as an idea whose time has come."
Victor Hugo

"The young do not know enough to be prudent and therefore they attempt the impossible—and achieve it generation after generation."

Pearl Buck

And at age 93, Pablo Casals said,

"Each day I am reborn. Each day I must begin again. For the past 80 years I have started each day in the same manner. It is not a mechanical routine but something essential to my daily life. I go to the piano, and I play two preludes and a fugue of Bach. It is a sort of benediction on the house. But it also is a rediscovery of the world of which I have the joy of being a part. It fills me with awareness of the wonder of life, with a feeling of the incredible marvel of being a human being. The music is never the same for me, never. Each day it is something new, fantastic, and unbelievable."

quoted by Alber Kahn
in *Joys and Sorrows*

"For most of us, creativity is more of a dull glow than a divine spark. And the more fanning it receives, the brighter it will burn."

James Adams
in *Conceptual Blockbusting*

"To be nobody but yourself in a world that is trying its best night and day to make you everybody else is to fight the hardest battle any human being can fight and keep on fighting."

e. e. cummings

"If a man does not keep pace with his companions, perhaps it is because he hears a different drummer. Let him step to the music which he hears, however measured or far away."

Henry Thoreau

"There ain't no rules around here! We're trying to accomplish something."

Thomas Edison

"With each passage from one stage of human growth to the next we, too, must shed a protective structure. We are left exposed and vulnerable—but also yeasty and embryonic again, capable of stretching in ways we hadn't known before."

Gail Sheehy
Passages

CHAPTER II

Problem Solving:
Generating Creative
Alternatives for Action

The uncreative mind can spot wrong answers, but it takes a creative mind to spot wrong questions.

Anthony Jay

The following anecdote has been related about Dr. Henry Forbes:

One day Forbes had a vision of a long line of patients waiting to see him—a line extending far out of his office and into the street. He already knew what their diagnosis was: each had sprained an ankle stepping into a deep hole in the sidewalk outside. Forbes felt keenly the source of his own dilemma. It was simple: he was just so busy seeing patients in pain with sprained ankles that he never had an opportunity to go out and fill the hole.[1]

This is a graphic illustration of how too many managers function much of the time. They are so busy treating symptoms, they rarely get at the causes of their problems.

In an effort to combat this kind of "crisis band-aiding," I am beginning this chapter on problem solving by examining some of the problems themselves. What are some of the sweeping societal changes and trends impacting almost all of our organizations as we move toward the twenty-first century? How can we understand them and effectively help our organizations adapt and adjust? How can we learn to do preventive problem solving? How can we learn to be more creative, not only as individuals, but as groups as well?

LOOKING TO THE FUTURE

For any who doubt the changing nature of our world, I recommend reading Alvin Toffler's books *Future Shock* and *The Third Wave* and the rich array of books and articles in any public library today on *futurism*. Futurists seriously analyze trends (cultural, business, political, economic) and forecast the alternatives for the world of the future. Paul Dickson, in his book *The Future File*, claims that futurism is "the fastest-growing educational phenomenon in history, the most important new concept to hit government in a hundred years, an invaluable tool for industry, and a major breakthrough in human thinking . . . the Library of Congress has estimated that close to 100 private research institutions and think-tanks in the United States alone are involved in some aspect of futures research."[2] He goes on to state that we are, in fact, creating the future right now with today's decisions, discoveries, policies, actions, and inactions. This reaffirms the critical nature of our decision to conform or create. The future of society depends on it!

The inventor C.F. Kettering once said, "My interest is in the future, because I'm going to spend the rest of my life there." And Thomas Jefferson observed, "I like the dreams of the future better than the history of the past."

Obviously, most of us are not in a position to hire "think tanks" or futuristic researchers for our organizations. But we can do some serious examination of reports and articles available to us. Some of these are generated internally in the form of annual reports, needs assessments, cost-benefit analysis figures, evaluations, turnover studies, etc. And we all have access to libraries, chambers of commerce, state and federal commissions, and agencies that have rich resources to help us understand local, state, national, and worldwide trends. But do we care enough to even look for the information? And if we find it, do we go a step further and apply it to our own situation? It should serve as the basis for all our long-range plans.

The most helpful question you can ask whenever you read information relating to the future is "So what? How does it relate to our organization?" May I illustrate with a personal example. I am a consultant and trainer for human services agencies, primarily specializing in helping these organizations develop and manage more effective volunteer programs. In the course of my work, I have traveled across the United States and Canada and conducted workshops for well over 15,000 people. In these workshops, I began to notice a consistency of comments regarding trends in volunteerism that indicated major changes were occurring in who is volunteering and why. These trends seemed to be true for most parts of the continent, in both urban and rural areas (i.e., fewer traditional female housewife volunteers; more male, youth, and senior volunteers; increasing numbers of volunteers who also hold paid jobs, etc.). I decided to spend a morning in our city library to see if I could find some solid data relating to these apparent trends.

I discovered a fascinating publication entitled *The Statistical Abstract of the U.S.–1977.* It is data based on the 1976 census and was just what I needed. Some of the pertinent statistics I found were:

1. One in every three marriages in the United States ended in divorce in 1976.

2. There were 3 million more female heads of households in 1976 than in 1960. (Heads of households are defined as those who were responsible for themselves and/or themselves and children.)

3. The number of working women nearly doubled between 1950 and 1976. (Another resource indicated that in 1979, 47% of the total United States workforce was female and 49.4% of all married women worked outside the home.)

4. The number of two-person households almost doubled between 1960 and 1976. This represented both young couples not having children and older couples living longer.

5. The percentage of our population over forty-five years of age was 31% in 1976. It is projected to be 42.5% by 2050. A Denver *Post* article stated that by the year 2000, one in every eight Americans will be over the age of 65.

Dun's Review, May 1979, added these startling predictions:

1. By 1985 there will be more divorces annually than first marriages.
2. Almost one out of every three households will be headed by a single person by 1985.
3. By 1990 only half of the nation's children will live with both parents (two out of three do today.)

The Chicago *Tribune*, in an article published Sept. 18, 1979, added the following information: In 1900, the average woman lived 47 years and spent 18 of them in childbearing; in 1979, the average woman lives 77 years and spends less than ten exclusively raising children.

Now, to follow my own advice I had to ask, *So what for the field of volunteerism?* I think these few statistics help explain virtually all of the trends that had been identified by observation in the field. Take for example the fewer number of female volunteers:

Erma Bombeck, in a *TWA Ambassador* article in July 1978, sums it up beautifully:

> *I cover the utility room beat. You cannot imagine the changes that have affected the American housewife during the last 10-15 years.*
> *She's down ¼ of a child.*
> *Works outside the home.*
> *Her marriage made in heaven is virtually impossible to get parts for.*
> *The pushbuttons are fighting back.*
> *She is no longer being fulfilled by visiting her meat in the food locker and putting lids down.*
> *In fact, she is all but extinct. What has emerged as a brighter, more aware human being who does what she wants through choice.*[3]

With this sort of information, agency directors and their management groups can begin to look seriously and creatively at future implications regarding recruiting volunteers (who and where), types of volunteer assignments, when volunteers are available, length of assignments, reward systems, etc. The volunteer world has changed dramatically and only those agencies who know that, understand it, and ask the critical "so what" questions will survive. The same kind of information is vitally important for business leaders to utilize in planning for the future.

Many of you work in service institutions of one kind or another. Peter Drucker, in a most thought-provoking article entitled "Managing the Third Sector" (*Wall Street Journal*, October 3, 1978), made these important observations:

58

> *Service institutions have grown so big that they may now employ more people than federal, state, and local governments put together, and they are so important that we are beginning to talk of a "third sector."*[4] [The other two sectors are the *public* or governmental sector and the *private*, for-profit business sector.]

He includes in this vast third sector non-profit agencies, museums, libraries, orchestras, chambers of commerce, trade associations, professional associations, and public interest lobbies.

Mr. Drucker goes on to comment that so far, little attention has been paid to this third sector and its economics, management, performance, and impact— mostly because its growth is so recent. He then levels this charge at its managers:

> *After such explosive growth, yesterday's way of doing things has become inappropriate, if not counter-productive . . . yet by and large few service institutions attempt to think through the changed circumstances in which they operate. Most believe that all that is required is to run harder and to raise more money.*

Once again, we see the plea for more creativity and innovation in the workplace.

There is one common arena that all managers (whether of public, private, or third-sector organizations) need to examine carefully regarding the future. I am referring to the trends affecting the workforce and patterns of work in this country. In a keynote address to the national meeting of the Organization Development Network in May 1979, Jerome M. Rosow, President of Work in America Institute, made the observations listed below. He forecast five major shifts in the U.S. labor force in the decade of the 1980s. (He based these predictions on the work of Richard Freeman who wrote a chapter for the book entitled *Work in America: The Decade Ahead*, by Rosow and Kerr, New York: Van Nostrand Reinhold, 1979).[5]

Shift #1: The Coming Shortage of Youth. Because of the low birth rate in the 1960s, the number of young workers will drop sharply in the '80s. The 16-24-year-old group of workers will decline 6% or by 2.8 million youth between 1980 and 1985.

Shift #2: The Middle-Age Bulge. There will be an amazing demographic bunching of the 25-44-age workers in the 1980s. "In 1975, there were 39 million workers in this age bracket, and by 1990 there will be 60.5 million, *an extraordinary jump of 55%.*" They will comprise 52% of the total workforce. This would lead the experts to anticipate intense competition for promotions and severe disappointments due to limited opportunities for upward mobility. "Some of the major personnel and management problems of the eighties will revolve around this critical group in the workforce."

Shift #3: *The Expanding Role of Women.* The participation of women in the workforce is expected to increase until by 1990, 61% of all American women will be working for pay, outside their homes.

Shift #4: *Competition for Desirable Jobs.* The rise in the number of qualified minority and female workers will add to the competition referred to in Shift #2.

Shift #5: *Increased Employment of Older Workers.* American retirement patterns are changing primarily due to the extension of mandatory retirement to age 70, the increasing number of older persons, and the effects of double-digit inflation.

Rosow concluded with these summary observations:

1. The cross currents in the labor force in the 1980s will reflect the effects of the shortage of youth, the increasing role of women, and the continuing pressure to absorb the highly educated "bottleneck" generation. One of the most puzzling problems in the 1980s will relate to the increased role of older workers and the shifting preferences away from early retirement.

2. Changing employee attitudes and values have created an entirely new set of workplace expectations. The major sociological trends of the 1970s will persist in the coming decade: the challenge to authority, the persistent problems of confidence in our institutions, the trends towards increased leisure, and the growing demand for participation in decision making. Economic issues will become more severe because of persistent high inflation and the national problem of sustaining any improvements in the real standard of living for American workers.

3. The decline in the rate of productivity growth in the United States cannot be rationalized purely in terms of capital and research factors. The human factor in the productivity equation requires greater attention and provides one of the hopeful responses to the U.S. slowdown.

4. Finally, new patterns of work, which have evolved during this

60

decade, will grow in variety and scope in the period ahead. Work patterns will become more compatible with the changing composition of the workforce, the growing demands for family and leisure time, the urbanization of society, the over-dependence on the private automobile in a period of run-away energy costs, the emerging multiple-worker family, and the need to reduce occupational stress to improve productivity.[6]

It would be well for every organization to use information like this as a springboard for discussion at long-range planning meetings and management retreats. The agenda could be fashioned to allow for creative think time and problem solving based on the confrontation of "so what" questions related to each trend as it might impact your organization, its workers, and consumers in the decade ahead.

The following is an example of how relating data to the future plans of an organization helped foster significant insights.

A professor of business administration at the University of Colorado tells the story of how he once asked the head planner for a well-known fast food giant how his organization handled its planning. This executive reportedly said that they have a room at the top of their headquarters building that has nothing in it but a skylight and a waterbed. Each manager of a major department is required to spend a minimum of one hour per week in creative think-time on the waterbed. As chief of planning he stated he spent an hour per day there, allowing himself undisturbed planning time. He said it was during one of his "think sessions" a few years ago that the impact of zero population growth on their future became devastatingly clear to him. Until that time, all of their advertising had been aimed at youngsters and their primary sales campaign had revolved around a clown. From that point forward, their product line changed (including breakfasts and he-man burgers for the working man) and all advertising was redirected to adults or families (secretaries, school teachers, truck drivers, ball teams, families on an outing). Changing birth rates—this is a critical piece of information that could spell either growth or ruin for many organizations.

Many times organizations and the people in them are not creative simply because they are not aware that they need to be. Important information is neither gathered nor made available—so people assume everything is fine the way it is. I have repeatedly found that sharing the kind of information included in this chapter relating to changes and trends has a dynamic effect on groups. Once they know the facts, lively discussion inevitably follows. People begin to reexamine assumptions and redefine problems; and then creative problem solving can begin.

LINKING PERSONAL AND ORGANIZATIONAL NEEDS FOR CREATIVITY

It would seem that we have thus far articulated two critical needs facing almost every organization as we move into the 1980s and '90s.

1. The need for individuals who work in organizations to have more opportunity to be creative; and
2. The need for organizations to become more innovative in order to survive amidst the incredible changes that will impact them as they move into the twenty-first century.

I'd like to share a few more insights on both. At a recent national meeting of the American Society of Training Directors, the noted management authorities Bob Blake and Jane Mouton (authors of *The Managerial Grid*) stated that "our society is showing signs of going down the tubes. Productivity, creativity, education, job satisfaction and health care all show declines or serious problems . . . our nation faces critical issues in human factors."[7]

Don Scobel of Eaton Corporation has outlined three fundamental requirements to improve the quality of worklife in organizations today: (1) strip away the mistrusts and unnecessary regimentation of the workplace; (2) encourage greater involvement of employees in their jobs; and (3) foster participation by employees in decision-making processes.[8]

All three of these requirements address the need for managers to learn how to work more effectively with their people in group problem solving and decision-making situations. It is one thing *to say* you want to involve others in decisions affecting them. . . it is quite another *to do* that well. It is the intent of this chapter to help you develop both an understanding of the problem-solving process and the skills to help you do it more effectively.

If you have experienced difficulty in this area, rest assured that you have a great deal of company. Bradford observed,

Against this background of desperate need for understanding and skill in group productivity is the really tragic picture of the almost universal inability of people to operate effectively in group situations. Anyone familiar with the average committee, with its difficulty in reaching decisions, its incomplete discussions and immature ideas, its person-

ality clashes and emotional stress, its inability to move from decisions into actions should have no difficulty accepting this statement. [9]

As one pundit put it, a committee is often something you establish so you can share the blame!

Obviously the process your group chooses to solve its problems needs to be contingent upon several things:

—The nature of the problem

—The time restraints imposed (is a deadline imminent; are you in the middle of a crisis; or are you long-range or "preventive" planning?)

—The level of trust in the group

—The size of the group

—The levels and kinds of power within the group

—The history of past conflicts

—The type of leadership utilized

It is important to keep these in mind as we explore various problem-solving modes.

In his book *Management: Tasks, Responsibilities, Practices*, Peter Drucker sums up the critical importance of this topic:

An established company which in an age demanding innovation is not capable of innovation is doomed to decline and extinction. And a management which in such a period does not know how to manage innovation is incompetent and unequal to its task. Managing innovation will increasingly become a challenge to management, and especially to top management, and a touchstone of its competence. [10]

I rest my case for the need for more creative problem solving. We are now ready to examine some practical concepts and techniques for how to do it.

CREATIVE PROBLEM-SOLVING TECHNIQUES

One of the dangers many middle managers face (especially in human service agencies) is that they become so accustomed to people expecting the nearly impossible from them that they begin to believe they can and should be all things to all people. I recently saw this poster on the wall of a colleague's office:

We, the willing
Led by the unknowing
Are doing the impossible for the ungrateful
We have done so much for so long with so little
We're qualified to do anything with nothing.

This kind of attitude too often results in working harder and harder and faster and faster, until the manager either burns out or gives up. One of the antidotes is to become skilled at problem solving. Too much valuable time goes into solving the wrong problems, and dealing with things that should never have been allowed to become problems, or dealing with the results rather than the causes of problems.

James Adams, in his book *Conceptual Blockbusting*, identifies one of the crucial issues.

Few people like problems. Hence the natural tendency in problem solving is to pick the first solution that comes to mind and run with it. The disadvantage of this approach is that one may either run off a cliff or into a worse problem than the one started with. A better strategy in solving problems is to select the most attractive path from many ideas and concepts. [11]

The key to what he suggests lies in the ability of a group or person to conceptualize many possible solutions from which to choose. But he cautions, "A good conceptualizer must be a creative conceptualizer. The mental characteristics which seem to make one creative not only are valuable in idea-having, but also better equip one to find and define problems and implement the resulting solutions."

Again we see how badly creative individuals are needed within groups and organizations! Take a moment to review the characteristics of right- and left-brained thinkers (page 21). The logic of needing both in problem-solving situations becomes immediately apparent. Left-brained people are often referred to as *preceptive information-gatherers*: they begin working on a problem as if they already had a mental image of what they need to know, so they simply look for facts that fit their preconceived image. They also tend to pay close attention to the relationship among all the data gathered and have a need to tie it together in some logical sequence. They are usually thorough and organized.

Right-brained persons (often called *receptive thinkers*) approach a problem very differently. They usually do not begin with a pre-conceived picture of what is needed, so they do not try to fit their information and data into a scheme or system. They illicit, digest, and ponder all sorts of seemingly unrelated facts and clues. Part of the fun in problem solving for them is finding a whole that all these parts relate to, and that is more than likely something new and different from what has been before. They often have giant leaps of understanding or insights (the aha!)—rather than moving in a methodical, step-by-step fashion.

You can readily see why even though it makes sense to have both types of thinkers in a group, due to their unique perspectives and contributions to finding "best" solutions, it is very difficult to do so. Neither of them understands or really trusts the other. It is up to you, the manager or the group leader, to understand and value them both and to help build the bridge between them.

Creative problem solving has been defined simply as the degree to which one can think up different, more effective approaches. To do that, we definitely need the richness of both the preceptive and receptive thinkers in our organizations.

Each can learn from the other and in the process become more like the wise, well-rounded, truly creative person described by Robert Heinlein:

> A human being should be able to change a diaper, plan an invasion, butcher a hog, conn a ship, design a building, write a sonnet, balance accounts, build a wall, set a bone, comfort the dying, take orders, give orders, cooperate, act alone, solve equations, analyze a new problem, pitch manure, program a computer, cook a tasty meal, fight efficiently, die gallantly . . . specialization is for insects.

PROBLEM SOLVING MODELS

Moskowitz, in his *Creative Problem Solving Workbook*, visually depicts the interplay of right and left brain activity as follows:

The Creative and the Judgment Sides of Problem Solving

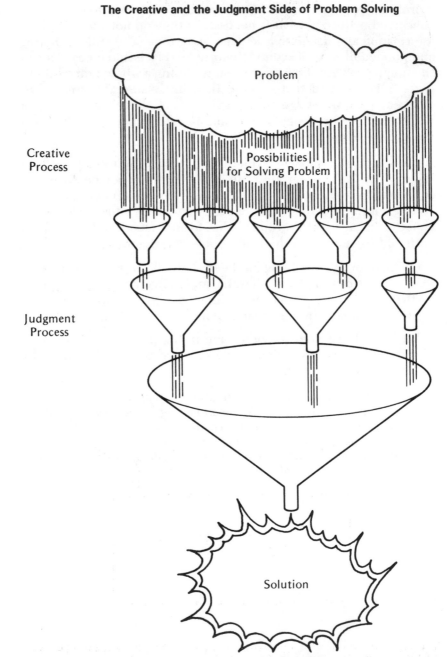

Problem

Creative Process

Possibilities for Solving Problem

Judgment Process

Solution

A Blend of Creativity and Judgment

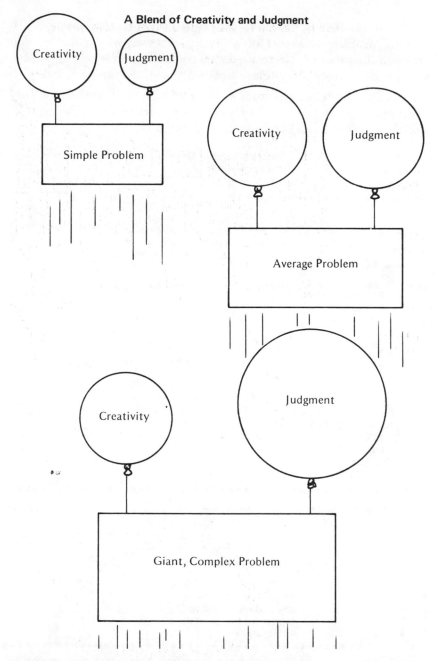

It is important to have a logical system to use in assessing and solving problems—a sort of analytical framework to guide you through the process. There are dozens of books and articles suggesting a wide variety of systems. Several have been helpful to me.

This first model comes from Koberg and Bagnall, authors of *The Universal Traveler. A Soft-Systems Guide to: Creativity, Problem-Solving and the Process of Design Goals.*

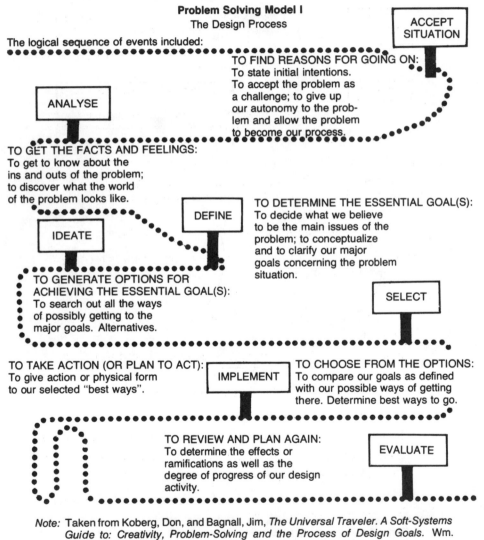

Problem Solving Model I
The Design Process

The logical sequence of events included:

ACCEPT SITUATION

TO FIND REASONS FOR GOING ON:
To state initial intentions.
To accept the problem as a challenge; to give up our autonomy to the problem and allow the problem to become our process.

ANALYSE

TO GET THE FACTS AND FEELINGS:
To get to know about the ins and outs of the problem; to discover what the world of the problem looks like.

DEFINE

TO DETERMINE THE ESSENTIAL GOAL(S):
To decide what we believe to be the main issues of the problem; to conceptualize and to clarify our major goals concerning the problem situation.

IDEATE

TO GENERATE OPTIONS FOR ACHIEVING THE ESSENTIAL GOAL(S):
To search out all the ways of possibly getting to the major goals. Alternatives.

SELECT

TO TAKE ACTION (OR PLAN TO ACT):
To give action or physical form to our selected "best ways".

IMPLEMENT

TO CHOOSE FROM THE OPTIONS:
To compare our goals as defined with our possible ways of getting there. Determine best ways to go.

TO REVIEW AND PLAN AGAIN:
To determine the effects or ramifications as well as the degree of progress of our design activity.

EVALUATE

Note: Taken from Koberg, Don, and Bagnall, Jim, *The Universal Traveler. A Soft-Systems Guide to: Creativity, Problem-Solving and the Process of Design Goals.* Wm. Kaufman, Inc., 1974, p. 17.

68

For those of you who are more comfortable with a left-brain version, let's restate it this way:

Accept Situation	To find reasons for going on. (Accept the problem as a challenge).
Analyze	To get the facts and feelings. (Size up the situation).
Define	To determine and clarify the essential goals and main issues of the problem. (Develop conceptual guidelines).
Ideate	To generate *options* for achieving the essential goals and alternatives. (Generate ideas).
Select	To choose from the options the best way to go. (Decide from all alternatives).
Implement	To take action on the decision. (Make idea happen).
Evaluate	To review and plan again. Determine the effects, ramifications, and progress toward stated goals. (Review progress—plan ahead).

A second model comes from the AFL-CIO's Department of Community Services. It offers some guidelines regarding both the intellectual and the psychological aspect of group problem solving:

The Intellectual Level of Problem Solving

1. *Define and describe the problem:* its symptoms and history. (How do we know there is a problem?)

2. *Search for causes*

   —Find the facts and classify them (who, what, where, when, and why?)

   —Search out the political, social, economic, and moral implications of the problem (so what?)

   —Discover the principle and values involved

   —Develop theories as to cause

   —Make predictions of what will happen if problem continues

3. *List alternative solutions* (What are all the possible solutions?)

   —Identify desired goals

   —Test proposed courses of action in terms of resources available and the consequences of the actions

   —Choose best solution

69

4. *Decide on means and methods of implementing the chosen solution* (who, what, how, etc.)

5. *Evaluate the outcome*

The problem-solving system most generally breaks down at point three—generating alternatives and choosing the best one. The Department of Community Services suggests the following steps to ensure that you get beyond (3) and move on to successful implementation.

Step 1–Production of an idea: withhold judgment on new options and ideas at this point (here is where the left brain people must learn to tolerate their right-brained co-workers).

Step 2–Evaluation of the idea: discuss ideas in the whole group and test out positive and negative consequences; seek all alternatives.

Step 3–Consensus: determine the criteria for selection of the solution; what are the critical factors in *this* situation?

Step 4–Planning for action: set realistic goals, objectives, and action steps; determine responsibilities regarding implementation; what is needed and who has it? What are the assignments?

Step 5–Implementation and Feedback: Be sure group has obtained the commitment of those carrying out the solution; be sensitive to feedback regarding positive and negative consequences and feelings at each stage.

The emotions, needs, beliefs, values, assumptions, and expectations of each group member have a decided effect on the outcome of the solution and how each person feels about the process.

The Psychological Level of Problem Solving

—*Personal assumptions.* Be wary of assuming everyone else shares your diagnosis of the problem and agrees with what is the best solution. (I learned this in a creative writing course. It was amazing how when a class of thirty students was given the same two-line phrase and instructed to write a story—no two were ever alike. Some would end up comedies; some tragedies; some factual news stories; some romances; some horror stories. We all had the same information but our assumptions about the data differed amazingly!)

—*Personal needs.* Some group members need more support and warmth; others want challenge and action; others control and power. The challenge in a group is to try to meet as many personal needs of the members through judicious assignments of roles and responsibilities as possible.

—*Self-Concept.* Members need to be encouraged to view themselves as valued contributors if their self-concept is to be enhanced in the problem-solving process. Watch for domineering, aggressive members who utilize "put downs" and "one-upsmanship" tactics.

INTRODUCING CREATIVITY INTO
THE PROBLEM-SOLVING PROCESS

No matter what system you use in your problem solving, the results can be greatly affected by how you approach the whole exercise. If you leave it up to your rational, "no nonsense" left brain alone, you will probably come up with a solution that works, but it will all too often be sterile, logical, and not very innovative. And, if you do think to involve others in the process, you will probably make sure it is done efficiently, with no unnecessary waste of time.

John Ingalls suggests he has frequently seen this kind of left-brain problem solving practiced in business and industry and summarizes the process as follows:

1. A problem situation arises;

2. A meeting or series of meetings is set up to discuss the problem. Facts, more facts, and counter facts are produced. Rebuttals to the counterfacts are then offered but are usually ignored;

3. A plan for resolution is formulated based on the beliefs of the senior manager presiding at the meeting(s). (Other beliefs are generally not discussed);

4. A solution is sought in accordance with the plan dictated;

5. A periodic review of progress is conducted; and

6. A decision is eventually made to change people or the organization's structure when the plan fails. [12]

Does this sound familiar? It is no wonder so little innovation occurs!

Let's explore some other options regarding how you can involve others in the process of problem solving, still using a method or system, but just incorporating some possibilities for creativity along the way.

71

First, try thinking of problems as opportunities . . . *situations in need of improvement* instead of something negative, painful, or frightening. Then go one step further and dare to view the process of finding a solution as an opportunity for your group to grow their creative muscles and even have fun together. In order to make this happen, I would like to summarize several critical factors you need to tend to:

—Identify the *real* problem—so you are working on the right thing;

—Involve the *right* people—those affected by the problem and outcome;

—Use a participative, enabling style of leadership in the group; encourage everyone to contribute;

—Create a comfortable, enthusiastic climate—so it is safe to participate;

—Consider feelings and attitudes about the problems, as well as facts;

—Use creative techniques to generate ideas and alternative solutions;

—Evaluate carefully—remember, you want the *best* answer, so have patience;

—Decide and act, involving the group affected in the planning and implementation; and

—Have fun!

(You may want to assess the strengths and weaknesses of your group right now. If so, the instrument included in the Appendix of this chapter will be of help.)

ANTICIPATE BLOCKS TO CREATIVE PROBLEM SOLVING

In Chapter I, we discussed the blocks we need to recognize and overcome to be creative as individuals. It might be helpful to spend a moment rereading those Sections (pp. 31 to 47). James Adams warns us in his book *Conceptual Blockbusting* that there are other blocks we need to understand because they affect our creativity within groups and organizations.[13]

PERCEPTUAL BLOCKS

How does this look? Perceptual blocks are obstacles that keep us from perceiving clearly what the problems really are and what information we need to solve them. Some manifestations of these blocks are that we delineate problems too narrowly (imposing too many assumed limits and boundaries); we are unable to see them from various points of view and therefore suffer from tunnel vision; we see what we expect and want to see; we think we already know all we need to know about them; or, we fail to use all our sensory inputs.

What can be done about it? First of all, we need to spend more time defining the problem and exploring alternative ways of stating it. (Is the problem two-hour lunch breaks, or employee boredom and frustration, or unclear goals and job definition?)

A good example of an exercise to help learn to delineate and state problems in a variety of ways is suggested in *Conceptual Blockbusting*:

Exercise: *The next time you have a problem, solve it. Then, at your leisure, list at least three different possible delimitations of the problem and answers you might have come up with in each case. For instance, suppose that you are in your late thirties, your children are well into school, your husband is establishing a name for himself in his profession, and you are bored.*

You might formulate your problems as "difficulty in establishing contact with the real world." You might contact several people you know and find a job as a secretary for a personable and rising young star in an interesting company. After a few exciting days in your new life, ask yourself how else you might have formulated your problem, and what might have happened. Perhaps:

1. *You might have considered your problem to be "difficulty in dispelling boredom during the day" (a more delimited statement). You might have taken up several crafts, involved yourself in many lunches, coffees, and volunteer activities, and attended many classes;*

or:

2. *You might have phrased your problem as "lack of a sufficiently challenging and productive career, now that the child-raising, home-establishing phase of life is under control" (a less delimited statement). You might then have spent a large amount of effort outlining your goals and deciding how to best accomplish them and ended up as a law student.*

or:

3. *You might have decided that the problem is "role stereotyping which does not result in natural fulfillment of women" (even less delimited).*

You might have talked to people you know, professional people, people in educational institutions, and others and decided that a large-scale social problem exists. You might have then organized a city-wide, state-wide, or even a national organization oriented toward helping women, such as you, to better enter the professional world. [14]

This example illustrates beautifully how radically different the solutions can be *depending on how you perceive the problem.*

Another concept that helps with this block is de Bono's notion about *lateral* versus *vertical* thinking that he discusses in his book *New Think.* He states that vertical thinking is when you start with a single idea or concept and just keep going with it until you reach a solution. Lateral thinking, on the other hand, causes you to generate several ways of seeing the problem before ever seeking a solution. He uses the process of digging holes to illustrate:

Logic is the tool that is used to dig holes deeper and bigger, to make them altogether better holes. But if the hole is in the wrong place, then no amount of improvement is going to put it in the right place. No matter how obvious this may seem to every digger, it is still easier to go on digging in the same place than to start all over again in a new place. Vertical thinking is digging in the same hole deeper; lateral thinking is trying again elsewhere . . . . Breakthroughs usually result from someone abandoning a partly-dug hole and beginning over in a different place. [15]

ENVIRONMENTAL BLOCKS

How does this look? These are restraints on creativity imposed on us by our social or physical environment in the workplace. They are manifested by lack of cooperation and trust among colleagues and co-workers; an autocratic boss who does not value others' ideas; physical distractions such as space and noise problems; or lack of support for actualizing new ideas.

What can be done about it? It is terribly important for us to realize the tremendous impact the *climate* of a group or organization has on its members and their feelings about their work. The basic question you need to ask yourself and others is "How does it feel to work here?" (That is basically what climate is.)

One of the best books I have found in helping me to understand and assess organizational climate and then determine ways to change it is *The Feel of the Work Place,* by Steele and Jenks. [16] Two of their questionnaires are particularly useful. I highly recommend that you take time out right now to complete them. It would be helpful to have your staff do so as well.

Following their questionnaires is an instrument I developed for my first book, *The Effective Management of Volunteer Programs*, that would be particularly useful for volunteer organizations to utilize as a preface to problem solving or yearly planning. It also examines climate from both the staff and volunteers' perspective.

A Climate Questionnaire

How is the weather in your organization? Stormy? Sunny? Constantly changing? By thinking of your organization in terms of a weather metaphor, it is sometimes easier to see more clearly the realities of its "climate." That is the combination of factors which sets the tone of an organization and so clearly affects its functioning.

It is important to diagnose the problems of an organization's climate in order to understand what might need to be changed or improved in it. The following questions can serve to foster fruitful discussions about the nature and needs of an organization's climate.

How much do I need to wear foul-weather gear here?

How changeable is the weather and what regular warning signs occur before it changes?

How comfortable is it for me here? For other people with different styles or roles?

Who are the weather forecasters that we rely on to predict what things will be like here?

Are there different zones within the organization that have very different climates? Who tends to end up in each of these zones?

When there are storms in this system, are they fast-moving or slow-moving?

Who can do something about the weather here, rather than just talk about it?

Which people and what kinds of ideas can grow in this climate, and which die out?

75

Who are the sources of energy in this system? Where are they located?

Is there enough breeze (emotional expressiveness) in this system?

Is there enough precipitation (conflict and challenge) in the system for people to grow?

Still another means of obtaining data about the climate of an organization is to move around in that system and observe settings and how people use them. The setting as a reflection of climate can be understood by asking questions such as:

Where do people tend to go in this space when they have free moments?

What kinds of things have people done to their places to reflect themselves as persons? (If there are few signs of this kind of influence, people may feel transient in this system.)

What do arrangements, locations, furniture, etc. say about relative status or power in this system?

Do the work areas look as if the people in them care about the areas (and also about themselves)?

Do the arrangements of furniture, movable walls, etc., say anything about how people want to relate to one another—close/distant, visible/hidden, free movement/controlled movement, and so on?

Do people use their settings in patterns that suggest they like spending time here? Do they choose to be here when they have an option?

What do facilities and layouts suggest about the norms of the system, and about how loose or constraining the whole normative system feels to members?

Similar questions can be asked when thinking about the physical setting as a cause of a particular climate. For example:

What kind of mood (institutional sameness, vitality, work orientation, etc.) do the arrangements and colors foster here?

Who can get together easily, given this arrangement, and can people develop connections with one another in this setting?

How elaborate are the rules about how the spaces and facilities can be used? To what extent do these rules present a "pressing down" climate, where people are visibly reminded of how little freedom of expression they have?

What do patterns set up by traffic (foot and vehicle), noise, lighting, etc. provide as a climate for existing or growing? Do they make it difficult to experiment, concentrate, demonstrate, and so on?

Note: Taken from Fritz Steele and Stephen Jenks, *The Feel of the Work Place*, Addison-Wesley Publishers, 1977, Chap. 12.

These tools can help you more accurately assess the group's feelings about the climate of your department or organization. But once you get these data, then what do you do? I suggest it be used as a basis for honest discussion at a staff meeting or retreat. Which norms (ways of work) are healthy and which are not? What changes would remove unnecessary blocks to more effective and satisfying functioning in this situation? Climate can be changed!

Steele and Jenks suggest there are three components of a successful change strategy:

The right targets are chosen for change. *Often people try to change climate by changing the wrong thing. For example, a change in formal policies is not likely to change the climate very much if the current climate is suffering from problems related to reward systems or informal norms.*

The right people are involved. *Who needs to be involved to ensure the proposed change is implemented? Do they have a sense of ownership of the change? Do they have the power to make the necessary behavioral or procedural changes?* [See Chapter III to help determine this.]

The right timing is used. *Most organizations have a kind of seasonality. Introducing change at the wrong time in the cycle can greatly increase resistance to change. Changes need to be accepted by those who will be affected by them.*[17]

PROFILE OF VOLUNTEER-STAFF CHARACTERISTICS*

Instructions:

1. Please mark each item below with an "n" at the point on the scale which in your experience best describes your organization *now*.

2. Then mark each item with a check (X) where you would like to have it be with regard to that item.

Note: Please check if you are: Paid Staff _____   Volunteer _____

I. LEADERSHIP:

	System 1 Virtually none	System 2 Some	System 3 Substantial amount	System 4 A great deal
1. How much confidence and trust does staff have in volunteers?	Virtually none	Some	Substantial amount	A great deal
2. How much confidence and trust do volunteers have in staff?				
3. How free do you feel to talk to your immediate volunteer or staff supervisor about your job?	Not very free	Somewhat free	Quite free	Very free
4. How often are your ideas sought and used constructively by your volunteer or staff supervisor?	Seldom	Sometimes	Often	Very frequently
5. How do you feel about delegation of authority?	Discouraged Almost never occurs	Occasionally occurs	Encouraged most levels	Good at all levels

*Adapted by Marlene Wilson from an instrument used in industry (Rensis Likert).

II. MOTIVATION:

	Minimal recognition, personal involvement and achievement	Moderate recognition, involvement and achievement	Frequent recognition, some involvement, marginal achievement	Optimum involvement, personal enrichment and achievement
1. The motivational forces used most in organization are:				
2. Who feels responsibility for achieving the goals of this organization?	Top administration	Top administration and Board volunteers	Most people who work here	Everyone—admin., staff and volunteers
3. How much cooperative team work exists	Very little	Relatively little	Moderate amount	Great deal
a. between members of paid staff?				
b. between volunteers and paid staff?				
c. between volunteers?				
4. How much satisfaction do you derive from your job and your achievements here?	Very little	Moderate amount	Adequate	Very high

III. COMMUNICATION:

1. What is the amount of interaction and communication aimed at achieving the goals?

Very little	Some	Quite a bit	Much, with both individuals & groups

2. What is the usual direction of the flow of information?

Downward	Mostly downward	Down & up	Down, up, and sideways

3. How well do supervisors comprehend problems faced by their volunteers and professional staff?

Not very well	Rather well	Quite well	Very well

4. How would you rate the general communications between staff & volunteers?

Poor	Need more	Adequate	Very good

IV. DECISIONS:

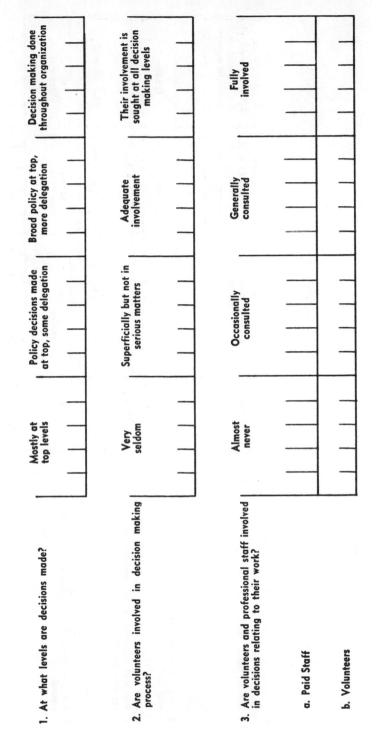

1. At what levels are decisions made?

| Mostly at top levels | Policy decisions made at top, some delegation | Broad policy at top, more delegation | Decision making done throughout organization |

2. Are volunteers involved in decision making process?

| Very seldom | Superficially but not in serious matters | Adequate involvement | Their involvement is sought at all decision making levels |

3. Are volunteers and professional staff involved in decisions relating to their work?

| Almost never | Occasionally consulted | Generally consulted | Fully involved |

a. Paid Staff

b. Volunteers

V. GOALS:

	By management and staff to volunteers in condescending manner	By Board volunteers to staff in an arbitrary manner	By select management, staff and volunteers in a controlling manner	By management, staff & volunteers in a democratic manner
1. How are agency goals established?				
2. Do you have the opportunity to set goals for your job?	Never	Seldom	Occasionally	Usually
3. How well informed are most members of this organization of the goals?	Know very little	Vague knowledge	Adequately informed	Well informed
4. Are your personal goals being met in your present job?	Not at all	Minimally	Adequately	Very well

VI. GENERAL KNOWLEDGE:

	Inhibits initiative and achievement	Sometimes conducive but with many restrictions	Adequately conducive	Extremely conducive
1. *Physical Facilities.* Extent to which the physical facilities and equipment within the office are conducive to creative initiative and achievement.				
2. Extent to which printed internal communications serve as information tool.	Inadequate information flow	Information flow adequate	Information flows very well	Keeps everyone well informed
3. Extent of my personal knowledge and understanding of:	Almost none	Limited	Adequate	Excellent
A. the programs of this agency				
B. mission and principles of this agency				
C. the policies				
4. *Image.* Within your personal contacts what response do you get regarding the image of this agency in the community?	Negative	Disinterested	Vague	Positive

INTELLECTUAL AND EXPRESSIVE BLOCKS

How does this look? We stumble over these blocks when we have an insufficient or ineffective repertoire of problem-solving strategies and tactics or when we are unable to communicate our ideas effectively to others. We may try to solve the problem by using the wrong language (i.e., using mathematical statistics, charts and graphs when an emotional appeal from the client would be more effective or using a verbal report when a visual approach such as a slide show could better depict the problem).

What can be done about it? Obviously, we need to expand and hone our problem-solving and communications skills however we can. Let's explore some of the well-known, but often under-utilized processes that stimulate a group to think creatively. We need to examine these techniques and to practice them.

From Interaction Associates' *Strategy Notebook*, here are sixty-six strategies that can be used to help a group keep from bogging down or overlooking possible alternative ways of looking at the problem.[18]

Build up	Display	Simulate
Eliminate	Organize	Test
Work Forward	List	Play
Work Backward	Check	Manipulate
Associate	Diagram	Copy
Classify	Chart	Interpret
Generalize	Verbalize	Transform
Exemplify	Visualize	Translate
Compare	Memorize	Expand
Relate	Recall	Reduce
Commit	Record	Exaggerate
Defer	Retrieve	Understate
Leap In	Search	Adapt
Hold Back	Select	Substitute
Focus	Plan	Combine
Release	Predict	Separate
Force	Assume	Change
Relax	Question	Vary
Dream	Hypothesize	Cycle
Imagine	Guess	Repeat
Purge	Define	Systemize
Incubate	Symbolize	Randomize

From Alex Osborn's classic book *Applied Imagination*, we get the notion that to help free up the right brain (the idea generator) and control the left brain (the idea filter) we can try two techniques:[19]

(1) *Brainstorming.* This was the brain-child Osborn introduced in 1952. It has now become a household word. We stated the rules of brainstorming on page 34, but let's review them again:

(a) No evaluation of any kind during the idea generation period; (b) Everyone is encouraged to think of the wildest ideas possible; (c) Quantity of ideas is the goal; (d) All participants are encouraged to build on the ideas of the others.

(2) *Check List for New Ideas.* This is another set of questions Osborn suggests for us to use in unlocking the flow of creative ideas:[20]

Put to other uses?
New ways to use as is? Other uses if modified?

Adapt?
What else is like this? What other ideas does this suggest? Does past offer a parallel? What could I copy? Whom could I emulate?

Modify?
New twist? Change meaning, color, motion, sound, odor, form, shape? Other changes?

Magnify?
What to add? More time? Greater frequency? Stronger? Higher? Longer? Thicker? Extra value? Plus ingredient? Duplicate? Multiply? Exaggerate?

Minify?
What to subtract? Smaller? Condensed? Miniature? Lower? Shorter? Lighter? Omit? Streamline? Split Up? Understate?

Substitute?
Who else instead? What else instead? Other ingredient? Other material? Other process? Other power? Other place? Other approach? Other tone of voice?

Rearrange?
Interchange components? Other pattern? Other layout? Other sequence? Transpose cause and effect? Change place? Change schedule?

Reverse?
Transpose positive and negative? How about opposites? Turn it backward? Turn it upside down? Reverse roles? Change shoes? Turn tables? Turn other cheek?

Combine?
How about a blend, an alloy, an assortment, an ensemble? Combine units? Combine purpose? Combine appeals? Combine ideas?

And from Robert A. Moskowitz, in the *Creative Problem Solving*

Workbook, we find we have a choice of four types of solutions to a problem:

FOUR TYPES OF SOLUTIONS TO PROBLEMS

– – – – – – – outline of solution
——————— outline of problem

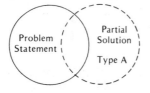

A Type A solution solves some of the aspects of the problem, but leaves others untouched, and brings with it factors that may cause unwanted side effects.

A Type B solution solves many aspects of the problem, but leaves others untouched. It brings no unwanted side effects.

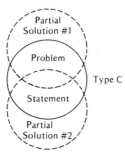

A Type C solution is a combination of solutions— two or more Type A solutions brought together and applied simultaneously. It may solve all or most aspects of the problem, but it usually brings unwanted side effects.

A Type D solution is a total solution. It covers the entire problem in all its aspects and, in some cases, extends beyond it to bring additional positive effects and benefits.

Note: Reprinted by permission of the publisher, from CREATIVE PROBLEM SOLVING WORKBOOK, by Robert A. Moskowitz, © 1978 by AMACOM, a division of American Management Associations p. 61.

Hopefully, this chapter has helped dispel the myth that solving problems is dull, difficult, or impossible. As we face the challenge of being managers in the challenging decade ahead let us remember:

Just as we use physical tools for physical tasks, we employ conceptual tools for conceptual tasks. To familiarize yourself with a tool, you may experiment with it, test it in different situations, and evaluate its usefulness. The same method can be applied to conceptual tools. Our ability as thinkers is dependent on our range and skill with our own tools. [21]

REFERENCES

1. Austin, James H. *Chase, Chance and Creativity*, Columbia University Press, 1978, p. 53.

2. Dickson, Paul, *The Future File*, Avon Publisher, 1977, p. 14.

3. *TWA Ambassador Magazine*, July 1978. Quote by Erma Bombeck.

4. Drucker, Peter, "Managing the Third Sector," *Wall Street Journal*, Oct. 3, 1978.

5. Rosow, Jerome M. "Organizational Issues in the 80's: Shifts in the Work Force, Changing Values, New Patterns of Work," *OD Practitioner*, Vol. 11, No. 2, July 1979.

6. Rosow, p. 14.

7. *National Report*, Vol. 5, No. H, ASTD, Sept. 5, 1979.

8. Ibid.

9. Bradford, L., "Introduction,"*Journal of Social Issues*, Vol. 4, No. 2 (1948), p. 3.

10. Drucker, Peter, *Management: Tasks, Responsibilities, Practices*, Harper and Row, 1973, p. 786.

11. Adams, James, *Conceptual Blockbusting*, W.H. Freeman & Co., 1974, Preface.

12. Ingalls, John D., *Human Energy*, Learning Concepts, 2501 N. Lamar, Austin, Texas 78705, 1976, p. 64.

13. Adams, Chapters 2-5.

14. Adams. pp. 21-22.

15. de Bono, Edward, *New Think*, Basic Books, 1967.

16. Steele, Fritz, and Jenks, Stephen, *Feel of the Work Place*, Addison-Wesley, 1977, p. 187.

17. Ibid.

18. *Strategy Notebook*, Interaction Associates, San Francisco, 1971.

19. Osborn, Alex, *Applied Imagination*, Charles Scribner & Sons, 1953.

20. Ibid.

21. *Strategy Notebook*, Introduction.

The text is arranged inside a circle formed by a procession of caterpillars. The caterpillars are labeled around the rim with the words: TRADITION, OPINIONS, PAST EXPERIENCE, THE BEATEN PATH, FILING PRACTICE, CUSTOM, FORMS, HABIT, PRESENT METHODS, RESISTANCE TO CHANGE, STANDARD PRACTICE.

PROCESSIONARY CATERPILLARS

Processionary Caterpillars feed upon pine needles. They move through the trees in a long procession, one leading and the others following — each with his eyes half closed and his head snugly fitted against the rear extremity of his predecessor.

Jean-Henri Fabre, the great French naturalist, after patiently experimenting with a group of the caterpillars, finally enticed them to the rim of a large flower pot. He succeeded in getting the first one connected up with the last one, thus forming a complete circle, which started moving around in a procession, with neither beginning nor end.

The naturalist expected that after a while they would catch on to the joke, get tired of their useless march, and start off in some new direction. But not so.

Through sheer force of habit, the living, creeping circle kept moving around the rim of the pot — around and around, keeping the same relentless pace for seven days and seven nights — and would doubtless have continued longer had it not been for sheer exhaustion and ultimate starvation.

Incidentally, an ample supply of food was close at hand and plainly visible, but it was outside the range of the circle so they continued along the beaten path.

They were following instinct — habit — custom — tradition — precedent — past experience — "standard practice" — or whatever you may choose to call it, but they were following it blindly.

They meant well — but got no place.

APPENDIX B: OUTLINE FOR PLANNED CHANGE

    I. WHAT I AM DOING NOW:

   II. WHAT I WOULD LIKE TO DO:

  III. GOAL STATEMENT
       (Specific, measurable, target)
       Example: To do a countywide 4-H program review using a six person task group
                 beginning in July with a report and recommendations to be presented at
                 the September 4-H Council meeting.

  IV. ACTION PLAN

1. Positive forces for doing this	Negative forces against doing this

2. Based on the forces for and forces against, what are the things I must do if I want to reach my goal?
   List as many as you can think of:

3. Now develop strategies. Which of the things listed to be done must be done first and by whom?
   (Check, are they all necessary?)

Action Steps	By Whom	Date to be Completed
1.		
2.		
3.		

4. How should I go about taking the action steps? Is this the best use of my resources and abilities?

How	Outcome is Worth Cost yes or no

V. EVALUATION

1. How and when will progress toward goal be checked?

2. What were the good results?

3. What were some poor results?

Developed by V. Milton Boyce, SEA/Extension, 3/78

PROBLEMS ON THE JOB

- Identify the 5 most serious difficulties that prevent you from performing at top effectiveness on your job.

- Then, list the reasons why these are the most serious difficulties. (Discuss these difficulties with others, especially if it will help you clarify the reasons for them.)

- Finally, list the resources (time, people, money, support services) you'll need to remedy the most serious problem(s).

Job Difficulties	Reasons	Needed Resources to Solve

Forest & Mulcahy, University of Wisconsin

APPENDIX D—EXAMPLES OF CREATIVE PROBLEM SOLVING
WHY NOT GIVE IT A TRY?[21]
by Kay Bixby

The "one answer" syndrome is an easy habit to develop—and usually the "one answer" is money. (It's needed, but not always.) There are, however, a variety of alternatives to problem-solving. Every person is a walking computer endowed with an unending supply of facts and ideas. If this wealth is properly tapped and linked, amazing solutions can be found to even the most complex needs.

Society tends to set up all sorts of barriers to creative approaches—bureaucracies, policies, turf protection, fear. As a result, people forget, or are too frustrated to use, the magnificent equipment of mind and memory which is unique in each of us.

The following examples illustrate the variety and extent of the problem-solving process when more than one individual or group is asked to find a solution. In other words, posing a question of need to any five people brings five different answers. Or, if the five people collaborate, one idea spurs another. The cases, though real, have been simplified.

PROBLEM: A children's section of a hospital had an immediate need for 80 pajama bottoms for their little boy patients. (The tops did not wear out as fast.)

ALTERNATIVES: One group felt that a fundraising event should be held to buy the pajamas. This solution, however, would take too much time. Another group discovered two members with power sewing machines, one who knew where to obtain donated remnants of cloth, and others who had thread and the time to help. This alternative allowed the hospital to have the pajama bottoms within a week.

PROBLEM: An agency was in deep financial straits. There was an obvious need for funds.

ALTERNATIVES: One suggestion was to ask for an immediate grant of money—a bandaid solution at best. Another was to obtain some management advisors. By instituting sound financial practices, the agency realized a surplus of funds within three months.

PROBLEM: A school was being constantly vandalized.

ALTERNATIVES: The school board considered proposals to hire more guards (another bandaid) or to enlist the support of parents as volunteers to watch the school during periods of heavy vandalism. Selecting the latter solution, parents and teachers saw vandalism disappear at the school in a period of four months.

PROBLEM: Emergency services were deleted from the city budget, creating a need for food, clothing and rooms for people in crisis.

ALTERNATIVES: Concerned citizens and groups thought of exerting political pressure for funds, but decided that soliciting community agencies and businesses for space, food and clothing would yield quicker results. They also ran a newspaper ad which resulted in the donation of a freezer, and recruited volunteers to run the centers and develop resources for housing.

PROBLEM: A forest was dying from smog pollution.

ALTERNATIVES: Conservationists refused to let it die. They should have demanded that the forestry department replant; instead, they discovered which types of trees are smog-resistant and how to obtain seedlings. Volunteers were recruited to plant and raise the seedlings.

There is a tendency to assume that certain individuals or groups, because of background or skill in a particular field, have all the answers and that it is unnecessary to ask others for their input. One example of a "non-expert" solution is the story of a truck getting jammed underneath an overpass where it couldn't be extricated. Engineers were summoned but could find no solution. In the crowd standing around the truck, a little boy studying the situation finally said, "Why don't you let the air out of the tires?" The non-expert saw the problem from a different perspective, and because the situation allowed for out-of-the-ordinary participation, he was able to solve the problem.

An awareness of the diversity of people is essential to obtaining creative answers to problems. Clues come from unexpected sources. The assumption that any part of the human family is without capability in any area builds another fence to obtaining valuable assistance.

Society often conditions us to be hesitant and fearful of presenting our own viewpoints and perspectives. Consequently, the habit of reticence is hard to break. The phrases "That's never been done before," "We have a policy against that," "That isn't possible," or "It's too much trouble," surround us and dampen our enthusiasm and freeze us into inactivity.

On the other hand, remarkable things happen when other phrases are used: "Of course I'd like to hear about it," "That's very interesting, what can we do to help?," "Let's try to see how it could be done," "Thank you for bringing the idea to me," or "Why didn't we think of that before! It's great." Minds open, hope returns and accomplishment begins for those who are met with such *sincere* interest.

The volunteer community offers a rare opportunity for the free flow of creativity without self-consciousness or restrictions. Volunteers are self-motivated and have eager expectations of accomplishment. If, in their chosen arena, they find access to decision-making and receive encouragement and support, the opening of ideas should result and benefit the activity.

The volunteer effort, no matter how small (a cup of soup brought to an ill neighbor) must be respected. All self-initiated, constructive and creative activities that are caring and problem-solving should meet appreciation.

Our nation has a multitude of problems, but it also has a remarkable people. If given belief and trust, their wisdom will find answers. Opening our systems, lessening our bureaucracies, and (perhaps most of all) listening and encouraging, we will find more and more "volunteered" participation and creativity.

People should have access to encouragement, undergirding and support in the volunteer community, as a means of gaining due credence for new ideas and problem-solving.

The "one answer" syndrome is a trap we can overcome. We need only to open the door to alternatives and options.

Reprinted with permission from *Voluntary Action Leadership*, Spring, 1977, NCVA, 1214 16th St., N.W. Washington, DC 20036.

APPENDIX E

A symphony group commissioned a marketing survey to find out why *Schubert's Unfinished Symphony* did not appear more frequently on concert programs. The market research consultant went completely in the wrong direction and submitted the following analysis: "I have surveyed the *Unfinished Symphony* and find it has myriad problems:

a. For considerable periods the four oboe players have nothing to do. The number should be reduced, and their work spread over the whole orchestra, thus eliminating peaks of activity.

b. All 12 violins play identical notes. This seems an unnecessary duplication and the staff of the section should be drastically cut. If a large volume of sound is really required this could be obtained through an electric amplifier.

c. Much effort is absorbed in the playing of demi-semi-quavers. This seems an excessive refinement, and it is recommended that all notes should be rounded out to the nearest semiquaver. If this is done, it should be possible to use trainees and lower grade operators.

d. No useful purpose is served by repeating with horns the passages that have already been handled by the strings. If all such redundant passages were eliminated, the concert could be reduced from two hours to 20 minutes. If Schubert had attended to these matters, he would probably have been able to finish his symphony after all."

Source Unknown

CHAPTER III

Power and Negotiation:
How To Make Ideas Happen

In doing what you love to do there will of course be difficulties, but that won't matter to you, it is part of life. . . . But don't battle against society, don't tackle dead tradition, unless you have this love in you, for your struggle will be meaningless and you will merely create more mischief. Whereas, if you deeply feel what is right and can therefore stand alone, then your action born of love will have extraordinary significance, it will have vitality and beauty.

J. Kreshnamurti
quoted by Elizabeth O'Connor
in *Eighth Day of Creation*

POWER

Some important questions to deal with as we step from the heady world of ideas into the harsh world of reality are these:

How much do you believe in what you are doing or want to do?

How badly do you want to see innovation and change occur?

How committed are you to accomplishing your goals?

My guess is that if your answers to these three questions are a tentative "sort of" or "it would be nice," you are not ready—or willing—to deal with the present topic. It will remain safer and easier to continue dreaming of "if only's" and feeling like a pawn or victim of what is happening.

May I illustrate with another word picture. When my family and I were recently in Hawaii, I was lying on the beach one afternoon watching a youngster about four or five years old happily engaged in building a sand castle. He spent nearly two hours erecting towers and walls and building moats and roads. It was obvious he was getting great joy and satisfaction from this creative effort. Then his mother called him in for dinner and he reluctantly left his masterpiece. I happened to be there the next morning when the little fellow came running down to resume work on his castle. All he found was a mound of sand. The tides had come in and destroyed his castle. He obviously felt angry, hurt, and betrayed. He could not understand how anyone could do such an awful thing. *No one had told him about the tides!*

I have seen many creative people in human services and industry suffer this same kind of rude awakening. Good ideas that seem so obviously right are rejected. Innovation that is desperately needed is time and again turned down. Projects that are imaginative and worthwhile are not funded. Tides people do not understand wash them away.

My belief is that most of these "forces" can be anticipated, understood, and often managed if we are willing to embark on a serious study of power, both personal and organizational. That is what this chapter will attempt to do.

In his excellent book *Power and Innocence*, Rollo May states:

I cannot recall a time during the last four decades when there was so much talk about the individual's capacities and potentialities, and so little actual confidence on the part of the individual about his power to make a difference. [1]

On the other hand, Harold Lasswell offers this observation:

Men do not need to live as resentful pawns in a game that no one bothers to explain. It is feasible for everyone to achieve some understanding of the whole chess board of nature, life and culture; to acquire some awareness of the rules of the game; to see where he can win or lose by abiding by the rules, or how he can most effectively act to change the rules. [2]

And Elizabeth O'Connor helps us know where to begin:

To be in earnest about a vision is to think about strategy—how to take what is out in the distance and bring it into the here and now where it can be perceived by ordinary sight.[3]

The one common denominator that runs through all of these statements is *power*.

DEFINING POWER

Since *power* is often considered a dirty word in our culture, it is important once again to define our terms.

Power: the ability of one person to influence another; the ability to *cause* or *prevent* change; having influence or impact on a person or situation. The word power comes from the Latin word meaning "to be able" and describes ways of influencing others and achieving a sense of the significance of oneself.

In other words, *powerful people influence outcomes*. Now is it apparent why the questions posed at the beginning of this chapter are so critical? How strongly do you feel about the outcomes? If you seriously want to and intend to influence them, you *must* exercise power of one form or another.

In their book *Synergic Power*, James and Marguerite Craig lay it out very clearly:

By denying power, I hope to affect others without openly trying to do so. To promote social change I must either seek and use power myself—or work to build the power of someone else who will use it to make the change I want.[4]

UNDERSTANDING POWER

To reinforce the critical link between creativity and power, let us reexamine two of the definitions we have used:

innovation: to make changes in anything established.
power: the ability to cause or prevent change.

Most management experts agree that change is not a sideline in the business of leadership; rather, it is integral to the whole idea. Changing things is central to leadership, and changing them before anyone else is creativity.

So, if initiating change is an essential ingredient of effective leadership, then power must be also. We must therefore understand and use it effectively if we want to survive as managers, at the same time encouraging creativity and avoiding "turn out."

First, it is important to examine your present feelings about your power situation. In the following useful diagram, try to identify which corner of the triangle most closely describes your feelings.

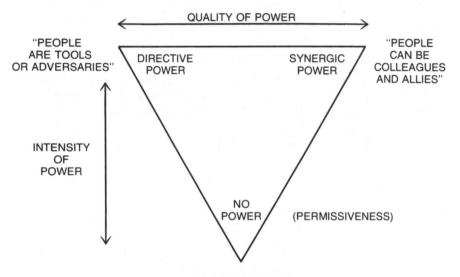

Note: Taken from *Synergic Power* by James H. and Marguerite Craig, 1979 (P.O. Box 296, Berkeley, CA 94701), p. 64.

No Power

The people in the No Power position are often the people who choose not to exercise power because they feel it is wrong to intentionally affect the behavior of others. Rollo May refers to this stance as *innocence* and warns that there is a difference between authentic and pseudo innocence:

    a. *Authentic innocence* is the preservation of childlike attitudes into adulthood without sacrificing the realism of one's perception of evil. Everything has a freshness, purity.

and newness that spawns awe and wonder. It leads to spirituality.

b. *Pseudo innocence* consists of blinders and naïveté. It is childish, rather than childlike, and makes things *seem* simple and easy. By denying power, there is no need to take responsibility for what is happening.[5] May states:

When young pseudo-innocent people are pressed for a statement of their values and one asks what they would make the center of a new world, one is often left with picayune or self-revolving items like never stepping on insects or never throwing away anything made of plastic. This is a blatant use of pseudo innocence. We look—often in vain—for a serious, responsible confrontation with the real problems: power, organization in national groups, fidelity in personal life . . . Innocence as a shield from responsibility is also a shield from growth. It protects us from new awareness and from identifying with the sufferings of mankind as well as with the joys, both of which are shut off from the pseudo-innocent person.[6]

No power is an option, but have we weighed the consequences to ourselves and others?

Directive Power

Directive power is the type of power that has given the word a bad name. Coercion, force, intimidation, and manipulation are often strategies employed. Others are viewed as either tools or adversaries, and the name all too frequently is "I Win-You Lose." It is because many people have suffered the slings and arrows of others who use this form of power that we have assumed power in and of itself is bad.

Synergic Power

Synergic power is the "capacity of an individual or group to increase the satisfactions of all participants by intentionally generating increased energy and creativity, all of which is used to co-create a more rewarding present and future." It differs dramatically from directive power particularly in the concern for and involvement with those led or influenced. A synergic power leader:

1) shares the vision of what might be;

2) shares knowledge and information relating to that vision;

3) encourages full and open sharing of the ideas and input of all those affected; and

4) "guides a synthesis of all of these toward creating and carrying out jointly devised programs."[7]

It becomes apparent how your style of management greatly affects your ability to develop synergic power. The autocratic authoritarian, or the "doer," almost inevitably falls into the directive power stance, whether that is his intent or not. The Craigs make the rather disillusioning observation that not many people ever try to use synergic power. To do so requires that we:

1) *Intend* to affect others' behavior and experience;
2) *Be open* about it;
3) *Value and cherish* the others involved; and
4) *Believe* the others are or can become responsible and effective allies and colleagues.[8]

The intriguing thing about synergic power leadership is that it gives the people led as much, if not more, freedom than when the leader is in the No Power corner of the diagram. Having no power limits options and visions of what could and should happen, and it also tends to make those led feel powerless. Synergic power, on the other hand, builds the self-esteem, capabilities, and incentives for the present and the future for everyone involved. Try it . . . you'll like it!

It might be helpful in attempting to gain a clearer understanding of the concept of power if we examine it from several perspectives. To do this, we will consider the theories of Rollo May and David McClelland relating to kinds of power and levels of power.

KINDS OF POWER

McClelland suggests that power's negative "face" is the one most of us think of when we hear the word.[9] This he entitles *personal power*. (It correlates with the Craigs' definition of directive power.) He contends, however, that we often neglect to recognize or appreciate another kind of power, and this he calls *social power* (similar to Craigs' synergic power). The people who are motivated by either of these kinds of power *want to have influence and impact on situations or persons*, but their methods and motives differ a great deal. A synopsis of the differences might be stated as follows:

Personal Power	*Social Power*
—"I win—You lose"	—"I win—You win"
—People viewed as pawns to be used	—People viewed as valuable colleagues

100

—Personal aggrandizement is the goal	—Wants to attain shared social goals
—Trappings of power are important, i.e., biggest title, desk, car, club	—Results of efforts are important—advocacy for a cause

McClelland warns that our country and our causes desperately need social power people to help influence outcomes. But we so often consider any power person negatively, and thus abuse people like city council, school board, state commission, and agency board members instead of understanding and valuing them.

The underlying message of the social power person is: Convince me of the value of your organization's goals and I will use money, expertise, connections, and/or influence to help us achieve those goals. What a godsend to struggling organizations! But so often, once these people are attracted to a board of directors, for example, they are given very little information and even less freedom to act, due to the fact the executive or other board members are threatened by them. It would seem that many organizations already have social power people in their ranks as staff, board members, or volunteers. They are very likely willing and able to act but are underutilized, ignored, or "turned out" . . . almost like an untapped gold mine.

To give you a personal example: In my opinion, both my husband, Harvey, and I have become social power people during the last few years. We are cause-oriented, like to influence outcomes and choose only those causes to become involved in that we strongly believe in and feel we have something positive to contribute to. Sounds easy enough, doesn't it? Here are some of the frustrations we have experienced.

Harvey is Vice President of Personnel and Administration for a corporation and has over twenty years of excellent experience in personnel and management development. Whenever he goes on an agency's board of directors, he makes a point of privately offering this expertise to the executive. In essence, he is volunteering to help that organization in matters relating to his field. (Remember—he only goes on a board if he believes in the cause and feels he has something to offer the organization.) You have no idea how few of these agencies have ever followed up on his offer. And yet most of them have had personnel problems; wage, salary and benefits difficulties; training needs; etc.

As I have mentioned earlier, I am a national consultant in management, specializing in the management of volunteer programs. A few years ago, I agreed to serve as a volunteer on the Citizen's Advisory Council of our local high school. I eagerly accepted the post, because I firmly believe in broader utilization of volunteers within the school system, as well as increased opportunities for high school students to become volunteers. After our first meeting, I stayed after and spoke to the chairman and principal. I gave them a copy of my book *The Effective Management of Volunteer Programs* and offered to help the school in any way I could with the whole issue of volunteers. In two years on the council, I was never asked anything relating to it, although I was (during that same period) hired as a consultant by the Los Angeles School District and several others to help them with their programs.

I am sure many of you have also experienced this extreme frustration of not being allowed to give what you do best to the organizations with which you are involved. My plea to you executive directors and board chairmen is this:

If you have social power people, allow them to function. If you do not have them—get them! The future of your organization and its effectiveness in meeting the needs of your clients may just depend on it.

Rollo May, in his book *Power and Innocence*, examines the kinds of power from a different perspective. He identifies five kinds of power:

1) *Exploitative*—power *using* another
2) *Manipulative*—power *over* another
3) *Competitive*—power *against* another
4) *Nutrient*—power *for*, or on behalf of another
5) *Integrative*—power *with* another[10]

Tying these two theories together, it would seem May's exploitative, manipulative, and competitive power definitions correlate closely with McClelland's personal power, whereas social power fits the nutrient and integrative definitions, i.e.:

$$
\text{Personal Power} \quad \left\{ \begin{array}{l} \text{Exploitative} \\ \text{Manipulative} \\ \text{Competitive} \end{array} \right.
$$

$$
\text{Social Power} \quad \left\{ \begin{array}{l} \text{Nutrient} \\ \text{Integrative} \end{array} \right.
$$

These definitions also correspond closely to McGregor's Theory "X" and "Y" assumptions about people and how to manage them:[10]

Theory X Managers: assume people are basically immature and irresponsible; work is distasteful; people want close direction and control in their work and want as little personal responsibility as possible. (A leader holding this set of assumptions is therefore very *directive* and *autocratic* in style.)

Theory Y Managers: assume people can and want to be basically self-directed and creative; they are responsible and ambitious and want to develop their skills and abilities. (A leader holding these assumptions tends to use a *participative* style of management and *enables* others to develop to their fullest potential.)

These statements reinforce those made earlier in this chapter indicating that power is neither good nor bad. It is what you do with it that is.

In an attempt to integrate all of the various notions about power that we have covered thus far, let's expand on the diagram on page 98.

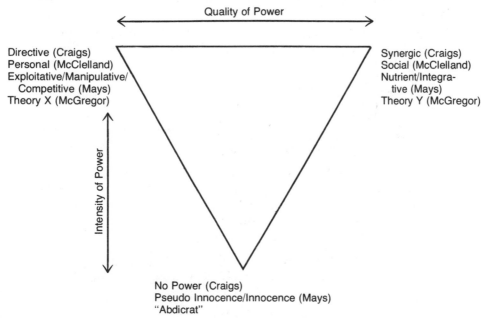

Quality of Power

Directive (Craigs)
Personal (McClelland)
Exploitative/Manipulative/
   Competitive (Mays)
Theory X (McGregor)

Synergic (Craigs)
Social (McClelland)
Nutrient/Integra-
   tive (Mays)
Theory Y (McGregor)

Intensity of Power

No Power (Craigs)
Pseudo Innocence/Innocence (Mays)
"Abdicrat"

LEVELS OF POWER

Let us now examine May's assertion that there are five levels of power that it is possible to use. These are:

1) Power to be
2) Self-affirmation
3) Self-assertion
4) Aggression
5) Violence[12]

It is important in determining power strategies to understand each level.

Power To Be

The "power to be" is the simple human cry for survival—the expression of a person's right to life. The ultimate impotence here is death. Newborn children come fighting into the world expressing their needs and experimenting with ways to get those needs met. ("When I cry, she holds me.")

Impoverished and disadvantaged persons around the world struggle so often at this level. Mere existence becomes a day-to-day battle. However, we must not believe this struggle exists only for the obviously downtrodden (the starving masses in Africa and India, or the minority ghetto dwellers in crowded cities). Statistics now indicate that the fastest growing poverty group in the United States is single women over fifty. The power struggle for these women has often changed from self-assertion or affirmation to survival.

Putting this concept into an organizational setting, this "power to be" might be the concern people have with just keeping their jobs. The greater their need for work, the more apt they are to use basic survival strategies, i.e., "Don't rock the boat," "Don't ask questions," "Just go along," "Live and let live."

Self-Affirmation

Self-affirmation is the need for recognition—to affirm one's own human worth. It is the longing to be valued as a person. The catch-word today is "I'm OK." If we cannot affirm our own value, we find it difficult to affirm others'. "Our attitudes toward others parallel our attitudes toward ourselves, and a basic love for ourselves is necessary if we are to love others."[13]

In your position as a manager, it is essential to recognize this need for self-esteem in your people. That is why feedback, evaluations, recognition, personal interviews, promotions, and title changes are all important. These are all ways of validating a person's worth. They help diminish a person's feelings of powerlessness.

May states that one mistake powerless people often make is to skip this level of self-affirmation and jump straight into aggression or violence. He warns that if self-affirmation is omitted, something of great value is lost, stating *"It is self-affirmation that gives the staying capacity and depth to one's power to be."*[14]

If you have any doubt as to the strength of this need for affirmation in people today, visit your local bookstore. The shelves are filled with such intriguing titles as:

—*Looking Out for # 1*

—*Power! How to Get It, How to Use It!*

—*Winning Through Intimidation*

—*The Magic of Thinking Big*

—*The Organization Gorilla*

—*Stand Up, Speak Out,* & *Talk Back*

The fact that these books are selling by the millions reflects that we have not felt very important or powerful as persons in this country—and people are fed up with it. I can empathize with the frustration, but I am very concerned with some of the advice people are getting via these pop bestsellers.[15]

Here are some examples:

- Wile, guile, manipulation and self-centered one-upsmanship are now the recommended route for rapid ascension in the business world.
- Learn to ignore your altruistic instincts.
- Do not concern yourself with honesty.
- It's OK to be greedy.
- Your interests are nobody else's concern. (If you lose, somebody else wins—and if you win, somebody else will be the loser.)

In other words, these books are pushing the directive, personal, exploitive type of power and ignoring the possibility of the synergic, social, nutrient kind of power, promulgating a grave disservice to their readers in my opinion.

As an antidote to this *me first* philosophy, let me share some thoughts of D.O. Smart.[16]

He suggests that you begin with a simple exercise. On a piece of paper, list the three persons who have had the most positive influence on your life. (Please stop and do this now.)

If you are typical of the many individuals he has worked with, you will list the following: (1) a relative; (2) a mentor: teacher, minister, leader; and (3) a close friend.

Next, answer the question "What was it about those people you listed that made them so influential in your life?"

The common denominator that almost always surfaces is—they *cared*! They cared about *you* as a person, and that is what made them so influential.

Smart's logical conclusion is:

If the job of a manager or supervisor is to influence, and the most influential persons are those who care, does it not follow that for supervisors to become more influential, they should become more caring?[17]

Think about it.

Self-Assertion

Self-assertion is a stronger, more overt expression of power. It often entails testing limits or checking out assumptions or rules. We test our personhood by pushing against opposition. People often *seek out* opposition at this stage just to practice assertiveness or try out their "psychological muscles." It is normal for it to occur when self-affirmation has been denied.

May suggests this level can be depicted as digging in our heels on what we believe, even against opposition. The message is "Here I stand; you can come this far and no further."[18] Another expression which depicts this level would be "standing up for my rights" as an employee or volunteer.

Aggression

As contrasted to the holding-fast stance of self-assertion, "Aggression is moving out, a thrust toward the person or thing seen as the adversary . . . the action that *moves into another's territory to accomplish a restructuring of power*."[19] Again it happens because the aggressor is convinced self-affirmation or assertion will not work (or has not worked) in a situation. An interesting way of understanding this is the saying "Some people change their ways when they see the light; others only when they feel the heat."

Aggression is the effort to seize some of the power for oneself or for one's cause. It is the stage or level on May's spectrum where *overt* conflict emerges and where the potentiality for use of force enters in. Thus, it is most often viewed with fear or condemnation. He points out there are, however, positive forms of aggression such as "cutting through barriers to initiate a relationship; confronting another without intent to hurt but with intent to penetrate into his consciousness; warding off powers that threaten one's integrity, actualizing one's own self and one's own ideas in a hostile environment."[20]

The negative manifestations of aggression, on the other hand, include physical fighting, with the intent to harm someone, or building up your own power by diminishing another person ("I win—You lose"). This can occur when a person subtly but consciously uses "put-downs" or "one-upsmanship" games to feel important by making others seem unimportant. This form of aggression is almost always destructive.

May states that aggression is always the result of frustration, and *wherever there is frustration there will be aggression.* The question is, if we are in a work situation fraught with frustration, are we and others expressing negative or positive forms of aggression?

Again, if we feel strongly about our ideas, beliefs, or causes and meet apathy, indifference, or opposition, we may very well need to employ aggressive strategies to ensure that we are heard. (Remember the passion, even rage, that creativity sometimes requires.) Implementing change, righting wrongs, or championing causes can rarely be accomplished without pain and some turmoil. We must learn positive aggressive techniques like conflict management, problem solving, negotiation, and positive confrontation to help us deal with frustration (our own and that of our people). Otherwise, the aggression will become destructive. These topics are all dealt with in this book.

I would recommend an excellent article entitled "The Abrasive Personality" by Harry Levinson which appeared in the May-June 1978 issue of *Harvard Business Review.*[21] It deals very effectively with the problems of working with or for a person who demonstrates aggression inappropriately in a work situation. Some words or phrases used to describe such a person are "perfectionist," "insecure," "bulldozer," "antagonist," "intellectual bully," "unwilling to compromise," "controlling," "humorless," "competitive," "often extremely intelligent," "poor delegater," "keenly analytical," "insensitive to others," "domineering," "pushes self and others too hard."

Levinson says, "These people puzzle, dismay, frustrate, and enrage others in organizations . . . in the long run they are a bane to themselves as well." This is a great description of unproductive and destructive aggression. If you or someone you work with is utilizing this style, it is essential for you to deal with it if positive, long-term results are to be achieved.

Violence

When all efforts at attaining power at any of the other levels fail there is very likely to be "the ultimate explosion, known as violence."[22] It is usually physical because the other levels of persuasion and influence have not worked, and this may be the only way left for the person or group "to get release from unbearable tension and achieve a sense of significance." May warns:

> We are going to have upheavals of violence for as long as experiences of significance are denied people. . . . When we consider contemporary man—insignificant, lonely, more isolated as mass communication becomes vaster, his ears and sensitivities dulled by ever-present transistor radios and by thousands of words hurled at him by TV and newspapers—aware of his identity only to the extent that he has lost it, yearning for community but feeling awkward and helpless as he finds it—when we consider this modern man, who will be surprised that he yearns for ecstasy even of the kind that violence and war may bring. . . The challenge before us is to find ways that people can achieve significance and recognition so that destructive violence may not be necessary.[23]

It is apparent to me that this challenge must be faced squarely by all managers, for they control to a large extent each employee's feelings of significance or insignificance for 2,080 hours per year.

Let us try to visualize May's five levels of power as follows:

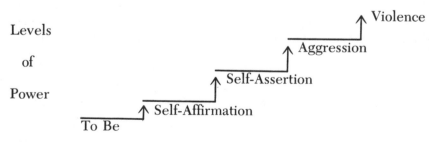

Levels

of

Power

108

It is normal to expect human beings to escalate from one level of power to the next until they attain a sense of personal significance. It would seem that if managers truly define their roles as being enablers of others, then their people would have more possibility of attaining this sense of personal worth at the first three levels without resorting to destructive aggression or violence. It is also important to remember that the critical level so often by-passed is self-affirmation. We *must* find legitimate and meaningful ways to affirm people, for that is at the root of much of the frustration and discontent in the workplaces of America today. And I keep emphasizing throughout this book that one way to affirm people is to involve them in the decisions that affect them.

It would seem to me that this is even more critical (and yet so frequently overlooked) in human services agencies and organizations. The irony is that even though these groups have as their avowed reason for being the alleviation of human suffering, they tend to almost totally ignore the suffering created within their own ranks of paid staff and volunteers by poor management and inappropriate uses of power. I am appalled at both the "burn out" and "turn out" rate in these organizations and am becoming convinced that it stems from ineffective and even sometimes inhumane management practices within them. An interesting contradiction of the term *human service*.

Someone once observed that a little kindness from person to person is better than a vast love of mankind.

STAGES OF POWER

May's levels of power correlate closely with some conclusions David McClelland reached relating to four modalities or stages of power orientations. He has defined these as follows:[24]

Stage I: It strengthens me

This stage is where we incorporate the strength and inspiration we get from others (parents, spouse, friends, leaders). Adults who stay at this stage will seek to work for powerful others, for this helps them feel a sense of power vicariously (similar to May's level "To be").

Stage II: I strengthen myself

This stage often sees people testing their own strength and ideas by saying "no" or pushing back. If an adult stays at this stage, he or

109

she often tries to enhance his feelings of being personally powerful by accumulating things—TV sets, cars, bigger desk, credit cards—or by demonstrating control over himself by dieting, yoga, jogging, exercises. McClelland says, "They are apostles for the doctrine of finding sources of strength in self to develop the self."[25] (This would seem to correlate with May"s self-affirmation and self-assertion levels.

Stage III: I have impact on others

At this stage, a person realizes the sense of power inherent in influencing or controlling other people. He or she develops skills in persuasion and bargaining to accomplish this. Two ways this is often expressed are, oddly enough, by competing with or helping others. Perhaps one of McClelland's most important yet disturbing contributions to understanding power (particularly as it relates to those of us in human services agencies or the helping professions) is his statement:

One way of looking at giving is to perceive that for help to be given, help must be received. And in accepting a gift or help, the receiver can be perceived as acknowledging that he is weaker, at least in this respect, than the person who is giving him help. . . . Americans have been so taught that helping others is a highly moral thing to do that they have been slow to recognize how such behavior can be used as a form of domination. It was with a start of surprise that white liberals found their efforts to help blacks proudly rejected. Why? The blacks recognized eventually that the more help they accepted, the more they were acknowledging their weakness or their inferior position. The whites could be viewed as satisfying their needs to feel powerful at the expense of blacks.[26]

This is a legitimate and sobering cause for honest self-examination on the part of each of us regarding our motives for helping. It need not mean, however, that we are automatically in the business of helping for totally selfish reasons. McClelland states that there is a nonmanipulative kind of giving that he calls sharing which is the nutrient and integrative kind of power (using power *for* and *with* others). Our motivation in giving is determined largely by how we philosophically view the recipients. Do we see them as a disembodied cause or needy persons (down-and-outers), or do we view people as able to help themselves if we remove the blocks? Do we see them as origins or pawns? Do we appreciate self-help as the most healthy and long-lasting or do we insist we know what is best?

Do we seek the input and counsel of those we serve in the planning, implementing, and evaluating of our programs? If not, we clearly state to them (and all the world) that *we* are the experts: *we* know what's best. (Remember, experts are simply people who are wrong for more sophisticated reasons!)

The levels of power utilized here are often positive or negative aggression and even violence—we consciously move out to affect the lives of others.

Stage IV: It moves me to do my duty

This is the stage of power that McClelland claims we have neglected to take seriously or acknowlege adequately in our society. He calls this "the most advanced stage of expressing the power drive in which the self drops out as a source of power and a person sees himself as an instrument of a higher authority which moves him to try to influence or serve others." These people frequently subordinate their own personal goals to the goals of the cause. "Great religious and political leaders from Jesus Christ to Abraham Lincoln and Malcolm X have felt that they were instruments of a higher power which is beyond self. Their goal was to act on others on behalf of this higher authority."[27]

As a deeply committed Christian, I can understand and appreciate McClelland's stance regarding this stage. He goes on to say,

Men and women who reach Stage IV expression of the need for Power are more fully actualized. They are more responsible in organizations, less ego-involved, more willing to seek expert help when appropriate, more open with intimates. . . . Maturity involves the ability to use whatever mode (of power) is appropriate to the situation. Immaturity involves using perhaps only one mode in all situations or using a mode inappropriate to a particular situation.[28]

In conclusion, we need to deal with McClelland's strong conviction that helping behavior implicitly involves a power goal (having influence or impact on a situation or person). We often discount or deny it—and therefore refuse to understand this power motivation. We must simply work towards a healthy, mature, and genuinely helpful use of power instead of denying or misusing it.

Once again, let us update our diagram to include the information just covered:

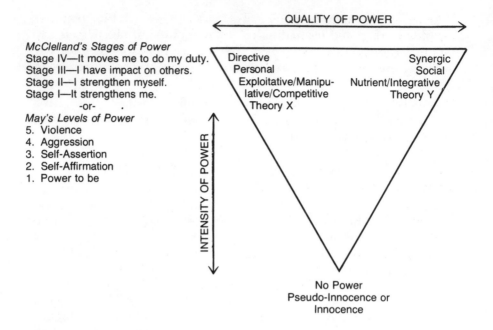

QUALITY OF POWER

McClelland's Stages of Power
Stage IV—It moves me to do my duty.
Stage III—I have impact on others.
Stage II—I strengthen myself.
Stage I—It strengthens me.
-or-
May's Levels of Power
5. Violence
4. Aggression
3. Self-Assertion
2. Self-Affirmation
1. Power to be

INTENSITY OF POWER

Directive
Personal
Exploitative/Manipu-
lative/Competitive
Theory X

Synergic
Social
Nutrient/Integrative
Theory Y

No Power
Pseudo-Innocence or
Innocence

THE PROCESS OF BEING AN INFLUENCER

How does a manager (steeped in the notions of powerlessness and the "badness" of power) begin? For those of you who answered the opening questions with strong affirmative convictions, perhaps I can help. Here is a sequence of steps to try:

1. Identify things "as they really are."

Your first task is to objectively evaluate the situation at hand. Here is where your programmatic or technical skills as a manager are important. You must isolate, assess, and articulate the pros and cons of the situation you want to change or the need you want to meet. Analytical or mathematical "left brain" thinking is needed here. Surveys, questionnaires, data gathering, research, documentation are all important. Be wary of hunches, vague feelings of unrest, and surmises without verifying them.

2. Project things as they might or should be.

Here is where your right brain goes to work, envisioning a better, more effective, and satisfying future. It is important to translate this vision into clearly understandable goals. Be specific as to outcomes desired.

112

In my book *The Effective Management of Volunteer Programs* I emphasize the need for managers to develop sound planning skills and to learn to distinguish between general, global goal statements and *specific, measurable*, and *achievable objectives*. Many times we cannot convince people of the value of what we are trying to accomplish because we are so vague and unclear ourselves.[29]

The problem can also be stated in terms of needing both long- and short-term goals and objectives. May I remind you of the illustration I used in Chapter I (page 43) regarding the mine hike—we keep forgetting the switchbacks and we wear ourselves out heading straight up the mountain!

3. Share this vision with others so that it comes alive for them as well.

Help others to share your vision. Someone once said *the key to willpower is wantpower*. People who want something badly enough can usually find the willpower to achieve it. This ability to inspire others is a test of your leadership abilities. Enthusiasm and commitment are contagious. Learn to be an effective communicator.

4. Carefully strategize how to get from "how things are" to "how they might be."

Build realistic bridges to help you and your people get there. This is considered to be the most common Achilles heel of managers. Perhaps that is because it is at this stage that utilizing power and influence is required to bring about the needed change and we have been unable or unwilling to deal with that. Hopefully by the end of this chapter that will no longer stop us.

Keats once observed, "In dreams begin responsibility," and Robert Greenleaf in his monograph *The Servant As Leader* stated:

> *The real enemy is fuzzy thinking on the part of good, intelligent, vital people and their failure to lead. . . . Too many people settle for being critics and experts. There is too much intellectual wheel spinning, too much retreating into research, too little preparation for and willingness to undertake the hard and high-risk tasks of building better institutions in an imperfect world.*[30]

It is at this juncture that I feel we need to understand more clearly some types of power and influence available to us in organizational settings. If we use the appropriate types of power in each situation, we are far more apt to succeed.

These types of power were identified by Raven and French and are divided into power we have as leaders or subordinates.[31]

LEADER POWER

1. Position Power

    Position in the organizational hierarchy (often called organizational chart power)
    Ability to set policy
    Possession of information

2. Coercive Power

    Followers' fear of punishment (leader *perceived* to be able to punish, i.e., fire, keep from promotion, exclude from decisions, etc.)

3. Reward Power

    Followers' expectation of positive rewards (leader *perceived* to be able to promote, give raise or praise, help subordinate to succeed)

4. Expert Power

    Leader's special knowledge or skills (subordinates look to the leader as mentor, enabler, source of expertise)

5. Identity Power

    Personal traits or characteristics of leader; "care power"; charisma

Note: Using the first two types of power is very tenuous, because people resent it and will try to sabotage your efforts whenever possible.

SUBORDINATE POWER

1. Collective Power

    Subordinates join together—can alter leader's behavior and affect organization's goals (i.e., unions, affirmative action, citizen action groups)

2. Legal Power

    Laws governing treatment of employees regarding selection, hours, pay, race, sex, national origin, religion, benefits, and working conditions (subordinates can at times use the courts to get what they need)

3. Identity Power

    Subordinates' influence on leader and co-workers due to personal traits (charisma—"care power")

4. Affluence Power

    Reduction of subordinate's dependence upon employing organization for economic reasons (not dependent on job for survival, i.e., volunteers and second-income jobs)

5. Expert Power

    Subordinates' special skills or knowledge (organization looks to you for expertise, information, advice due to past performance, personal accomplishments, and/or education)

114

In deciding which of these kinds of power are appropriate to any given situation, these words of wisdom from Samuel Butler may help—"Life is like music. It must be composed by ear, feeling, and instinct, not by rule."

A modified version of a chart the Craigs use in their book *Synergic Power* illustrates the four steps involved in bringing about change.[32]

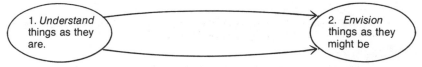

3. *Create* motivation in others to change

1. *Understand* things as they are.

2. *Envision* things as they might be

4. *Build* connecting bridges and *implement* strategies of change

Skipping any of these four steps most often leads to failure. For example:

—we may be trying to change something we do not completely understand because we have not done our homework; or

—we may be clear about the need for change, but have failed to do the necessary envisioning and problem solving to determine what the needed change should entail or produce; or

—we may have done both of the above, but failed to share our vision with others in a way that encourages them to join our cause; or

—if we have (1) evaluated, (2) determined clear alternatives, (3) created motivation that others share, we can still fail if we do not (4) strategize effectively, utilizing both management and power skills to make it possible to achieve the desired goals.

Rollo May reiterates the need to *both* care about and influence outcomes:

The cooperative loving side of existence goes hand in hand with coping and power, but neither the one nor the other can be neglected if life is to be gratifying . . . if we neglect the factor of power, as is the tendency in our day of reaction against the destructive effect of the misuse of power,

115

we shall lose values that are essential to our existence as humans . . . for man asserts his powers in creativity. One product of this is civilization. [33]

Once again our concern must be with the practical consideration of *how*. One key may be in the varying roles we must play in actualizing the four steps outlined on page 115. I would suggest these roles are as follows:

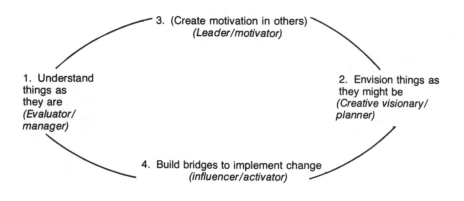

Antony Jay, in his interesting book *Management and Machiavelli*, suggests that a creative leader needs to be both "yogi and commissar." He says, "The yogi is the contemplative man, the thinker. . . . The commissar, on the other hand, is the man of action who does not need to be chased or prodded. . . . These are the people who can lead creative groups, by virtue of the dual insight which the combination of these qualities gives them."[34]

He goes on to say this kind of leader has the one thing none of the rest possess and that is an understanding of both the yogis and commissars who work there and also an understanding of the *whole operation*. He warns that such people are rare, but are around in most organizations "but the great corporations do not want them. Or do not deserve them." Once again, the phenomenon of "turn out" is all too often a reality. What a waste!

Let's now complete our power diagram, integrating this final information.

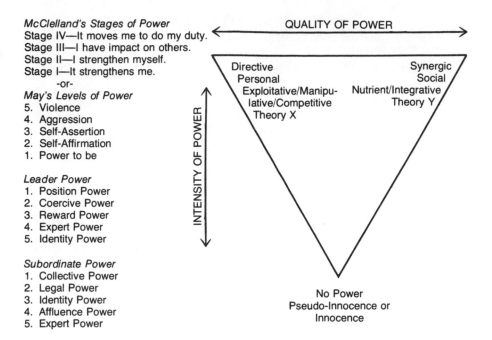

McClelland's Stages of Power
Stage IV—It moves me to do my duty.
Stage III—I have impact on others.
Stage II—I strengthen myself.
Stage I—It strengthens me.
        -or-
May's Levels of Power
5. Violence
4. Aggression
3. Self-Assertion
2. Self-Affirmation
1. Power to be

Leader Power
1. Position Power
2. Coercive Power
3. Reward Power
4. Expert Power
5. Identity Power

Subordinate Power
1. Collective Power
2. Legal Power
3. Identity Power
4. Affluence Power
5. Expert Power

QUALITY OF POWER

INTENSITY OF POWER

Directive
Personal
Exploitative/Manipu-
lative/Competitive
Theory X

Synergic
Social
Nutrient/Integrative
Theory Y

No Power
Pseudo-Innocence or
Innocence

We are now ready to move from a theoretical understanding of power and influence to practical application. It is essential that you learn to assess power (yours and that of other people) in order to create workable strategies to implement your creative ideas or problem solutions.

I would like to share a very practical tool developed by my husband which will help you work through power/influence situations in a planned, step-by-step fashion. We have both used this instrument on numerous occasions with gratifying results. It is important to work through *each step* carefully and honestly. This may be done individually or with your group when you reach the stage of implementation in the problem-solving process. It would also be helpful for you to utilize the chart on this page to help you review all of the power dynamics that may apply in this situation relating to kinds of power, levels and stages of power, and quality of power, as these relate both to you and the person(s) you are trying to influence.

117

INFLUENCE—ACHIEVEMENT WORKSHEET

Following are questions which should be answered when planning how to achieve a goal that involves influencing others:

Definition of the influence problem (define clearly and concisely):

1. What outcome(s) would you like to see occur?

2. Who must be influenced to have the desired outcome(s) occur?

3. What is your source of influence (power) with the person(s) identified above? (Consider the following kinds of power: reward, coercive, expert, identity, position.)

4. What will the person(s) do if you have been successful in your attempt to influence?

5. What is your strategy for influencing the person(s) to work toward the desired outcome?

6. What action must occur to achieve the desired outcome? By whom?

7. What is the "pay off" if the desired outcome occurs?

      to you?

      to·the person(s) you're attempting to influence?

to others?

8. What happens if the desired outcome fails to occur?

to you?

to the person(s) you're attempting to influence?

to others?

9. What obstacles, real and potential, must be overcome? (Consider obstacles in influencing others along with obstacles to achieving the desired outcome.)

10. What can be done to avert or minimize the obstacles?

11. How intensely do you want the desired outcome to occur?

Developed by: Harvey Wilson, Volunteer Management Associates, 1976.

One strategy that is useful to consider if you seem blocked or in an unfavorable power position with the person you need to influence is what I call an "end run." This is when you then ask yourself the question, "Can I influence someone else who can in turn influence this person?"

May I cite an example. Early in my husband's career, he worked for a large corporation on the West Coast. Since he had been hired to do management development and training, he assessed their current training programs and concluded some innovation was desperately needed. Most of the existing programs were sadly outmoded.

Harvey first attempted to influence his immediate supervisor, who flatly rejected all of his ideas. (It later became evident that many of the current programs had been instituted by this person.) So Harvey analyzed the situation and realized that one of the most influential people in the department was the secretary of a manager three levels above him on the organization chart. He became acquainted with her and at an appropriate time shared an outline of his training ideas with her. (He wisely left his name off the outline.) She was very impressed, took the outline and shared it with her boss. About two weeks later, Harvey's suggested changes came through channels, with her boss's signature on them. The changes happened because the needed innovation was more important than who got the credit. Two valuable concepts: end-runs and not caring who gets the credit!

NEGOTIATION

There is still one critical step left in the influence process and that is to actually present it to or "negotiate" it with the person or group who can say "yes" or "no."

As I think of the images that come to mind when I hear the term "negotiations," I realize they are also mostly negative:

Students at a university in the '60s locked in the president's office, with police surrounding the building;

Frantic parents awaiting a call from kidnappers;

Deadlocks at the negotiating tables in Korea and Viet Nam;

Stalled negotiations regarding the United States' hostages in Iran;

Union workers on strike.

In almost all of these cases, the situation became newsworthy because "negotiations had broken down" at some point and the result was high drama—anger, frustration, threats, fear.

In an attempt to gain a more healthy and optimistic perspective of the process of negotiation, it is important for us to realize that we all negotiate every day of our lives, when we

Buy a new house, car, or appliance;

Decide on family vacation plans;

Determine work assignments for staff and volunteers;

Change a child's eating, sleeping, or studying routine;

Agree on the salary for a new job; or

Write goals and objectives for a group.

The dictionary defines negotiating as *arranging for or bringing about a settlement of terms by discussion.* Chester Karrass offers another definition. It is "the exchange of ideas for the purpose of influencing behavior. . . . Wishes are converted into reality through the cold water of bargaining."[35] In other words, negotiation is the tool or mechanism we must go through to have other people say "yes" to our innovative ideas and changes.

Koberg and Bagnall state the case beautifully: "Don't fall in love with an idea. There are so many of them; they are truly expendable. *It is only after an idea is translated into reality that it becomes valuable.*"[36]

As we review our previous model of change on page 115, we realize negotiating helps us create a motivational need in others and to build bridges between things as they are and things as they might be. One of my favorite definitions of a leader is "someone who dreams dreams and has visions and can communicate those dreams and visions to others in such a way that they say yes."

Sometimes this process requires strategies, ceremonies, and rituals which we need to know about. (Think of the mating dance of some exotic birds. What a display of bravado, coyness, prescribed choreography; and ritual before the coveted *yes* is obtained.)

In this section we will continue to examine some notions about the strategies, rituals, and techniques of making good ideas happen. To do this, we will explore some resistance to change we may experience from groups and organizations and some tips regarding effective negotiating.

UNDERSTANDING RESISTANCE TO CHANGE

In the first two chapters of this book we consistently dealt with the concept of change. The very essence of creativity and innovation is introducing new ideas or processes into a situation, which automatically requires changing the old. We have defined power as the ability to cause or prevent change. We are now at the point in our journey "where the rubber hits the road." Can we convince others to accept and implement those changes?

Margulies and Wallace clearly articulate the challenge.

Planned organizational change requires effort and imagination. It isn't an easy business. Aside from the effort and imagination it requires knowledge and understanding [i.e., both right and left brain functions are involved once again]. And it is our conviction that it is the latter two factors that are often missing. Even in organizations that are willing and ready for change, change will not magically happen. Somebody must know how to make it happen, initiate it, manage it, and see that it occurs smoothly and effectively. [37]

It sounds a bit overwhelming. What we need to do is decide first of all, is the idea still worth pursuing? Here is where the work you have done on the Influence/Achievement Worksheet (page 118) will help you. How did you respond to the last question, "How intensely do you want the desired outcome to occur?" If your answer was strongly affirmative and not a tentative "sort-of," then it deserves the time and effort to try to implement it.

One important strategy to consider in avoiding or reducing the resistance of others to your idea or change is to attempt to analyze and understand *who* might resist and *why*. We so often short-circuit this step. We get an idea, tell it to others, and expect it to happen. Wismer calls this the "vending machine" approach to change—put a quarter in the machine and out comes the candy; write a memo and out comes the desired solution to a problem. Not true!

Types of changes that cause resistance

Human nature being what it is, we know people tend to resist change. What we do not often consider is *why* this is so. Hodge and Johnson shed some needed light on the subject by identifying eight types of changes that people will very likely resist. Those are:

1. Changes that they *perceive* will lower their status or prestige;

2. Changes that cause fear;

3. Changes that affect their job content and/or pay;

4. Changes that reduce their authority or freedom to act;

5. Changes that disrupt established work routines;

6. Changes that rearrange formal or informal group relationships;

7. Changes that are forced without explanation or employee participation; and

8. Changes that come at a time of mental and/or physical lethargy (sometimes called "system's overload")[38]

This information can be extremely useful if we use it to assess each change situation individually. Try putting yourself (through fantasy if possible) in the other party's situation. If you were that person or group, how would you feel about this idea or change? Which of these reasons for resistance would come into play? Be sure to try to experience not only what others may *think* about your idea, but also what they might *feel* about it.

Barriers that stimulate resistance

Gordon Lippitt reminds us that *the way a change is implemented sometimes stimulates more resistance than the change itself.* "Resistance to change is not inevitable. People may fear it as a threat to their security and their way of doing things. On the other hand, the idea of change can also produce pleasant anticipation of new experiences and benefits." He suggests there are nine barriers to change that managers create or reinforce:

1. Failing to be specific about a change.
2. Failing to show why a change is necessary.
3. Failing to allow those affected by change to have a say in the planning.
4. Using a personal appeal to gain acceptance of a change.
5. Disregarding a work group's habit patterns.
6. Failing to keep employees informed about a change.
7. Failing to allay employees' worries about possible failure.
8. Creating excessive work pressure during a change.
9. Failing to deal with anxiety over job security.[39]

Ways to minimize resistance and encourage support for change

It would seem, then, that it is essential for us to carefully consider (1) the idea itself; (2) those affected by that idea; and (3) the way we introduce it to others.

In an excellent article, "Organizational Change: How to Understand It and Deal with It," author Jack N. Wismer sums it up neatly.

People can accept an organizational change, if they are:

1. *involved* in the process;
2. *asked* to contribute their feelings, opinions, and suggestions;
3. *told* the reasons and advantages that will mitigate the uncertainty and anxiety about a change;

4. *provided* honest communication and feedback to create an atmosphere of confidence and trust;

5. *respected* for their feelings, even though they may oppose change;

6. *asked* what assistance is necessary to facilitate the effects of a change on-the-job; and

7. *given* appropriate and deserved recognition for their contribution in implementing the change.[40]

In each instance, action is required on the part of the change agent or manager. We must initiate those actions of involving, asking, telling, providing, informing, etc. Once again, change does not just happen, it has to be carefully managed.

It might be useful to try to exercise these concepts on some theoretical situations before applying them to your own specific influence/change problem. In each of these cases, answer the following questions:

1. Who will be affected by these suggested changes?

2. Which reasons for resistance could be anticipated for each affected group? Why?

3. What methods could be used in introducing the change that could minimize these resistances?

Case I: You have just been hired as director of volunteers for a juvenile detention center in a large city. The executive director created your position because he wants to add a number of volunteer counselors to the staff since the need for counselors far exceeds the allotted budget for paid staff. He has had positive experiences with volunteer counselors at another agency, although he has never utilized them in this facility. He gives you free rein to recruit community volunteers, stating, "It has been shown that volunteers are able to relate better to troubled kids than paid staff because the kids know volunteers are not being paid to be there and consequently they know the volunteers *really* care about them." The paid staff is given this same message as a rationale for adding the volunteers.

Case II: You are on the board of directors of a firm that manufactures parts for large, luxury automobiles. The board has just determined that the recent decline of sales due to energy-conscious consumers

124

purchasing small, economy cars necessitates a drastic cutback in plant operations and a search for new product lines.

Case III: You are the administrator of a rapidly expanding hospital in a metropolitan area. Your administrative staff has decided to introduce a computerized system throughout the hospital. It will affect how doctors, nurses, aides, support staff, administrative staff, and volunteers will carry out procedures for reporting, admissions and discharge, billing, scheduling, and record keeping.

Case IV: You are a senior staff member of a mental health facility and thus on the executive committee. This facility received a very large federal grant five years ago which enabled the staff to extend services to several outlying areas of the county. The grant period is now over and local funding sources have been unable or unwilling to provide the finances to continue these outreach services. Therefore it looks as though it will be necessary to curtail all service to outlying areas.

These are difficult situations, but not unlike those faced by managers in communities across the country every day of the week. (It would seem pleasant at times not to have to deal with such constant change. As Sidney Harris once said, most people both love and hate change. What we'd really like is for things to stay the same and get better!)

After these practice situations, you are now ready to return to your own Influence/Achievement Worksheet and deal with the same questions:

1. Who will be affected by your suggested change?
2. Which reasons for resistance to change can you anticipate for each affected group? Explain.
3. What methods could be used in introducing the change that could minimize these resistances?

SOME TIPS TO IMPROVE NEGOTIATING SKILLS

Probably all of us have had the experience many times in our lives of sitting helplessly by while an idea or project we have invested a great deal of time, energy, and commitment in was shot down. Someone else managed to convince the decisionmakers that their idea was better. A win/lose negotiation had taken place and we were probably not even aware that we had been in a negotiation.

We have all heard the old saw "Nice guys can't win"—but Chester Karrass (one of the nation's leading authorities on negotiations) says nice guys can win, *if they know what they're doing!*[41]

Karrass claims more than good intentions and commitment are needed. He identifies seven traits he feels are important for effective negotiators:

1. Planning skills;

2. Ability to think clearly under stress;

3. Ability to use common sense;

4. Verbal ability;

5. Program or product knowledge;

6. Personal integrity; and

7. Ability to perceive and use power.

He summarizes by stating a good negotiator must have a good self-image, as well as a high tolerance for ambiguity and uncertainty, openmindedness, courage, and a real desire "to achieve, to aspire, to take that sensible but extra measure of risk that represents a commitment to one's strivings."[42]

Karrass has written three excellent publications intended primarily for professional negotiators: *Give and Take*, *The Negotiating Game*, and *The Effective Negotiations Workbook*. In these books he identifies the three basic ingredients of any negotiations as *power, aspirations, and skill*.

We have discussed *power* extensively and need only reiterate here that the important thing in negotiations is how each party *perceives* the power of the other, whether that is accurate or not.

There have been experiments which clearly indicate that one's *aspirations* are perhaps the most critical predictor of success in negotiations. Persons with higher aspiration levels win higher awards. Those with high aspirations get high settlements; those who want little get little. In other words, don't just ask for what you think the other party will accept—ask for what you really need to accomplish your goals, and expect to get it!

With regard to *skill*, these same studies showed most unskilled negotiators were losers except when they had a high degree of power *and* high aspirations. When both parties were equally matched in power and aspirations, the most skilled always gained more. To illustrate:

Once upon a time there was a bear who was hungry and a man who was cold, so they decided to negotiate in a neutral cave. After several hours a settlement was reached. When they emerged the man had a fur coat and the bear was no longer hungry![43]

To help improve our skills in negotiating, the experts suggest these common-sense hints:

1. Carefully select the person(s) who will be your negotiator(s) (keeping in mind the traits mentioned on page 126);
2. Be conscious of the importance of timing (almost no new idea will look good to the boss in the midst of an audit, grant deadline, or annual meeting);
3. Check out your assumptions throughout the entire process;
4. Remember—time and patience are power, so do not be forced into unwanted or unwise deadlines;
5. Understand the sources of power and the needs—theirs and yours;
6. Clarify the outcomes you want;
7. Avoid "take it or leave it" tactics or conflict too soon (you can always escalate);
8. Dare to risk;
9. Try not to have too great a need to be loved by all;
10. Do your homework;
11. Examine *all* alternatives—(most people do not and often fight for less than the best);
12. Be a bit unpredictable; and
13. Have high aspirations.

I would like to close this chapter with a true story that illustrates many of these concepts on power and negotiating.

Our home is located in the foothills just outside of Boulder, Colorado. We have two acres of beautiful, rugged terrain surrounding our alpine house. We chose this location for the peace, quiet, and beauty offered by that environment.

About a year ago, the president of the local Water District Board paid us a visit. She informed us that due to the steady increase in the number of homes being built in this area, present water supplies were critically insufficient. The Water Board had hired geologists to locate new sources of water and they had "happily" found an excel-

127

lent underground spring—right in the middle of our backyard. The purpose of her visit was to announce that the Board wanted to build a pumping station about ten feet from our kitchen windows.

Needless to say, this presented us with a very difficult dilemma. On the one hand, we possessed water that was clearly needed by our neighbors. On the other hand, the prospect of the sights and sounds of a pumping station in our backyard seemed totally unacceptable. What to do!

My husband, Harvey, a very skilled negotiator, took over. He announced we would consider it and get back with them. In the meantime, we met with our next-door neighbors who had been informed that the Water District planned to plow an access road right through their yard. (They were as upset as we were.) Together, we laid out our joint strategy: We both adamantly opposed the pump and road, but if they had to be built we said we would agree under these conditions:

1) Insist on free water for both properties forever;

2) Charge a royalty on water pumped; and

3) Require the Board to provide landscaping to minimize the environmental disruptions of both the road and the pump.

Since I tend to "want to be loved by all," I really had problems with (2)—charging our neighbors for water—but Harvey said we had to make the demands tough enough to force them to examine other alternatives. Remember—our goal was not the money, it was to avoid having the well in our backyard.

We met with the full Board a few days later. Our two families announced the stated conditions of acceptance. The Board was furious and stated they could get an injunction and claim the water, even though it was on our property. The meeting ended with them implying we needed to reconsider, and they gave us a deadline of two weeks. They claimed work had to start by then in order to avoid an imminent shortage and that they might have to take legal action if we did not consent by then. We replied that we would be happy to go to court if necessary. Harvey counseled that we just wait them out. He reasoned they were trying to use the pressure of a critical deadline to rush us into a decision in their favor. So . . . we waited. Two weeks turned into six and we had not heard.

In the meantime, the Board decided it needed to be sure there were no other, less costly options, so they had their geologists do

128

further checking. They found an excellent source of water right next to the county road below our property, completely apart from anyone's home. No disruption of the environment was needed to build the pump or have easy access to it.

This is a perfect example of a win/win. The area got the needed water while the privacy and beauty of our property was preserved.

How frequently we settle for less than the best solution, either because we fail to explore all alternatives or because we do not know how to negotiate effectively.

REFERENCES

1. May, Rollo, *Power and Innocence*, W.W. Norton and Co., 1972, p. 21.

2. Lasswell, Harold, *American Psychologist*, 1970, p. 122ff, © 1971 by the American Psychological Association. Reprinted by permission.

3. O'Connor, Elizabeth, *Search for Silence*, Word Books, 1972-74, p. 106.

4. Craig, James H., and Marguerite, *Synergic Power*, Proactive Press, 2nd Edition, 1979 (P.O. Box 296, Berkeley, CA 94701), p. 44.

5. May, pp. 48, 49.

6. May, pp. 60, 64.

7. Craig, p. 62.

8. Ibid, p. 69.

9. McClelland, David, "The Two Faces of Power," *Journal of International Affairs*, Vol. 24, No. 1, 1970.

10. May, p. 105 ff.

11. McGregor, Douglas, *The Human Side of Enterprise*, McGraw-Hill, 1960.

12. May, pp. 40-44.

13. Ibid, p. 138.

14. Ibid.

15. Abramson, Martin, "The Success Merchants," *TWA Ambassador Magazine*, Vol. 11, No. 5, May 1978, p. 31 ff.

16. Smart, D.O., *Care Power: A Bridge to Increased Productivity*, The Calibre Group, 3435 Broadway, Kansas City, MO 64111, pp. 4, 5.

17. Smart, p. 5.

18. May, pp. 142-145.

19. Ibid, p. 148 ff.

20. Ibid, p. 151.

21. Levinson, Harry, "The Abrasive Personality," *Harvard Business Review*, May-June, 1978, pp. 86-94.

22. May, p. 43 ff.

23. Ibid, pp. 177-179.

24. McClelland, David, *Power: The Inner Experience*, Irvington Publishers, John Wiley & Sons, 1975, p. 13 ff.

25. Ibid, p. 16.

26. Ibid, pp. 18, 19.

27. Ibid, p. 20.

28. Ibid, p. 23.

29. Wilson, Marlene, *The Effective Management of Volunteer Programs*, Volunteer Management Associates, 1976.

30. Greenleaf, Robert, *The Servant as Leader*, Center for Applied Studies, Windy Row Press, 43 Grove St., Peterborough, NH 03458, 1972, p. 35.

31. French, J.R.P., and Raven, B.H., "The Basis of Social Power," *Studies in Social Power*, University of Michigan Press, 1959.

32. Craig, p. 47.

33. May, pp. 19, 20.

34. Jay, Antony, *Management and Machiavelli*, Holt, Rinehart and Winston, 1967, p. 114 ff.

35. Karrass, Chester, *Negotiating Game*, Thomas Y. Crowell Co., 1970, p. 4.

36. Koberg, Don, and Bagnall, Jim, *The Universal Traveler. A Soft-Systems Guide to Creativity, Problem-Solving and the Process of Reaching Goals*, Wm. Kaufman, Inc., 1972-1976.

37. Margulies, N., and Wallace, J., *Organizational Change: Techniques and Applications*, Scott, Foresman & Co., 1973, Preface.

38. Hodge, Billy J., and Johnson, Herbert J., *Management and Organizational Behavior*, John Wiley and Sons, 1970, pp. 432, 433.

39. Wismer, Jack, "Organizational Change: How to Understand and Deal with It," *Training*, May 1979, p. 28.

40. Ibid, p. 31.

41. Karrass, p. 11.

42. Ibid, p. 36.

43. Ibid, p. 3.

CHAPTER IV

Conflict Management: Managing It Instead of It Managing You

Conflict within the organization is a sign of a healthy organization— up to a point. A good manager doesn't try to eliminate conflict; he [she] tries to keep it from wasting the energies of people. Conviction is a flame that must burn itself out—in trying an idea or fighting for a chance to try it. If bottled up inside, it will eat a person's heart away. If you're the boss and your people fight you openly when they think you're wrong— that's healthy. If they fight each other openly in your presence for what they believe in–that's healthy. But keep all conflict eyeball to eyeball. [1]

. . . Robert Townsend

Friendly competition is a healthy thing. It makes the adrenalin flow, increases levels of achievement, and creates enthusiasm and excitement. Our culture has fostered competition in almost all arenas of human activity: business; sports; politics; and the arts. We love a good contest!

But have you ever observed when friendly competition crosses over some important, though invisible, line? All of a sudden you have a "win at any cost" situation, which can then become open conflict. It is no longer fun or friendly and the stakes are incredibly high.

131

I have seen this happen in little league baseball, bridge or monopoly games, tennis, jogging, elementary school art contests, sales competitions, and a hundred other places. It is understandable, because in all of those situations there are winners and losers. Everyone loves a winner (and we bestow accolades, promotions, trophies, ribbons, and attention to prove it). But how about the losers? How often are they blamed, ridiculed, by-passed, or just plain ignored? Yes, winning definitely feels better than losing.

When we look at competitive situations within work groups and organizations, the stakes are even higher. Our very livelihood and professional futures might be on the line. Is it any wonder that we find competition turning into conflict in many inter- and intra-organizational situations. We often wish we could just pout and go home when we lose, but the reality is that we must face the winners at 8:00 o'clock the next morning and oftentimes spend many of the next 2,080 working hours with them in the year ahead. So we often find ourselves shuffling papers, staring out the window, or immersing ourselves in nonproductive, but furious activity in an effort to cope.

It therefore seems prudent for us to ask, are there any other options relating to disagreements and conflicts than this win/lose one? If so, what are they and how can we utilize them to minimize destructive or divisive outcomes in our interactions as persons, groups, and organizations?

DEFINING AND UNDERSTANDING CONFLICT

First, let's see if we can come to a common understanding of what we mean by conflict:

Conflict is an expressed struggle between at least two inter-dependent parties, who perceive incompatible goals, scarce rewards or resources, and interference from the other party in achieving their goals.[2]

Most authorities claim some conflict is inevitable in human relationships where people or groups are interdependent. Often the clash occurs more over *perceived* differences than real ones . . . people anticipate blocks to achieving their goals that may or may not be there.

A more simple way of stating this definition is:

Two or more people perceive that what each one wants is incompatible with the other.

There is a normal process of development in any conflict and this

132

process tends to be cyclical, repeating itself over a series of episodes:

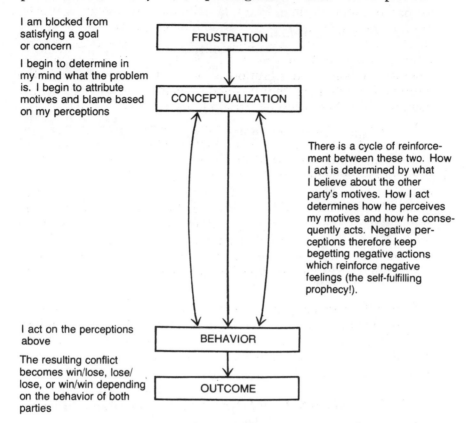

I am blocked from
satisfying a goal
or concern

I begin to determine in
my mind what the problem
is. I begin to attribute
motives and blame based
on my perceptions

FRUSTRATION

CONCEPTUALIZATION

There is a cycle of reinforcement between these two. How
I act is determined by what
I believe about the other
party's motives. How I act
determines how he perceives
my motives and how he consequently acts. Negative perceptions therefore keep
begetting negative actions
which reinforce negative
feelings (the self-fulfilling
prophecy!).

I act on the perceptions
above

The resulting conflict
becomes win/lose, lose/
lose, or win/win depending
on the behavior of both
parties

BEHAVIOR

OUTCOME

This diagram illustrates how important it is to check out our perceptions and assumptions about the other party's attitudes and motives. Our subsequent behavior and the outcome of the conflict is directly determined by the conceptualization phase.

We act on our beliefs about the other party. For example, I may have decided that the person has rejected my idea because he or she is threatened by me or does not like me when, in fact, I did not communicate clearly or give them enough information. How differently I would respond depending on which of these I believed to be true.

ANTECEDENTS TO CONFLICT

Filley has identified nine characteristics of social relationships that can lead to conflict. These can serve as our early warning signs if we pay attention to them:[3]

1. *Ambiguous jurisdictions.*

   If boundaries of responsibility and authority are unclear, the possibility of conflict increases. Clear role definitions are therefore very important.

2. *Conflict of interest.*

   Competition for perceived scarce resources (or rewards) escalates conflict possibilities. Both parties want the same things.

3. *Communications barriers.*

   Time and space separations can divide people into groupings which tend to compete with one another. This diminished ability for sub-groups to interact on a regular basis increases the possibilites of misunderstandings, which can readily escalate into conflicts. (It is also important to clarify assumptions and definitions of terms, for often people mean the same thing but use different terminology to define it.)

4. *Overdependency of one party.*

   If one party depends too heavily on the other for resources or tasks, conflict is more apt to occur. (We will say more about this later.)

5. *Differentiation in organization.*

   The greater the degree of differentiation in an organization (i.e., levels of authority, types, and numbers of specific tasks), the greater the potential for conflict.

6. *Association of the parties.*

   The more the parties interact both in decision-making situations and informally, the more the opportunities for conflict increase. However, *major incidences of conflict decrease as participation increases.*

7. *Need for consensus.*

   When all parties *must* agree to the outcome, disagreements tend to escalate.

8. *Behavior regulations.*

   Conflicts are greater when controls, i.e., rules, regulations, formal policies are imposed.

9. *Unresolved prior conflicts.*

   As the number of past *unresolved* conflicts increases, so

does the possibility for more conflicts in the future. (This underlines the importance of managing conflicts at their earliest stages since they do not go away!)

When you consider that all work groups are made up of *individuals* who each come to a situation with different experiences, knowledge, capabilities, and emotional characteristics, it is no wonder that there are conflicts. As McGregor points out, "On the one hand these differences provide the essential ingredients of innovation, creative problem solving, organizational achievement. On the other hand, these same differences are the source of *inevitable* conflict and disagreement that may interfere with effective group and organizational accomplishment. They can lead to major inefficiency, delay and frustration and to the least common denominator decisions and highly unsatisfactory solutions."[4] (Sounds like we can't live with differences . . . and can't live without them . . . at least not very creatively or productively.)

One of the things that has caused many of us to shy away from or deny conflict is the memories of past conflicts that still hurt. I have acquired an impressive array of "conflict scars" over the years (as I am sure each of you has). Only my most intimate confidants have been allowed to see most of them and I have never revealed some to anyone. I would like to deny they even exist. The most hurtful, and therefore lasting, scars have most frequently been caused by conflicts with those who are closest and dearest to me:

—family
—husband
—children
—close friends
—trusted colleagues and work groups
—church and other causes I've cared most about

Some of these scars came as a result of denying or avoiding conflicts which should have been dealt with and resolved. Others were produced by destructive, unproductive "fights." Almost none of the conflicts I have had that were managed constructively have any residue or scar tissue left at all. With resolution comes release.

Perhaps the most stressful times are when we find ourselves engaged in conflicts on more than one front at the same time (i.e., work and marriage; cause, work, and children; or friend and colleagues). That is when we need to take seriously the business of stress management (see next chapter). We are then very close to "system's overload" and steps must be taken to change the situation before we burn out.

COMMON MISCONCEPTIONS REGARDING CONFLICT

Frost and Wilmot suggest that one reason people still hold very negative opinions about "doing conflict" is the following *misconceptions* which seem to be perpetuated:[5]

a. *Harmony is normal and conflict is abnormal.* This is untrue. It is very normal, in fact inevitable, that conflicts emerge, subside, and reemerge in any on-going relationship.

b. *Conflicts and disagreements are the same phenomena.* Conflicts are, in fact, more serious than disagreements and usually involve incompatible goals.

c. *Conflict is pathological.* (If so—we're all sick.)

d. *It is only o.k. to manage, reduce, or avoid conflict, never to escalate or incite it when the cause seems right.* Again—not so.

e. *Conflict is the result of "personality problems."* Personalities do not conflict—people's behaviors conflict!

f. *Conflict and anger are closely merged in most people's minds.* Conflict involves issues as well as emotions and the issue and the participants determine the emotions generated. They may feel fear, excitement, sadness, frustration, and other emotions as well as anger.

CONFLICT AS IT RELATES TO CREATIVITY, PROBLEM SOLVING, AND POWER

This topic of conflict is also very closely related to our previous subjects: creativity, problem solving, and power.

Conflict and Creativity
Douglas McGregor states,

> *Virtually every successful innovation—technical or social—is the outcome of conflict between the new and old; competition and conflict are pervasive in all social interaction. One more important reason lies in the very nature of man. Winning, overcoming obstacles, solving problems are the source of fundamentally important rewards. On the other hand, many if not all human beings deplore, even hate, certain forms of conflict.* [6]

(Remember May's emphasis on the value of conflict in creating the heightened awareness, sometimes rage, required for creativity.)

136

Conflict and Problem Solving

"The opposite of conflict is problem solving."[7] It is important for persons, groups, and organizations to learn how to turn conflict into problem solving situations. Conflict usually ends in loss for one or both parties whereas problem solving helps participants feel like and become winners, with increased energy and creativity, as opposed to feeling defeat and disillusionment.

Conflict and Power

"One of the fundamental concepts in conflict theory is power. It is central to the study of conflict."[8] In any conflict situation we try to exert influence (power) to move others to help us accomplish our goals. According to Frost and Wilmot, power operates in interpersonal conflicts as follows:

1. *Parties are interdependent.*

2. *Parties have resources that another is dependent upon to reach their goals.*

3. *The ability to influence the goal attainment of the other is the power you have over him or her.*

4. *Each person in a conflict has some degree of power. Power is always a relative judgment:*

   a. *One party may have more power compared to the other party's power, and*

   b. *Power bases can shift during the course of conflict.*

5. *Persons in conflict can make choices that define power either equally or unequally. High power persons can choose to share power by changing the structure of the power relationship.*

6. *Using power productively to achieve both individual and relational goals is a skill that can be learned.*[9]

Over the long run, conflict seems to be more productive and outcomes more satisfying to both parties when power is more evenly distributed. People are more committed to outcomes they have the power to help determine.

CONFLICT IS BOTH AFFECTIVE AND SUBSTANTIVE

Another dimension of conflict that we must understand is that it has both affective (feelings) and substantive (issues) aspects. The balance varies depending on the situation, but both are involved in *any* conflict.

This can be viewed from the perspective of the usual struggle

137

between our right and left brain thinking. The left brain's normal striving for logic, structure, reason, and order often creates conflict. We want quick solutions to bring order out of the chaos of differences. Our inability to tolerate ambiguity too often plunges us headlong into win/lose conflicts rather than taking the time and patience needed for creative problem solving. When we develop and encourage more right-brained thinking, we learn to play with options and seek more input before deciding. We are more conscious of relationships and consider them as important as the issues.

We must learn to deal with both the affective and substantive aspects of conflict. It often seems less difficult to tackle the issue or task than the feelings. But the feelings everyone has—about themselves, the others, the problem, and the outcome—will greatly impact the *long-term results* of the solution. (We may just win the battle and lose the war.)

LEVELS OF CONFLICT

One of the things that determines the depth and complexity of a conflict is the basic issue(s) at stake. Most experts identify four areas of disagreement which are involved in conflict situations. Each one gets more complex and thus more difficult to resolve:

Level   I—*Facts or Data:* the parties simply have different information. This is often a basic communications problem and when all pertinent information is shared with those concerned, differences disappear.

Level   II—*Processes or Methods:* the parties disagree over the best way to achieve a goal or solve a problem. This becomes somewhat more difficult, but by utilizing sound problem-solving techniques it can usually be settled.

Level III—*Goals or Purpose:* the parties cannot agree on what the group's basic purpose or mission is or what they would like it to be. Negotiating goals takes patience and skill, but it is vital if collaboration is ever to be attained.

Level IV—*Values:* the parties disagree about the basic meanings of the situation and the things they hold dear. They are, in fact, coming from very different and alien places. These conflicts are extremely difficult and can best be dealt with by an expert third party. (Have you ever tried to change someone's value system?)

Let's take a look at a typical example of each:

Facts: Only one department in a welfare agency failed to receive a memo from the director informing them that a new grant had been received for a child abuse program.

Process: At the next staff meeting, this oversight was corrected and plans were begun to implement the program. However, disagreements arose regarding allocation of staff and funds. Many of the staff were already feeling overworked and priorities became an issue.

Goals: The Supervisor of Adult Services felt strongly that the basic intent of the new program should be to help abusing parents. The Supervisor of Children's Services adamantly insisted it was obviously meant to aid abused children.

Values: Two very conservative members of the board of directors became extremely upset about the grant itself, since they felt the agency had no business getting involved in "that whole sordid mess."

As you see, each level becomes more complex and sensitive to deal with, so it is important that we are clear what the conflict is about. Remember, in problem solving, the most critical phase is *problem definition.*

The following questionnaire may help you begin to determine the level of the conflict and some steps to take to manage it.

CONFLICT QUESTIONNAIRE

Question #1—What is the difference between what is being done versus what is desired?

Question #2—Where does the difference originate?

( ) A. Disagreement over facts?

If so:

- Assist in *mutual* validation of data.
- Begin with factual data that has high likelihood of agreement by both parties.
- Ask *both* parties what additional information would obviously help resolve the issues.

( ) B. Disagreement over methods? Procedures? Policies? Rules?

139

If so:

- Start with factual analysis as above.
- Begin focusing both parties on common objectives, conveying that conflict is over means not ends.
- With the help of both parties, develop a list of criteria by which a mutually acceptable method or procedure could be achieved.
- With both parties, generate a list of alternate methods which meet the established criteria.

( ) C. Disagreement over goals, aims, purposes?

If so:

- Start with factual analysis as above.
- Determine if the *cause* is really a goal difference or a method difference.
- With both parties, gain an agreement over what is the "super-ordinate" goal (that goal that rises above differences).
- Find what each is willing to concede as a last resort to achieve the super-ordinate goal.

( ) D. Disagreement over values, philosophies, life styles?

If so:

- Start with factual analysis as above.
- With the help of both parties, obtain a clear working statement of the problem in behavioral, or operating terms, then solve as above. You may need the help of a third party intervener.

Question #3—At what stage of conflict are the disputants at?

( ) A. One or both sides anticipate a change which will likely lead to conflict.

( ) B. A conflict implicitly exists that as yet has not been expressed.

( ) C. Discussions have occurred which indicate a conflict exists.

( ) D. An open dispute or difference has occurred which has pinpointed opposing points of view.

( ) E. Open conflict exists wherein one or both sides have firmly committed themselves to an opposing positon and are working to increase their position.

Question #4—At what stage of problem-solving effectiveness are the disputants at?

( ) A. Both sides ignore or deny that a problem exists.

( )   One side only.

( ) B. Both sides admit to a problem but are unwilling to meet.
( )   One side only.

( ) C. Both sides are willing to meet but are blaming the other.

( )   One side only.

( ) D. Both sides accept part of the responsibility for the problem.

( )   One side only.

( ) E. Both sides are willing to test new approaches to solve the problem.

( )   One side only.

Some additional thoughts:

1. After problem analysis, always begin by looking for "win-win" solutions.

2. Get both involved in creating solutions. People become committed to the things they help create.

3. New commitments are best achieved when:

  - Both commit to a mutually agreed upon plan in the presence of a trusted third party.

  - A built-in review is agreed upon, involving the third party.

  - No exceptions are considered or taken by either side.

  - Both sides agree to take the first opportunity to show "good faith" in the agreement.

  - Both sides meet in a neutral, informal place.

  - *Conflict is caught at the earliest stage.*

KINDS OF CONFLICT

For our purposes we will deal with three types of conflicts:

—*Intrapersonal*

—*Interpersonal*

—*Inter-group*

INTRAPERSONAL CONFLICT

Intrapersonal conflict is the internal clash caused by the various roles, needs, and expectations we have as persons. (It is "me fighting with myself.") It is when our roles of manager, spouse or lover, parent, subordinate, citizen, and professional conflict for our time, attention, and commitment.

In some workshops I have conducted, we have demonstrated this conflict very graphically by utilizing an adaptation of a Virginia Satir exercise. We call it "Multiple Role Schizophrenia." It consists of physically binding a manager role-player with ropes representing the different systems he/she must interact with and respond to during the course of his or her job. These include parents, spouse, children, supervisor, subordinates, clients, board, community-at-large, and the hierarchy of their profession. We then attach "actors" along each of the ropes representing all of these persons who have claims and petitions for the manager's time and energy. At one point, we give the instruction for all 20-30 people to get what they need from the manager—any way they can. (They are still all bound together by the various ropes.) The chaos and frustration experienced by all, but especially the manager, are profound! It serves as a very graphic example of the "pulls and tugs" we all feel when our "roles" collide.

Douglas McGregor observed,

The role of the manager can be visualized as a dynamic interplay between environmental forces and pressures operating on the manager and forces originating from within the manager, his values, personality, and aspirations. Role conflict is inescapable, for there is really no way that a manager can harmonize perfectly the competing pressures emanating from within and from without . . . finding a way to cope with tension and to confront and grow from conflict is a genuine challenge. [10]

(We will deal in depth with coping with these tensions in the Stress Management chapter.)

Sometimes this conflict regarding roles is strictly job related. This occurs when your written job description and your own expectations differ markedly from the situation as it actually is either because of your supervisor's actions (or inaction) or the realities of the work group or organization. Things are just not what you thought they would be and the frustration mounts daily. In this case, a model for planned renegotiation suggested by Sherwood and Glidwell may be useful:[11]

PLANNED RENEGOTIATION MODEL

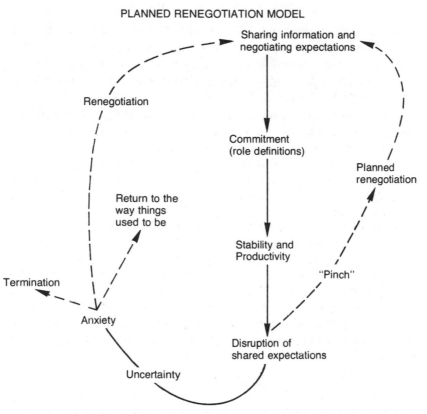

The model describes how roles are established and changed. Relationships cycle through:

(1) the sharing of information and the negotiation of expectations; then

(2) commitment to a set of expectations, which governs behavior during a period

(3) of stability and productivity, when, for the most part you do what I expect of you and I do what you expect of me, until

(4) disruption occurs and the possibility of change enters the system.

Planned renegotiation is a norm-setting intervention featuring concepts which provide a way to introduce controlled change by anticipating disruption and renegotiating in advance. A relationship is established so that "whenever I feel a pinch," that pinch is shared, and the possibility of renegotiation is raised before disruption occurs.

An example of the importance of this model occurred in my own worklife a few years ago:

I was hired as the first director of a small fledgling agency which a consortium of agencies and volunteers had founded. (It was the county's Volunteer Bureau and Information and Referral Agency.) I accepted the position with the understanding that it would be a half-time job. (My children were still in elementary school.) The first couple of years I worked on the stage of "productivity and stability," forming a strong team of volunteer staff to assist in the management of the agency. The agency flourished, and gradually my negotiated half-time job was becoming closer and closer to full time (with no increase in salary). I still did not want a full-time job due to family commitments, yet I loved the work I was doing. I hesitated to say anything, for I was afraid they would say the job now required a full-time director. The reality of unfairness (greater expectations and longer hours with no corresponding rewards) led to the "uncertainty and anxiety stage." When I finally called *pinch* and asked for renegotiation of the job, my board cooperated beautifully. We worked out a compromise of a three-quarter-time position and a corresponding increase in salary. From this experience I learned to yell *pinch* when feelings of unrest and dissatisfaction first occur.

INTERPERSONAL CONFLICT

Interpersonal conflict is a struggle between two parties who are interdependent and perceive that their goals on an issue are incompatible. They also believe that there are scarce resources (money, time, attention) and also scarce rewards (usually self-esteem and power)—so they begin by competing for them and all too often end in conflict.

The severity and repercussions of this conflict are often determined both by the level of the conflict issue (facts, process, goals, or values) and the level of dependence each party feels toward the

144

other. This is especially important to understand in conflicts involving spouses, parents and children, friends, or managers and subordinates.

The normal stages we go through relating to dependence and interdependence are:[12]

Dependency

We all start off life (and relationships) in a condition of dependency. It is nice to have someone care for (or take care of) us. If someone tries to move us out of this stage too soon, too suddenly, we get restive and frightened. (Unfortunately, some people never mature enough to ever fully move out of this stage.)

Counter-dependency

Counter-dependency is the natural breaking away process. It occurs as we grow out of the dependency stage and as our need for independence surfaces. At this point, the solicitousness and controls that we used to feel were comforting begin to smother us and we resist them.

This is a very uncomfortable stage for everyone, because it is often marked by combative and aggressive behavior. Anyone who has parented teenagers knows this to be true. The prevailing pitfall of this stage (as parents or supervisors) is to become either overly rigid or too permissive. Neither is helpful. (This is the move toward self-affirmation.)

Independence

Gradually we emerge into new-found freedoms. It feels good to be free at last and "stand on our own two feet." It feels like a glorious release.

But then this feeling of independence begins to subtly turn into a vague feeling of unrest. Loneliness and uncertainty are the flip side of the coin of total independence and are often a bit unnerving.

Interdependence

If a person was not too damaged in the counter-dependent phase, a healthy, mutually collaborative relationship emerges based on reciprocal rights and responsibilities. This, of course, is what true maturity is all about.

145

Now, as we look at these stages of dependency, it is easy to see how the content, structure, and style of the conflict are greatly affected by where each party is in relation to its dependency on the other. The closer they both are to mature interdependence, the more productive the problem solving is apt to be.

One hard lesson I have learned (time and again) is how seductive it is to become the "rescuer" in situations where the other party is either dependent or counter-dependent. It almost always backfires! I now try to remember, before falling into that temptation, a concept I once heard at a workshop:

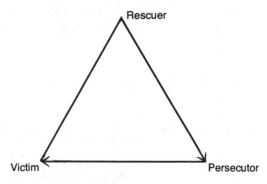

A rescuer almost always ends up being viewed as a persecutor and then becomes a victim.

PERSONAL CONFLICT STYLES

Just as boxers in the ring have different styles of fighting, so each of us has personal styles of doing conflict. These range all the way from tough battler, to fancy footwork artist, to avoider, to hit and run attacker, and so on.

Let's examine a theory that may help you gain some understanding of your own style and that of others.

This theory comes from Kilmann and Thomas (1975) and is based on the notion that each style is composed of two partially competing goals—*concern for self* and *concern for others*.[13]

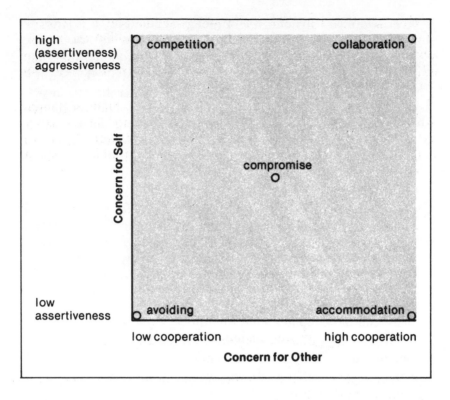

(assertiveness)
aggressiveness

competition   collaboration

Concern for Self

compromise

low
assertiveness   avoiding   accommodation

low cooperation   high cooperation

Concern for Other

Reprinted with permission of authors and publisher from: Kilmann, R.H., & Thomas, K.W. Interpersonal conflict-handling behavior as reflections of Jungian personality dimensions. PSYCHOLOGICAL REPORTS, 1975, 37, 971-980, Table 1.

Let's look more closely at each style:[14]

1. *Competing.* A person's competitiveness represents a high concern for your own goals and low concern for the goals of others. It is characterized by being assertive (sometimes aggressive) and often uncooperative. You are apt to pursue your goals at the expense of others. One often uses whatever power is available (rank, economic sanction, etc.) to win. Winning is very important.

2. *Accommodating.* This represents a high concern for the goals of others, but a low concern for your own. It is characterized by being unassertive, pliable, and cooperative, the very opposite of competing. (So you can see who wins when these two are matched in a conflict.) There is a bit of a martyr tendency here. You almost always sacrifice your concerns for the good of others

147

(even when you do not agree or feel good about it). It is appropriate at times, obviously, but how often do you use this style?

3. *Avoiding*. This represents a low concern for your goals and a low concern for the goals of others. They are just not worth a "fight." It is an unassertive, uncooperative style, for you refuse to engage in the process of conflict or problem solving. Differences are denied or ignored (and it can be "crazy making" for the other party). Again, this style is appropriate at times—when time lines are too short, emotions too high, etc. But be careful if this is your normal style. It makes creative problem solving impossible because the problem is denied.

4. *Compromising*. This represents some concern for your goals and some concern for others. It is a sort of "half-a-loaf is better than none" approach. It is an intermediate stance between assertiveness and cooperativeness. You like to get along with everyone, so tend to look for a quick solution that will be all right with everyone. (Someone once said, "Compromise is simply changing the question to fit the answer.") It is easy to come out with "least common denominator," mediocre solutions that really do not fully satisfy anyone, including you.

5. *Collaborating*. This represents a high concern for your goals and a high concern for the goals of others. You are both assertive and cooperative. This style is the opposite of avoidance. Collaborating involves attempting to work *with* the other person(s) to find some new and better solution that satisfies the needs of both parties as fully as possible. It entails digging into the problem to find the underlying issues and then exploring all alternative solutions to find one that best meets the needs of both. It takes longer, and requires more trust, but it is by far the most effective conflict style in most cases. (This is when you use lateral thinking to help you dig a new hole rather than making the one you have deeper.)

CONTINGENCY CONFLICT STYLES

As in other aspects of management, it is important for a person to have a repertoire of styles so that your actions can be appropriate to the situation, person, and time restraints. The key word is flexibility! Each of these styles is appropriate in certain situations. Let's explore some possibilities:

148

1. *Competing*

    —when unpopular decisions have to be enforced

    —when grants, funding, or sales are involved

    —when you believe strongly that you are right and the out-
    come is very important (usually relates to goals or values)

    —in crisis situations where quick action is needed

2. *Avoiding*

    —when parties are over-emotional and need a "cooling off"
    period

    —when you agree to disagree

    —when it really is not your problem

    —when the cost is greater than the benefits or rewards

    —when you really cannot do anything about the situation and
    decide not to waste energy worrying about it

    —when priorities dictate that it is not wise to get sidetracked
    on less important issues

3. *Accommodating*

    —when the relationship is more important than the issue

    —when you perceive the other party's need is greater than
    yours

    —when the balance of power is clearly in their favor (i.e., you
    could get fired and you are not sure this one is worth it)

    —when the other party is trying out some new skills (decision
    making, problem solving) and you can live with the outcome
    even though it is not your first choice

4. *Compromising*

    —when the situation is stalemated or deadlocked and you
    need to avoid a win/lose outcome

    —when half a loaf would truly be better than none at all

    —when shortness of time does not allow for further problem
    solving (as long as you are aware that the cost is probably a
    "less than best" answer)

    —when you want to preserve the relationship, and further
    conflict on this issue would be too damaging

5. *Collaborating*

   —when the issue is of real significance

   —when the outcome has major implications for the future of the group, the organization, or the relationship

   —when you can commit the time and energy to do creative problem solving, seeking the best solution from among all possible alternatives

   —when you are committed to win/win solutions

   —when all persons involved must be committed to the outcome and help to implement it

It is important to continually evaluate our own effectiveness in conflict situations. Ask yourself: Did I correctly assess the problem and the other person's motives and actions? Did I choose the conflict style appropriate for that situation? How well did we "do conflict"? To answer these questions, I suggest you evaluate the outcome of each conflict as follows:

1. *What was the quality of the decison or solution regarding results?*

2. *What was the psychological and physical condition of both conflicting parties after it was over?*

3. *What is the status of the relationship? (Did I win the battle and lose the war?)*

PASSIVE AGGRESSORS

A far too-common phenomenon in our society, where conflict and aggressive encounters have been viewed as taboo or "bad," is what is called hidden or passive aggressors. These people avoid overt conflict but the end result is often confused, destructive, and unauthentic interactions. Hidden aggressors often inflict hurt indirectly (and sometimes unconsciously) and sometimes even with loving or friendly motives.

One of the common complaints and frustrations I hear from employees is trying to deal with "nice bosses" who pretend to be in a "no power" stance, but who use this as a totally controlling device. This is a form of *passive aggressiveness* and it needs to be understood, because it can be emotionally and psychologically draining.

Passive aggressors have often grown up in very authoritarian, repressive home environments, where expressing feelings (especially anger) was not allowed. Some of the behaviors they develop to compensate are:[15]

1. *Forgetting.*

   The passive aggressor consistently "forgets" things he or she agreed to do, especially those things the intended victim of the hostility asks him to do and is depending on him for. By consistently forgetting what he really does not want to do but does not have nerve to refuse, the forgetter eventually gets out of the obligation to do it again. It becomes known that he cannot be counted upon. To help understand the possible hidden motives of chronic forgetting, substitute the words "did not want to" in place of the word "forgot."

2. *Misunderstanding.*

   Misunderstanding is a type of aggression which can be cloaked behind great sincerity. "I could have sworn you said you didn't need this report until *next* week. I'm really sorry!" or "I thought you really wanted me to tell Jane you were upset with her." Supposedly innocent errors have sabotaged more than one project or relationship.

3. *Procrastinating.*

   Procrastination creates exasperating and often unnecessary delays. The aggressor then tries to create guilt feelings in the victim by accusing him of being too "uptight, impatient, or pushy." The procrastination is usually done very selectively. It is a way to "get the goat" of the intended victim.

4. *Coming late.*

   Individuals who are *chronically* late for meetings, dates, or appointments are often expressing their hidden hostility towards those kept waiting. It is sometimes a socially acceptable way they have to express resentment. (Have you ever had an employee consistently arrive late with imaginative and totally plausible alibis several times a week? Watch it; he or she is attempting to get at you for some reason.)

5. *Refusing to carry over learning.*

   This behavior is characterized by consistent thoughtlessness of the victim's needs and wishes which forces you to request what you need or want anew each time. This makes you feel frustrated and hurt because the aggressors never seem to remember what you like or how you want something

151

done. They innocently state, "Don't get so uptight. If you want something, just tell me!"

What can you do when confronted with chronic passive aggressors? Bach and Goldberg, in their book *Creative Aggression*,[16] suggest that you ask yourself two questions: (1) Am I overly controlling or dominating with this person and therefore making it impossible for him/her to assert himself more directly? (2) Am I actually more comfortable with passive aggression and even though it is frustrating and annoying, I'd rather have that than having this person express his feelings openly to me?

If the answer is "no" to both questions, then I must be willing to:

1) Avoid being seduced by my own guilt or anger created by this situation and be willing to express *my* feelings about the behavior.

2) Try to surface the hidden hostility behind these behaviors by talking about and trying to understand the causes.

3) Deal with the problem of *misunderstanding* by having the aggressor repeat back the instruction or message *before* he leaves to perform it.

4) Deal with the problem of *procrastinating* by setting precise, clear deadlines and establishing penalties for delays, being sure those are carried out when deadlines are missed. (When the boss consistently brings letters to be typed at five minutes before quitting time, unless it is an emergency, firmly assure him you will get at them first thing in the morning and leave.)

5) With *latecomers*, set deadlines and clarify outcomes. ("If you are not here in ten minutes, I'll leave," or "We will start all meetings on time and not repeat information for latecomers.")

Once a stand has been taken to combat a passive aggressor, failure to carry out one's position is disastrous. That is, passive aggression is an indirect way of expressing hostility and the more the passive aggressor gets away with it, the more likely it is that he will continue doing it.[17]

Firm self assertion of your own rights, feelings, and expectations would seem to be your best solution.

Some Helpful Hints Regarding Doing Interpersonal Conflict Constructively

Avoid these habits:

1. Refusing to take the conflict seriously by sneering, scoffing, or smiling when the other party is obviously distressed.
2. Giving them the "silent treatment" by walking away, falling asleep, or withdrawing into silence.
3. Bringing up all of the old hurts even when they have nothing to do with the present situation.
4. Attacking the *person* of the other party by name-calling or character assassination.
5. Second guessing the other person by speaking for him or telling him what he means.
6. Blackmailing them by withholding affection, approval, recognition, or anything which makes their life easier or more pleasant.

Develop these habits:
1. Programming conflicts at special times so they can be private and allow plenty of time to handle feelings.
2. Encouraging one another to express the positive feelings you have for each other, what you appreciate about the relationship.
3. Encouraging one another to be able to give full expression to the negative feelings toward one another in this situation . . . without fixing blame.
4. Restating in your own words what you thought the other party said; checking out assumptions carefully.
5. Accepting honest feedback thoughtfully.
6. Dealing with behaviors, not personalities.
7. Taking responsibility for your role in the conflict.
8. Striving for a win/win solution.

Remember: Conflict can be creative. It is difficult, to be sure, but with both partners working constructively, the outcome can be a more rewarding and authentic relationship.

INTER-GROUP CONFLICT

According to Blake, Shepard, and Mouton, groups tend to have one of the following sets of assumptions regarding disagreements and a resulting style for dealing with them:[18]

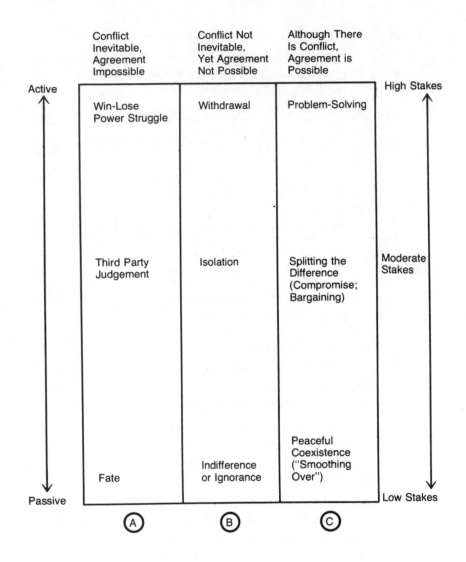

Conflict Inevitable, Agreement Impossible	Conflict Not Inevitable, Yet Agreement Not Possible	Although There Is Conflict, Agreement is Possible	
Active ↑			**High Stakes** ↑
Win-Lose Power Struggle	Withdrawal	Problem-Solving	
Third Party Judgement	Isolation	Splitting the Difference (Compromise; Bargaining)	**Moderate Stakes**
Fate	Indifference or Ignorance	Peaceful Coexistence ("Smoothing Over")	
Passive ↓			**Low Stakes** ↓
Ⓐ	Ⓑ	Ⓒ	

Let's examine each of these tracks more closely.[19]

Track A:

Assumptions: A pessimistic view that disagreement is inevitable; agreement seems impossible but resolution is compelling.

Options of actions to be taken:

154

1. *Fate*

    —Turn to purely mechanical techniques to settle the conflict, e.g., flip a coin or draw straws.

    —Used when stakes are low.

    —Fighting it out is no longer possible.

    —Continuing the conflict would be repugnant to those concerned.

    —Often have a super-ordinant goal (mission that rises above differences) that makes it important to resolve the conflict and move on.

    —Helps save face for both parties.

    —The outcome is often lose/lose, as winners know the outcome had nothing to do with their position or "rightness," so feel cheated. (Losers are still losers and resent it. It often sets the stage for greater problems later, as nothing was really resolved.)

2. *Third-Party Intervention*

    —Power is shifted to a third party and both groups become "powerless."

    —Used when stakes are moderately important.

    —Two conflicting groups have reached a deadlock or impasse and they want to shorten or end the conflict.

    —Third party should be impartial, objective, and free from conflict of interest.

    —Usually one group wins more than the other in the settlement and thus the groups feel differently about the process:

    Winners: Consider the arbitrator fair and unbiased; their position is reinforced as they have been proven right.

    Losers: Go along with the decision without really altering their stand on the issues; view the arbitrator as biased, unfair, or incompetent; blaming, splintering, and disruption occur.

3. *Win-Lose Power Struggle*

    —Leaders of each group emerge and become representatives or spokespersons for their groups.

—Used when the stakes are high.

—Competition between the parties develops and escalates as each group develops their own cohesiveness and conformity to their position and attack the other parties' stance.

—Leaders are viewed as "hero" by their own group and "enemy" by opponents; group pressure to win soon tends to overshadow the representatives' personal logic and objectivity so their perceptions are impaired.

—Interaction between the groups tends to minimize their commonalities and maximize their differences; each group begins to rationalize and support their own position and downgrade or attack their adversaries' position.

—The win/lose outcome has different effects on the winning and losing groups:

Winners: The leader is a hero and his/her power is strengthened; the group becomes more dependent on the leader and tends to become complacent; and they often fail to objectively critique their efforts.

Losers: The leader is often replaced; blaming occurs; cliques and factions form; the group often becomes "lean and hungry" and tries to understand their failure so they can win next time.

They both tend to continue to view each other as antagonists in future interactions.

Track B:

Assumptions: Conflict is not inevitable, yet agreement does not seem possible on this issue; belief that reducing interaction between the conflicting groups will reduce the need to have agreement and therefore reduce the possibility of conflict between them.

Options of actions to be taken:

1. *Indifference or Ignorance*

—Groups see no reason for their trying to be interdependent.

—Used when stakes are low.

—Separation seems logical and sensible since they feel they do not need or want one another.

—Take neutral positions on issues that could lead to a conflict.

—Represents ultimate passiveness.

—Denies or avoids conflicts, does not solve them.

2. *Isolation*

—Opportunity for contact between the conflicting parties is diminished.

—Need to receive or give input to the other group is eliminated.

—Each group goes their own way.

—Both fail to recognize (or decide to deny) their need to be interdependent with the other and thus lose the opportunity for valuable interchange of ideas.

3. *Withdrawal*

—Used when stakes are high.

—Different reasons for withdrawing are utilized by repeated winners than by repeated losers in win/lose conflicts:

Repeated winners:

—choose isolation due to feelings of superiority;

—let their traditions become "sacred cows"; and

—begin to feel they do not need others.

Repeated losers:

—limit contact with others to cut down the possibility of losing again;

—view others as threats and hazards;

—see others as sources of competition; and

—develop a loss of initiative and respond only to orders.

Track C:

Assumptions: Optimistic view that although conflict or disagreement is present, agreement is possible; believe that some common values can be achieved through the interdependency of their groups.

Options of actions to be taken:

1. *Peaceful Coexistence*
   —Emphasize commonalities and avoid or play down differences.
   —Used when stakes are low.
   —Conflicting groups are required to cooperate.
   —Tolerance and "looking the other way" become norms.
   —Potential conflict issues that could result in win/lose are avoided or denied.
   —Effort is made to generate and maintain harmony between the groups by initiating social interactions, e.g., parties, bowling clubs, picnics.
   —Adopted when it seems the cost of a win/lose struggle is too great and the rewards for appearing to collaborate are high.
   —Often entails much sham and play-acting and therefore rarely results in real problem solving or collaboration.

2. *Splitting the Difference*
   —Bargaining, compromise, or trading favors are the methods utilized.
   —Used when stakes are moderately high.
   —Usually both groups have fairly equal power and by necessity are dependent on one another.
   —Occurs frequently when there are scarce resources and both groups decide to share what there is rather than take the chance of losing everything.
   —Continued disagreement is too costly, so partial agreement seems more desirable.
   —The solution is an intermediate one that can be acceptable to both; neither party really wins, but they do not lose everything either.
   —This is the most common approach utilized by groups.

3. *Mutual Problem Solving*
   —Used when stakes are very high
   —Pre-conditions necessary are:

a) an optimistic belief in the capacities and capabilities of others;

b) both groups have a vested interest in the outcome; and

c) the conviction that the final outcome will represent the best interests of both.

—Emphasis is placed on solving the problem, not in accommodating differences.

—Both parties have faith that a better solution can be reached through real collaboration.

—Behavior consists of understanding, trust, respect, and confidence instead of competition.

—Causes of the disagreement/problem are identified and the definition is carefully arrived at jointly.

—All alternative solutions are explored and tested (*the final solution is usually different from the original one proposed by either group*).

—Identification of super-ordinate goals is key.

—Leaders serve as "linking pins" (persons who understand and are accepted by both groups) rather than representatives with vested interests to defend.

—Sometimes collaboration occurs so both groups can fight a threatening "common enemy."

—Creative problem-solving methods are utilized (see Chapter II).

—This is the most successful and long-lasting approach to solving inter-group conflicts.

EFFECTS OF MANAGERIAL STYLE ON GROUP CONFLICTS

How does a group determine which of these strategies to utilize in a given conflict situation? The choice is strongly influenced by their basic assumptions about people, groups, and problems. And here is where you, as a manager, come in, for the manager strongly influences the assumptions a group holds:

—Your basic assumptions about people (theory X or Y)
                          will
    —determine your management style
                       which

—influences how they feel about themselves and others
which
—causes the group to decide on their conflict strategies

Blake and Mouton have done extensive work in helping managers understand managerial styles. Their book *The Managerial Grid* has become a classic.[20] This grid serves to identify a person's management style with regard to two basic elements: *concern for people and concern for results.*

MANAGERIAL GRID

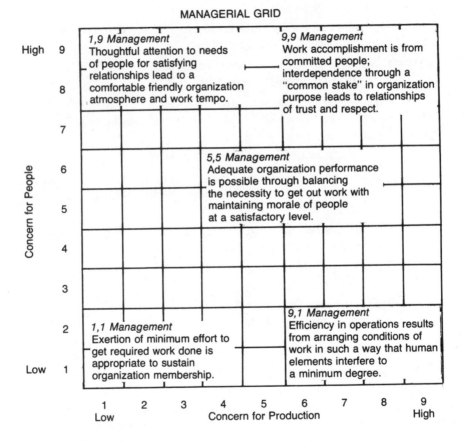

In an article entitled "The Fifth Achievement," Blake and Mouton link a manager's style of managing conflict to his basic philosophy of managment (based on the grid) as follows:[21]

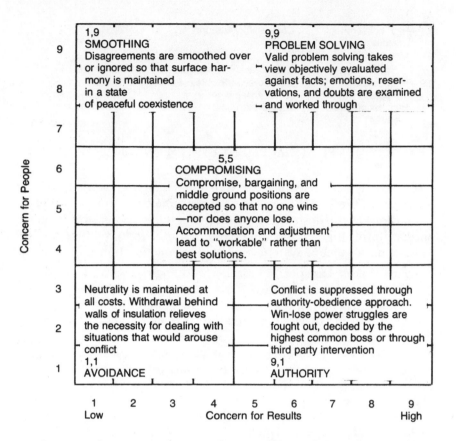

Since we have now discussed personal conflict styles (p. 146), group conflict strategies (p. 153), and now managerial styles of leadership and conflict (p. 159), let's attempt to integrate all three:

Managerial Style	Personal Conflict Style	Resulting Conflict Strategy for Group
1,1—Low concern for people Low concern for results	Avoidance	Withdrawal Isolation Indifference/ Ignorance
1,9—High concern for people Low concern for results	Accommodating/Smoothing	Peaceful Coexistence
5,5—Moderate concern for people Moderate concern for results	Compromising	Splitting the Difference Fate

161

9,1—High concern for results Low concern for people	Competition/Authority	Win-lose Third party judgement
9,9—High concern for people High concern for results	Collaboration/Problem Solving (other styles when appropriate)	Problem solving (other styles when appropriate)

EFFECTS OF THE MANAGEMENT SYSTEM ON GROUP CONFLICT

By now it would seem clear that our challenge as managers is enormous. We are the key to more productive problem-solving resolutions in the destructive conflicts raging in groups and organizations in this time of constant change. But how do we develop the kind of management system that makes collaboration possible?

Rensis Likert has spent a lifetime studying organizations and has published his findings relating to the elements that are necessary to make managers both successful and humane in his book *The Human Organization.* [22] He has identified four management systems prevalent in organizations, System I is totally autocratic, moving through II and III (each becoming more participative) until we arrive at System IV, which in Likert's view is the answer to truly effective and humane management. He identifies the basic ingredients of System IV management as follows:

Supervisory (Managerial) Leadership

Support: *Friendly, pays attention to what you are saying; listens to subordinate's problems.*

Team building: *Encourages subordinates to work as a team; encourages exchanges of opinions and ideas.*

Goal emphasis: *Encourages best efforts; maintains high standards.*

Help with work: *Shows ways to do a better job; helps subordinate plan, organize, and schedule; offers new ideas, solutions and problems.*

Organizational Climate

Communication flow: *subordinates know what is going on; superiors are receptive; subordinates are given information to do jobs well.*

Decision-making practices: *Subordinates are involved in setting goals; decisions are made at levels of accurate information; persons affected by decisions are asked for their ideas; know-how of people at all levels is used.*

162

Concern for persons: *The organization is interested in the individual's welfare; tries to improve working conditions; organizes work activities sensibly.*

Influence on department: *From lower-level supervisors and from employees who have no subordinates.*

Technology adequacy: *Improved methods are quickly adopted; equipment and resources are well managed.*

Motivation: *Differences and disagreements are accepted and worked through; people in organization work hard for money, promotion, job satisfaction, and to meet high expectations from others and are encouraged to do so by policies, working conditions, and people.*[23]

As I read this description, it strikes me as a picture of "organizational nirvana"—the absolute ultimate one would like to have in the way of an organizational setting. But having worked in several real-life situations, both in industry and human services, I also know that most managers and organizations fall short of the mark in many categories. I am sure your experience has been similar. So what do we do—give up in frustration because what we have to work with is less than ideal? I hope not. Instead, I would suggest we seriously assess where we are and determine where we want to be and then get on with building the bridges to get us there.

Since one of the greatest tests of groups' and leaders' health is in their ability to make good decisions and effectively solve problems, I suggest we start there. The Likerts (Rensis and Jane) in their book *New Ways of Managing Conflict* have devised some excellent tools to help us assess leadership behavior, group member behavior, personal behavior, and the group's problem-solving process. They are included in the Appendix of this chapter. I urge you to utilize them personally and with your group.

If we are really serious about improving our personal and group skills regarding managing problems and conflict, it can be done. But *we* must do it. It will not just happen. Remember to utilize the information, insights, and strategies suggested in the Power and Problem Solving chapters of this book. John Gardner once said that no organization or system moves unless it is pushed . . . so start pushing!

ORGANIZATIONAL GAMES THAT ARE NEITHER FUN NOR FUNNY

According to the proponents of Transactional Analysis (TA), people in organizations can play psychological games just like people do anywhere else.

163

When people play games, they fail to come through for others, blame others, make mistakes, complain a lot, and catch others in errors whenever possible. Psychological games can be a powerful negative force in organizations.

When people are bored or fail to get positive "strokes" (verbal, financial, psychic rewards), they tend to be more prone to game playing.

Frost and Wilmot describe some of the most common games:[24]

Name of the Game	Payoff
"If it weren't for you" "See what you made me do"	Blaming others for one's own behavior
"I'm only trying to help you"	To see oneself as "savior"— whether the person wants to be saved or not
"Blemish"	Picking out faults of others so you feel "one up"
"Now I've got you, you SOB"	Maneuvering someone into a position where you have surprise high power
"Kick me"; "Stupid"	Proving you can never do anything right, therefore you aren't responsible for your actions
"Poor me"	Getting others to help you enjoy your misery
"Harried"	Copping out and getting permission to not be responsible for what you do because you're so overwhelmed by the workload
"Yes but," "Ain't it awful"	Seeking others' help and advice but having no intention of taking it or really solving the problem. (It feels so good to feel so bad!)

(There is also one called the "Game-Game"—when people spend all of their time and energy trying to figure out everyone else's game.)

If you or those you work with are wasting precious time and energy on these kinds of non-productive games, you can give them up if you:

1. *refuse to buy into someone else's game, since it takes two to play;*
2. *learn to give people the positive reinforcement they need to make games unnecessary;*
3. *encourage open and honest communicaiton and practice it yourself;*
4. *emphasize the positive instead of the negative in both people and situations. Remember most people try games as a means of attaining self-affirmation, so affirm them!*

Robert Townsend, in *Up the Organization*, warns of one other popular, but destructive game in many organizations . . . "memo wars."

When two of your departments or divisions start arguing by memo and copying you, call them in and make them swear never to write another memo on that subject. Then listen to both sides and if they won't work it out then and there, decide it. . . . When the conflict between the State and Defense departments was at its peak, it was rumored that 20 percent of the employees of each department were there just to throw memo grenades at the other.[25]

Eliminating games frees everyone up to channel his energies into solving current problems, making decisions, and developing his talents and potentials.

TOOLS THAT HELP YOU MANAGE CONFLICT MORE EFFECTIVELY

It seems apparent by now that though conflict in interpersonal and intergroup relationships is inevitable, there are great differences in the outcomes of these conflicts.

Warren Schmidt, in an article in *Management Review*, points out some of the possible positive and negative outcomes:[26]

Positive Outcomes:

1. Better ideas are produced;
2. People are forced to search for new approaches;
3. Long-standing problems surface and are dealt with;

4. People are forced to clarify their views;

5. Tension often stimulates interest and creativity; and

6. People have a chance to test their capacities.

Negative Outcomes:

1. Some people feel defeated and demeaned;

2. Distance between people often increases;

3. A climate of distrust and suspicion develops;

4. People and departments that need to cooperate look only after their own narrow best interests;

5. Resistance—either active or passive—develops where teamwork is needed; and

6. Some people leave because of the turmoil.

This illustrates what we stressed in the very beginning. Conflict, like power, is neither good nor bad. It is what we do with it that is.

I would like to end this chapter by sharing some tools with you that will help you "do" conflict more effectively so the results may more frequently be positive rather than negative.

THE PRACTICES OF A GOOD LISTENER

1. Listens to understand what is meant, not to ready himself to reply, contradict, or refute. This is extremely important as a general attitude.

2. Knows that what is meant involves more than the dictionary meaning of the words that are used. It involves, among other things, the tone of the voice, the facial expressions, and the overall behavior of the speaker.

3. Is careful not to interpret too quickly but looks for clues as to what the other person is trying to say, putting himself (as best he can) in the speaker's shoes, seeing the world as the speaker sees it, accepting the speaker's feelings as facts that have to be taken into account—whether the listener shares them or not.

4. Puts aside own views and opinions for the time being. Realizes that one cannot listen to himself inwardly and at the same time outwardly to the speaker.

5. Controls impatience, knowing that listening is faster than talking. (The average person speaks about 125 words a minute, but

can listen to about 400 words a minute.) The effective listener does not jump ahead of the speaker; but gives him time to tell his story. What the speaker will say next may not be what the listener expects him to say.

6. Does not prepare an answer while listening but wants to get the whole message before deciding what to say in turn. The last sentence of the speaker may give a new slant to what was said before.

7. Shows interest and alertness. This stimulates the speaker and improves performance.

8. Does not interrupt. When asking questions it is to secure more information, not to trap the speaker or force him into a corner.

9. Expects the speaker's language to differ from the way he would say the same thing himself. Does not quibble about words but tries to get at what is meant.

10. Purpose is the opposite of a debater's. Looks for areas of agreement, not for weak spots to attack and blast with an artillery of counter-arguments.

AID FOR GIVING AND RECEIVING FEEDBACK

Some of the most important data you can receive from others (or give to others) consists of feedback related to behavior. Such feedback can provide learning opportunities if you can use the reactions of others as a mirror for observing the consequences of your behavior. Such personal feedback helps to make you more aware of *what you do* and *how you do it*, thus increasing your ability to modify and change your behavior and to become more effective in your interactions with others.

To help you develop and use the techniques of feedback for personal growth, it is necessary to understand certain characteristics of the process. The following is a brief outline of some factors which may assist you in making better use of feedback, both as the giver and the receiver of feedback. This list is only a starting point. You may wish to add further items.

1. Focus feedback on behavior rather than the person.

   It is important that you refer to what a person does rather than comment on what you imagine he is. This focus on behavior further implies that you use adverbs (which relate to actions) rather than adjectives (which relate to qualities) when referring to a person. Thus you might say a person "talked a lot in this meeting," rather than this person "is a loudmouth." When you talk in terms of "personality traits," it implies inherited constant qualities, difficult, if not impossible, to change. Focusing on behavior implies that it is something related to a specific situation that might be changed. It is less threatening to a person to hear comments about his behavior than his "traits."

2. Focus feedback on observations rather than inferences.

   Observations refer to what you can see or hear in the behavior of another person, while inferences refer to interpretations and conclusions which you make from what you see or hear. In a sense, inferences or conclusions about a person contaminate your observations, thus clouding the feedback for another person. When inferences or conclusions are shared (and it may be valuable to have these data), it is important they be so identified.

3. Focus feedback on description rather than judgment.

   The effort to describe represents a process for reporting what occurred, while judgment refers to an evaluation in terms of good or bad, right or wrong, nice or not nice. The judgments arise out of a personal frame of reference or values, whereas description represents neutral (as far as possible) reporting.

4. Focus feedback on descriptions of behavior which are in terms of "more or less" rather than in terms of "either-or."

   The "more or less" terminology implies a continuum on which any behavior may fall, stressing quantity (which is objective and measurable) rather than quality (which is subjective and judgmental). Thus, participation of a person may fall on a continuum from low participation to high participation, rather than "good" or "bad" participation. Not to think in terms of "more or less" and the use of continua is to trap yourself into thinking in categories, which may then represent serious distortions of reality.

5. Focus feedback on behavior related to a specific situation, preferably to the "here and now," rather than to behavior in the abstract, placing it in the "there and then."

   What you and I do is always tied in some way to time and place, and you increase your understanding of behavior by keeping it tied to time and place. Feedback is generally more meaningful if given as soon as appropriate after the observation or reaction occurs, thus keeping it concrete and relatively free of distortions that come with the lapse of time.

6. Focus feedback on the sharing of ideas and information rather than on giving advice.

By sharing ideas and information you leave the person free to decide for himself (in the light of his own goals in a particular situation at a particular time) how to use the ideas and information. When you give advice you tell him what to do with the information, and in that sense take away his freedom to determine for himself what is the most appropriate course of action.

7. Focus feedback on exploration of alternatives rather than on answers or solutions.

The more you can focus on a variety of procedures and means for the attainment of a particular goal, the less likely you are to accept prematurely a particular answer or solution, which may or may not fit your particular problem. Many of us go around with a collection of answers and solutions for which there are no problems.

8. Focus feedback on the value it may have to the recipient, not the value of "release" that it provides the person giving the feedback.

The feedback provided should serve the needs of the recipient rather than the needs of the giver. Help and feedback need to be given and heard as an offer, not an imposition.

9. Focus feedback on the amount of information that the person receiving it can use, rather than on the amount that you have which you might like to give.

To overload a person with feedback is to reduce the possibility that he may use what he receives effectively. When you give more than can be used, you may be satisfying some need for yourself rather than helping the other person.

10. Focus feedback on time and place so that personal data can be shared at appropriate times.

Because the reception and use of personal feedback involve many possible emotional reactions, it is important to be sensitive to when it is appropriate to provide feedback. Excellent feedback presented at an inappropriate time may do more harm than good.

11. Focus feedback on what is said rather than why it is said.

   The aspects of feedback which relate to the what, how, when, and where, of what is said are observable characteristics. The why of what is said takes you from the observable to the inferred, and brings up questions of motive or intent.

   It may be helpful to think of "why" in terms of a specifiable goal or goals—which can be considered in terms of time, place, procedures, and probabilities of attainment. To make assumptions about the motives of the person giving feedback may prevent you from hearing or cause you to distort what is said. In short, if I question "why" a person gives me feedback, I may not hear what he says.

In short, the giving (and receiving) of feedback requires courage, skill, understanding, and respect for the self and others.

Note: Adapted by Elaine Yarbrough, Ph.D., Associate Professor of Communications at the University of Colorado (Boulder) from lecture materials used in laboratory training by George F. Lehner, Ph.D., Professor of Psychology, University of California, Los Angeles.

ISSUE IDENTIFICATION IN CONFLICT SITUATIONS

1. *Clarify the content and feelings* of the conflict participants by paraphrasing them before speaking. Check out your clarifications with the persons(s) you are paraphrasing: your perceptions could be inaccurate, especially in a tense situation.

2. *Make observations (not interpretations)* of the conflict participants' words (how they talk about the conflict) and nonverbals for a more accurate assessment of the issues and for feedback to self and others about the effects each is having on the conflict process. For example, someone who calls the conflict a "battle" will be viewing the conflict and its consequences differently from the one who labels it a "disagreement." A voice that indicates anger along with words that do not should give you clues that you can not have all the information from the other that you need. Ask the person for clarification.

3. *Focus on the incongruities between verbals and nonverbals* to surface issues in the conflict.

170

4. *Focus on and make observations of the communication patterns participants are using*, e.g., blaming, placating, computing, and distracting patterns. Ask yourself and others how the communication patterns are proliferating the conflict issues and affecting the management of the conflict.

5. *Focus on the effects the conflict process is having on the participants.* Verbalize the effects as you interpret them and/or ask other participants to verbalize the effects. Often the way people behave in a conflict is indicative of the way they behave that created the conflict in the first place; and it is easier to deal with information that is being generated at the moment than to argue about who did what in the past.

6. *Focus on dyad or group themes*, e.g., trust, acceptance, control of information, perception and feelings.

7. *In every conflict there are requests of the others in the conflict.* State your requests clearly and ask what the other(s) is requesting of you, both materially and emotionally.

8. *Ask yourself what all conflict participants are feeling in terms of their self esteem and power*, two common issues in a conflict. People must have a feeling of power (an ability to influence) and confidence in order to cooperate authentically.

9. *Clarify the events that typically trigger the actual conflict.* Those events may give you clues about the conflict issues.

Note: Adapted by Elaine Yarbrough, Ph.D., Associate Professor of Communications at the University of Colorado (Boulder) from lecture materials used in laboratory training by George F. Lehner, Ph.D., Professor of Psychology, University of California, Los Angeles.

GOAL NEGOTIATIONS IN CONFLICT SITUATIONS

Below are several suggestions about how to negotiate goals productively in a conflict. Identifying issues *and* dealing with them effectively are two of the most important skills to develop in conflict management.

1. *Begin the negotiation session* (even an informal one) *with the points of agreement*, no matter how vague, instead of the points of disagreement. This helps give people common goals and some sense of the interdependence they share.

2. *Try to make choices available to the parties involved.* People

171

tend to become defensive when they are being controlled by having no options available to them. In destructive conflict behavior, options are closed off instead of opened up.

3. *Treat other persons as persons and not as things only.* Make choices based on an appreciation of the other's role instead of just thinking that the person is a "thing" blocking your goals. A good way to keep the conflict interpersonal is to keep clear the differences between your guesses about the meaning of certain behavior of participants and the behavior that you can actually observe. Telling another that you know what he/she is feeling or thinking is a "sure" way to escalate the conflict. BE RESPECT-FUL OF THE OTHER.

4. *Discriminate as to when and where control is to be exercised.* People who always try to exercise power, especially coercively, are conflict "gangsters," trying to be one-up on others. A low level of trust is usually generated, and later conflict will likely emerge because of the low trust.

5. *Take responsibility for the accuracy of your communication.* That is, take responsibility for your part in the conflict and own the feelings and perceptions you have about the situation. If you are in the conflict, you must have had a part in creating it, even if that part was withdrawal.

6. *State goals in terms of do-ables.* When goals are do-able, you can tell whether they are being achieved or not, and adjust accordingly. In the case of a job, a do-able goal would be to increase sales by 40 percent over last year as opposed to saying "I want to improve."

7. *Deal with both content and relationship goals in the conflict.* Participants want certain beliefs advanced, certain behavior changed, tasks performed, and promises made, but they also want to define the conflict differently, e.g., how they go about conflict, who has control, etc. Remember that the dual goals in most conflict are to: 1) reach agreement; and 2) enhance the relationship for future communication. Both are equally important.

8. *Include emotional data as well as "objective" data when goals are formulated.* People always have reasons for what they do, even though their reasons may not be your reasons. Therefore, discounting some reasons because they are "only emotional" is not productive for the relationship. Talk about your feelings

and encourage others to talk about theirs. If this is not done, the agreements reached are likely to be shallow.

9. *Try to avoid polarizing* into separate groups too early, or polarizing your position too early in the goal negotiations. There is nothing inherently wrong with polarizing, but the practice does not work very well. If groups get identified as totally aligned with one point of view, and refuse to listen to other points of view, they will have less chance for compromise if compromise is necessary. When people get ego-involved with a position, they change much less over time.

10. *Decide which goals are actually incompatible* at the moment and which ones only seem to be incompatible. Some incompatibilities never change. People feel so strongly about their side of the issue that they are unchangeable. Sometimes these conflict goals can be sidestepped or tabled for another time and the goals that are negotiable can be dealt with. Try to discourage the attitude of "If you don't agree with me about this important issue, then you can't agree with me about anything."

11. *Avoid reaching easy agreement on goals by premature voting, by giving away your power to some authority, or by using chance measures (flipping coins) when the seriousness of the conflict suggests more careful attention to the negotiation.* Often a group has to redo a conflict because the resolution reached the first time around was totally unrealistic, or did not take into account the deep feelings of the participants involved.

12. If you seem to be stuck, and no one can agree on anything, discuss the extent to which you are related as groups or as individuals in the group. Sometimes *reminding each other of your interdependence* serves the function of breaking down excessive stubbornness that gets in the way of advancement of new goals. Remind others that if everyone could get exactly what he or she wants, you would not be in conflict—it would already be happily resolved. Groups that do not need each other, and individuals that are not interdependent, seldom are involved in conflict, since the activity of conflict is so stressful and uncomfortable to many people.

13. In personal conflict, it is usually a good idea to *avoid making stands and then giving in as a ploy.* People catch on to the ruse, and your credibility is then lowered.

14. *Avoid stating goals in terms of winning and losing. Talk in*

terms of what is best for the common good. If a win-lose orientation seems inevitable, before final decisions are made, assess again the degree of interdependence of the participants. What is "lost" in the future by "winning" now?

15. *State emphatic feelings when you have them.* Show understanding of the other point of view when you feel it even if you make it clear that you disagree with the other side. Your understanding enhances the productive nature of the negotiations and does not decrease your chances of getting what you want.

16. *Suggest outside assistance when you feel this might be necessary and acceptable to other parties in the conflict.* Sometimes participants in a conflict are too close to the situation to suggest any more productive avenues. This is the time to ask for help from an appropriate third party.

17. *Observe the rules of giving and receiving feedback.*

Note: Adapted in large part from *Interpersonal Conflict* (W. C. Brown, publishers) by Joyce Frost and William Wilmot.

SUMMARY REMARKS ABOUT CONFLICT

In the preface of this book, I stated that there are subtle, undeclared and destructive wars going on in almost all organizations. The astonishing rate of divorce in this country today would also indicate similar wars are raging out of control in many personal relationships.

The tragedy is that these wars usually have victims. Sometimes the victim is you . . . or someone close to you. The intent of this chapter has been to help you understand that the stance of victim is a choice and hopefully one that you will carefully reexamine. Conflicts can be managed humanely and productively if you invest the time and effort to understand them and then learn the skills suggested to help you handle them well.

The other option is to continue the "poor me" and "ain't it awful" games and disclaim your own contribution to the conflict. The cost of unresolved conflicts is astronomical, both to organizations and to persons. As we move into the study of stress, this will become even more apparent.

I would like to leave this topic of conflict by sharing some poems with you that were written by Lyman Randall, a good friend of my husband and me. Lyman is a loving husband and father, as well as a corporate executive who has survived the organizational battleground for twenty years. [27]

THE GREAT GOTTCHA WAR

The last Great Gottcha War
Between departments
Was triggered by electric typewriter
After a double-manhattan project lunch.

    Old hurts were fed,
    Fattened and fermented
    Til they burst the stitches
    Of corporate propriety.

The first missiles looked innocent enough.
Disguised as interoffice memos,
They landed inside enemy lines.
But booby-trapped words
Soon blasted buried tempers.

    "Although discussed before, you've failed to. . . ."
    (Our only failure was trusting them!)

    "We cannot meet our commitment due to your. . . ."
    (I'd like to get him committed to the mental ward.)

The first casualty regained consciousness
In an unemployment line,
Sacrificed to superior strategy,
Losses mounted:

    Five fallen middle managers,
    Two ruptured ulcers,
    One mild coronary
    And a downtrend in sales and profits.

Three hundred twelve memos,
Sixty secret meetings,
And forty-five maneuvers later
The winners of the Great Gottcha War emerged.

"My loyal colleagues," the V.P. said,
"Here's to us and the work ahead.
We must rebuild what THEY destroyed!
Here's to us, the still-employed."

But they weren't for long.
First they were merged
Then later purged
In the Great Gottcha War #2.

                        . . . Lyman K. Randall

OF COURSE I BELIEVE

Trust you?
Sure, I trust you!
(I wonder what he's after now.)

Be open with you?
Of course, I'm open with you!
(I'm as open as I can be with a guy like you.)

Level with you?
You know I level with you!
(I'd like to more, but you can't take it.)

Accept you?
Naturally I accept you—just like you do me
(And when you learn to accept me, then I might accept you more.)

Self-direction?
I've always believed in self-direction.
(And someday this company may let us use some.)

What's the hang-up?
Not a damn thing!
What could ever hang-up
    Two self-directing,
    Open, trusting,
    Leveling, and accepting.
    Guys like us?

        . . . Lyman K. Randall

TURNING POINT

Like a soldier in the midst of battle,
A manager also faces that secret moment
When a person with human history
Can become a faceless number
To be dealt with in abstract terms—
To be rationalized
In order for his sacrifice
To be less painful and unforgiving.
    And once the killing is done,
    In the name of victory or profit,
    And proper rewards bestowed,
    The next occasions become less difficult
    Until human considerations

Are obscured in the shadows
Of persons who used to be
But are no more.

                              . . . Lyman K. Randall

BATTLE HYMN FOR TWO

Our minds converge along the hours
Occupied by routines of shopping,
Eating and cleaning out the garage.
Then from this smooth, quiet path of sameness
They suddenly veer in opposite directions.

Affection ruptures into anger.
Cutting words,
Whetted on the hardness
Of recent day's events,
Are drawn from secret scabbards
Of our minds
To throw across the widening battlefield.

Each knows the other too well
To escape unhurt.
Old wounds easily reopen.
Old pain festers into new hurting.

We each strengthen our positions
With granite blocks of indignant logic
Chiseled into special truths
The other somehow fails to grasp—
Thus proving his stupidity
Of which he is urgently reminded.

Each finally retreats
Under dark moods and fatigue
To lonely outposts of silence
Overlooking the enemy.
We listen and wait
For a sign of new fighting or surrender.

Something in the stillness
Then begins to pull us

From our opposing trenches
Toward a point of being
We recently abandoned in heat of battle.

Barricades of logic,
So carefully constructed
To hide our vulnerabilities,
Crumble easily before the superior force
Of two people once again uniting
Against a common enemy of loneliness.

. . . Lyman K. Randall

REFERENCES

1. Townsend, Robert, *Up the Organization*, Fawcett Crest, 1970, p. 21.

2. From Frost, Joyce Hocker, and Wilmot, William W., *Interpersonal Conflict*, © 1978, Wm.C. Brown Company Publishers, Dubuque, Iowa. pp. 8, 9. Reprinted by permission.

3. Filley, Alan, *Interpersonal Conflict Resolution*, Scott Foresman and Co., 1975, pp. 10-12.

4. McGregor, Douglas, *The Professional Manager*, McGraw-Hill, 1967, p. 185.

5. Frost and Wilmot, pp. 6-8.

6. McGregor, p. 184.

7. Filley, Preface.

8. Frost and Wilmot, pp. 47-52.

9. Ibid., p. 52.

10. McGregor, p. 55.

11. Sherwood, John, and Glidwell, John, "Planned Renegotiation," *Interpersonal Dynamics*, edited by Bennis, Berlow, Schein, and Steele, The Dorsey Press, 1973, pp. 480-487.

12. Ingalls, John, *Human Energy*, Addison-Wesley, 1976, p. 184.

13. Kilmann, H., and Thomas, K.W., "Interpersonal Conflict-Handling Behavior as Reflections of Jungian Personality Dimensions," *Psychology Reports*, 1975, 37, pp. 971-980.

14. Frost and Wilmot, pp. 28-31.

15. Bach, George R., and Goldberg, Herb, *Creative Aggression*, Doubleday and Co., 1974.

16. Ibid, p. 149.

17. Ibid, p. 150.

18. Blake, Robert; Shepard, Herbert; and Mouton, Jane, *Managing Intergroup Conflict in Industry*, Gulf Publishing Co., 1964, p. 13.

19. Ibid.

20. Blake, Robert, and Mouton, Jane, *The Managerial Grid*, Gulf Publishing Co., 1964.

21. Blake, Robert, and Mouton, Jane, "The Fifth Achievement," *Journal of Applied Behavioral Science*, Vol. 6, No. 4, 1970.

22. Likert, Rensis, *The Human Organization*, McGraw-Hill, 1967.

23. Likert, Rensis, and Likert, Jane Gibson, *New Ways of Managing Conflict*, McGraw-Hill Book Co., 1976, p. 73.

24. Frost and Wilmot, p. 79.

25. Townsend, p. 92.

26. Schmidt, Warren H., "Conflict: A Powerful Process for (Good or Bad) Change," *Management Review*, December 1974 (New York: AMACOM, a division of American Management Associations), p. 5.

27. Randall, Lyman K., "The Great Gottcha War," "Of Course I Believe," "Turning Point," and "Battle Hymn for Two" (unpublished).

APPENDIX A

By Rensis and Jane Gibson Likert in *New Ways of Managing Conflict* McGraw-Hill, 1976. (Reprinted with permission).

Profile of leadership behavior (Form LB)

This questionnaire is designed to describe the behavior of the leader in any group engaged in problem solving.

In completing the questionnaire, it is important that you answer each question as thoughtfully and frankly as possible. There are no right or wrong answers.

The answers will be summarized in statistical form so that individuals cannot be identified. To ensure complete confidentiality, please do not write your name anywhere on this questionnaire.

Please indicate your answer to each question by filling in the circle under the choice that best describes your view on that question.

For example, suppose the question were:

	Rarely		Sometimes		Often		Very often	
How often does the sun shine in your town?	①	②	③	④	⑤	⑥	⑦	⑧

If you think that the sun shines often, you would fill in ⑤ or ⑥. You would fill in ⑤ if you feel that the situation is closer to "sometimes" than to "very often." You would fill in ⑥ if you feel that the situation is closer to "very often."

To what extent do you feel that your leader:

	Very little		Some		Considerable		Very great	
1. Is friendly and easy to talk to	①	②	③	④	⑤	⑥	⑦	⑧
2. Listens well to you and others whether she or he agrees or disagrees	①	②	③	④	⑤	⑥	⑦	⑧
3. States your point of view as well or better than you can even though she or he disagrees	①	②	③	④	⑤	⑥	⑦	⑧
4. Encourages you and others to express your ideas fully and frankly	①	②	③	④	⑤	⑥	⑦	⑧
5. Encourages you and others to express your feelings frankly	①	②	③	④	⑤	⑥	⑦	⑧
6. Displays confidence and trust in you and others whether or not she or he agrees	①	②	③	④	⑤	⑥	⑦	⑧

180

To what extent do you feel that
your leader:

	Very little		Some		Considerable		Very great	
7. Shares information frankly	①	②	③	④	⑤	⑥	⑦	⑧
8. Expects each member to do her or his very best	①	②	③	④	⑤	⑥	⑦	⑧
9. Expects a high-quality job from herself or himself	①	②	③	④	⑤	⑥	⑦	⑧
10. Thinks what she or he and the group are doing is important	①	②	③	④	⑤	⑥	⑦	⑧
11. Encourages innovative and creative ideas	①	②	③	④	⑤	⑥	⑦	⑧

	Very little		Some		Considerable		Very great	
12. Is willing to take risks	①	②	③	④	⑤	⑥	⑦	⑧
13. Is not defensive when criticized	①	②	③	④	⑤	⑥	⑦	⑧
14. Avoids treating you and others in a condescending manner	①	②	③	④	⑤	⑥	⑦	⑧
15. Avoids pontificating	①	②	③	④	⑤	⑥	⑦	⑧
16. Avoids stating her or his views dogmatically	①	②	③	④	⑤	⑥	⑦	⑧
17. Avoids being impatient with the progress being made by the group	①	②	③	④	⑤	⑥	⑦	⑧

	Very little		Some		Considerable		Very great	
18. Avoids dominating the discussion	①	②	③	④	⑤	⑥	⑦	⑧
19. Encourages group to work through disagreements, not suppress them	①	②	③	④	⑤	⑥	⑦	⑧
20. Uses "we" and "our" rather than "I" or "my"	①	②	③	④	⑤	⑥	⑦	⑧
21. Shows no favorites; treats all members equally	①	②	③	④	⑤	⑥	⑦	⑧
22. Gives credit and recognition generously	①	②	③	④	⑤	⑥	⑦	⑧
23. Accepts more blame than may be warranted for any failure or mistake	①	②	③	④	⑤	⑥	⑦	⑧

181

To what extent do you feel that
your leader:

	Very little		Some		Considerable		Very great	
24. Avoids imposing a decision upon the group	①	②	③	④	⑤	⑥	⑦	⑧
25. Waits until members of the group have stated their positions before stating hers or his	①	②	③	④	⑤	⑥	⑦	⑧
26. Presents own contribution tentatively or as questions	①	②	③	④	⑤	⑥	⑦	⑧

Profile of group members' behavior (Form GMB)

This questionnaire is designed to describe the overall behavior of the members of any group engaged in problem solving.

In completing the questionnaire, it is important that you answer each question as thoughtfully and frankly as possible. There are no right or wrong answers.

The answers will be summarized in statistical form so that individuals cannot be identified. To ensure complete confidentiality, please do not write your name anywhere on this questionnaire.

Please indicate your answer to each question by filling in the circle under the choice that best describes your view on that question.

For example, suppose the question were:

	Rarely		Sometimes		Often		Very often	
How often does the sun shine in your town?	①	②	③	④	⑤	⑥	⑦	⑧

If you think that the sun shines often, you would fill in ⑤ or ⑥. You would fill in ⑤ if you feel that the situation is closer to "sometimes" than to "very often." You would fill in ⑥ if you feel that the situation is closer to "very often."

To what extent do you feel that
the members of your group:

	Very little		Some		Considerable		Very great	
1. Are friendly and easy to talk to	①	②	③	④	⑤	⑥	⑦	⑧
2. Listen well to you and others whether they agree or disagree	①	②	③	④	⑤	⑥	⑦	⑧
3. State your point of view as well or better than you can even though they disagree	①	②	③	④	⑤	⑥	⑦	⑧

182

To what extent do you feel that
the members of your group:

4. Encourage you and others
   to express ideas fully and
   frankly

Very little		Some		Considerable		Very great	
①	②	③	④	⑤	⑥	⑦	⑧

5. Encourage you and others
   to express feelings frankly

①	②	③	④	⑤	⑥	⑦	⑧

6. Display confidence and
   trust in you and others
   whether or not they agree

①	②	③	④	⑤	⑥	⑦	⑧

7. Share information frankly

①	②	③	④	⑤	⑥	⑦	⑧

8. Expect you to do your very
   best

①	②	③	④	⑤	⑥	⑦	⑧

9. Expect a high-quality job
   from themselves

①	②	③	④	⑤	⑥	⑦	⑧

10. Think what the group is
    doing is important

①	②	③	④	⑤	⑥	⑦	⑧

11. Encourage innovative and
    creative ideas

①	②	③	④	⑤	⑥	⑦	⑧

12. Are willing to take risks

①	②	③	④	⑤	⑥	⑦	⑧

13. Are not defensive when
    criticized

①	②	③	④	⑤	⑥	⑦	⑧

14. Avoid treating others in a
    condescending manner

①	②	③	④	⑤	⑥	⑦	⑧

15. Avoid pontificating

①	②	③	④	⑤	⑥	⑦	⑧

16. Avoid stating their views
    dogmatically

Very little		Some		Considerable		Very great	
①	②	③	④	⑤	⑥	⑦	⑧

17. Avoid being impatient with
    the progress being made by
    the group

①	②	③	④	⑤	⑥	⑦	⑧

18. Avoid dominating the
    discussion

①	②	③	④	⑤	⑥	⑦	⑧

19. Encourage group to work
    through disagreements,
    not suppress them

①	②	③	④	⑤	⑥	⑦	⑧

20. Use "we" and "our" rather
    than "I" or "my"

①	②	③	④	⑤	⑥	⑦	⑧

21. Show no favorites; treat all
    members equally

①	②	③	④	⑤	⑥	⑦	⑧

183

To what extent do you feel that
the members of your group:

	Very little		Some		Considerable		Very great	

22. Give credit and recognition
    generously
    ① ② ③ ④ ⑤ ⑥ ⑦ ⑧

23. Accept more blame than
    may be warranted for any
    failure or mistake
    ① ② ③ ④ ⑤ ⑥ ⑦ ⑧

24. Avoid imposing a decision
    upon the group
    ① ② ③ ④ ⑤ ⑥ ⑦ ⑧

This questionnaire is designed to enable a member of a group engaged in problem solving to describe his/her own behavior.

In completing the questionnaire, it is important that you answer each question as thoughtfully and frankly as possible. There are no right or wrong answers.

The answers will be summarized in statistical form so that individuals cannot be identified. To ensure complete confidentiality, please do not write your name anywhere on this questionnaire.

Please indicate your answer to each question by filling in the circle under the choice that best describes your view on that question.

For example, suppose the question were:

	Rarely		Sometimes		Often		Very often	

How often does the sun shine in
your town?
① ② ③ ④ ⑤ ⑥ ⑦ ⑧

If you think that the sun shines often, you would fill in ⑤ or ⑥. You would fill in ⑤ if you feel that the situation is closer to "sometimes" than to "very often." You would fill in ⑥ if you feel that the situation is closer to "very often."

To what extent do you feel that
you:

	Very little		Some		Considerable		Very great	

1. Are friendly and easy to
   talk to
   ① ② ③ ④ ⑤ ⑥ ⑦ ⑧

2. Listen well to others
   whether you agree or
   disagree
   ① ② ③ ④ ⑤ ⑥ ⑦ ⑧

3. State the points of view of
   others as well or better than
   they can even though you
   disagree
   ① ② ③ ④ ⑤ ⑥ ⑦ ⑧

184

To what extent do you feel that you:

4. Encourage others to express their ideas fully and frankly

Very little   Some   Considerable Very great

① ② ③ ④ ⑤ ⑥ ⑦ ⑧

5. Encourage others to express their feelings frankly

① ② ③ ④ ⑤ ⑥ ⑦ ⑧

6. Display confidence and trust in others whether or not you agree

① ② ③ ④ ⑤ ⑥ ⑦ ⑧

7. Share information frankly

① ② ③ ④ ⑤ ⑥ ⑦ ⑧

8. Expect others to do their very best

① ② ③ ④ ⑤ ⑥ ⑦ ⑧

9. Expect a high-quality job from yourself

① ② ③ ④ ⑤ ⑥ ⑦ ⑧

10. Think what you and the group are doing is important

① ② ③ ④ ⑤ ⑥ ⑦ ⑧

11. Encourage innovative and creative ideas

① ② ③ ④ ⑤ ⑥ ⑦ ⑧

Very little   Some   Considerable Very great

12. Are willing to take risks

① ② ③ ④ ⑤ ⑥ ⑦ ⑧

13. Are not defensive when criticized

① ② ③ ④ ⑤ ⑥ ⑦ ⑧

14. Avoid treating others in a condescending manner

① ② ③ ④ ⑤ ⑥ ⑦ ⑧

15. Avoid pontificating

Very little   Some   Considerable Very great

16. Avoid stating your views dogmatically

① ② ③ ④ ⑤ ⑥ ⑦ ⑧

17. Avoid being impatient with the progress being made by the group

① ② ③ ④ ⑤ ⑥ ⑦ ⑧

18. Avoid dominating the discussion

① ② ③ ④ ⑤ ⑥ ⑦ ⑧

19. Encourage group to work through disagreements, not suppress them

① ② ③ ④ ⑤ ⑥ ⑦ ⑧

185

To what extent do you feel that you:

	Very little		Some		Considerable		Very great	
20. Use "we" and "our" rather than "I" or "my"	①	②	③	④	⑤	⑥	⑦	⑧
21. Show no favorites; treat all members equally	①	②	③	④	⑤	⑥	⑦	⑧
22. Give credit and recognition generously	①	②	③	④	⑤	⑥	⑦	⑧
23. Accept more blame than may be warranted for any failure or mistake	①	②	③	④	⑤	⑥	⑦	⑧
24. Avoid imposing a decision upon the group	①	②	③	④	⑤	⑥	⑦	⑧

Profile of group problem solving (Form GP)

This questionnaire is designed to enable each member to describe the group's problem-solving behavior.

In completing the questionnaire, it is important that you answer each question as thoughtfully and frankly as possible. There are no right or wrong answers.

The answers will be summarized in statistical form so that individuals cannot be identified. To ensure complete confidentiality, please do not write your name anywhere on this questionnaire.

Please indicate your answer to each question by filling in the circle under the choice that best describes your view on that question.

For example, suppose the question were:

	Rarely		Sometimes		Often		Very often	
How often does the sun shine in your town?	①	②	③	④	⑤	⑥	⑦	⑧

If you think that the sun shines often, you would fill in ⑤ or ⑥. You would fill in ⑤ if you feel that the situation is closer to "sometimes" than to "very often." You would fill in ⑥ if you feel that the situation is closer to "very often."

In our problem solving, to what extent are we:

	Very little		Some		Considerable		Very great	
1. Selecting problems that we can do something about	①	②	③	④	⑤	⑥	⑦	⑧
2. Making sure that we are discussing the real problem	①	②	③	④	⑤	⑥	⑦	⑧
3. Stating the problem clearly	①	②	③	④	⑤	⑥	⑦	⑧

In our problem solving, to what extent are we:

	Very little		Some		Considerable		Very great	
4. Searching for and stating situational requirements	①	②	③	④	⑤	⑥	⑦	⑧
5. Avoiding solution-mindedness	①	②	③	④	⑤	⑥	⑦	⑧
6. Searching for and using integrative goals	①	②	③	④	⑤	⑥	⑦	⑧
7. Realistically facing hard facts rather than just being nice to each other	①	②	③	④	⑤	⑥	⑦	⑧
8. Using "win-win," not "win-lose" procedures	①	②	③	④	⑤	⑥	⑦	⑧
9. Depersonalizing problem solving, e.g., by not identifying contributions with persons	①	②	③	④	⑤	⑥	⑦	⑧
10. Building group cohesiveness prior to tackling hard problems, e.g., tackling easy problems first	①	②	③	④	⑤	⑥	⑦	⑧
11. Candidly dealing with "hidden agenda"	①	②	③	④	⑤	⑥	⑦	⑧

	Very little		Some		Considerable		Very great	
12. Applying the principle of supportive relationships, e.g., listening supportively	①	②	③	④	⑤	⑥	⑦	⑧
13. Encouraging members who hold differing points of view to express themselves freely and fully	①	②	③	④	⑤	⑥	⑦	⑧
14. Deemphasizing status	①	②	③	④	⑤	⑥	⑦	⑧
15. Using consensus	①	②	③	④	⑤	⑥	⑦	⑧
16. Using the authority of facts rather than the authority of persons	①	②	③	④	⑤	⑥	⑦	⑧
17. Taking each problem-solving step in sequence	①	②	③	④	⑤	⑥	⑦	⑧
18. Taking adequate time for each problem-solving step	①	②	③	④	⑤	⑥	⑦	⑧
19. Not wasting time by dawdling	①	②	③	④	⑤	⑥	⑦	⑧

187

In our problem solving, to what extent are we:

		Very little		Some		Considerable		Very great
20.	Solving general problem before tackling specific cases	①	②	③	④	⑤	⑥	⑦	⑧
21.	Defining conditions that a solution must meet to be acceptable	①	②	③	④	⑤	⑥	⑦	⑧
22.	Evaluating all suggested conditions as to whether they are merely desirable or are essential	①	②	③	④	⑤	⑥	⑦	⑧
23.	Separating the discovery and listing of alternative solutions from their evaluation	①	②	③	④	⑤	⑥	⑦	⑧
24.	Searching innovatively for all reasonably promising solutions and listing them	①	②	③	④	⑤	⑥	⑦	⑧
25.	Seeking innovative solutions by using different frames of reference and through brainstorming	①	②	③	④	⑤	⑥	⑦	⑧
26.	Obtaining facts to check whether the proposed solutions meet the conditions for acceptability	①	②	③	④	⑤	⑥	⑦	⑧

		Very little		Some		Considerable		Very great
27.	Selecting the solutions that best meet the conditions for acceptability	①	②	③	④	⑤	⑥	⑦	⑧
28.	Using backup and recycling technique when group cannot reach consensus	①	②	③	④	⑤	⑥	⑦	⑧
29.	Checking the solution against the problem as stated to be sure that it really solves the problem	①	②	③	④	⑤	⑥	⑦	⑧
30.	Rechecking the solution for undesirable side effects	①	②	③	④	⑤	⑥	⑦	⑧
31.	Specifying how, by whom, and when action is to be taken	①	②	③	④	⑤	⑥	⑦	⑧
32.	Establishing review procedures to be sure agreed-upon action will be taken	①	②	③	④	⑤	⑥	⑦	⑧

Note: from *New Ways of Managing Conflict*, Rensis and Jane Gibson Likert, McGraw-Hill Book Co., 1976.

CHAPTER V

Stress Management:
Taming the Quiet Killer

The older I grow, the more clearly I perceive the dignity and winning beauty of simplicity in thought, conduct and speech; a desire to simplify all that is complicated and to treat everything with the greatest natural-ness and clarity.

. . . Pope John XXIII
Journey of a Soul

The following is an excerpt from my personal journal, August 15, 1979:

I am still at the condominium I rented at Keystone Lodge. I awoke about 6:30 to sun streaming through my window. Unhappily I missed the sunrise which I'd enjoyed yesterday. I spent a half hour in devotions and meditation. Somehow God seems within such easy reach here.

Before breakfast, I decided to take a walk around the lake. What a contrast this walk was to the one I'd taken my first day here. Was it really only two days ago? That walk was "driven"! I knew "I needed exercise," that "walking reduces tension," that it was more practical for me than jogging due to my weight and temperament—and finally,

189

maybe after a walk, I'd be able to settle down to some serious thinking. After all . . . that's why I am really here. So I walked . . . briskly, blindly and with grim determination.

This morning I walked briskly . . . between stops. The stops were to enjoy a beaver, a chipmunk eating a lifesaver, five kinds of birds, a flock of ducks, several varieties of wild flowers, a dandelion floating on the lake and a school of trout swimming by the shore. The lake and the path are the same . . . only I have changed. My senses are alive and sharpened to sounds, smells and sights I've missed these past few months. How sad to go through life too busy to enjoy it—allowing perceptual blinders to filter out the world's beauty!

Now I'm sitting on a bench between the lake and a stream, writing while enjoying the warmth of the sun. I find it almost impossible to put into words the tremendous difference these three days have made in how I feel—about myself, others, and my work. Perhaps the best way is to contrast the emotions and feelings I experienced the last several weeks before this retreat and those I am experiencing now. Both may sound extreme . . . even exaggerated but they were very real to me:

Before	After
Overwhelmed	Centered
Out of control	Renewed energy
Loss of energy (very rare for me)	Values-goals clarified
No enthusiasm	Rested
Resentful	Relaxed
Distrustful	Productive
Martyred	Eager
Trouble with words (and words are my business)	Calm
	Vigorous
Loss of sensory perception	Senses sharp
Fatigue	Humor returned
Trouble sleeping	Ready for whatever comes
Annoyed at small things	Hopeful
Eating-drinking too much	I like me better!
Loss of humor	
Pain in the neck!	

The amazing thing to me is that I also got so much productive, creative work accomplished. It was far from only "navel gazing." Some of the tangible outcomes of these three days are:

—A statement of my values and an action plan to implement changes

—Reorganization of my company

—A rewrite of Chapter I of my book

—A book on power read

—One-half of a novel read and enjoyed

—A training session planned and outlined

In other words, I accomplished in three short days several projects I'd been floundering with for weeks. How about that for cost-effectiveness!

I now realize I had been on the edge of a precipice—with only a toe hold to keep me from crashing into a physical or emotional collapse. That has never happened to me before and now that I know how frightening and debilitating it can be, I vow never to let it happen again. I also realize it is my problem to see that it doesn't.

When I look at the results of these few short days, I realize this has been one of the smartest investments of my life. There is no such thing as not being able to afford the time or the money to do this when needed. I can never again afford not to!

What I had experienced was a full-fledged assault by the subtle killer known as stress. It is quietly and relentlessly waging its war on people of all ages across this country. It buries its victims daily—but it carefully hides behind the declared villains of heart disease, strokes, cancer, ulcers, etc. Therefore, few know of its deadly nature.

Only in the past few years have researchers, psychologists, and scientists decided the phenomenon of stress warrants their serious attention. Unfortunately, most of the medical profession is still ignoring it.

Norman Vincent Peale is said to have remarked in the '70s, "Americans have become so tense and nervous that it's been years since I've seen anyone fall asleep in church . . . and that's a sad situation!"

Stress unquestionably has great implications for today's managers, both as it affects themselves and their workers. In the insightful book *Stress and the Manager*, Karl Albrecht states:

Although one must probably tolerate a certain amount of stress discomfort, it is clear that chronic stress, prolonged beyond reasonable bounds, not only creates intolerable levels of discomfort, but it can steadily degrade one's health to the danger point. Once the health level has reached the danger point, continued chronic stress can precipitate a major health breakdown . . . the symptoms range from minor discomfort to death, from headache to heart attack, from indigestion to stroke,

191

from fatigue to high blood pressure and organ failure, from dermatitis to bleeding ulcers . . . it is indeed a fact of life for twentieth-century Americans that stress can kill. [1]

It then seems imperative that we as managers of others, try to gain more understanding of stress—its nature, effects, and remedies.

DEFINING STRESS

Woolfolk and Richardson define stress as follows:

Stress is a perception of threat or expectation of future discomfort that arouses, alerts, or otherwise activates the organism. [2]

In an article, "How to Manage Stress," Jennifer Bolch simply calls stress "a physiological response to the pressures of daily living."[3]

Most experts agree there are basically three components or stages of stress:

1. *The environment* or *stressor* (that incident or component of life that triggers a stress response);

2. *One's personal appraisal or perception* of the stressor; and

3. Based on this appraisal, *the emotional and physical arousal or response* . . . how the body reacts.

The most critical step seems to be the second one, for unless we interpret or perceive the stressor as a threat to our well-being, the physical and emotional response (that causes health problems) does not occur. That is why people respond so differently to the same seemingly stressful situations. Some people become extremely anxious (another term for stressed) when attending a party, giving a speech, or trying a new hobby. Others find each of these to be exciting and challenging. It is all in the eye of the perceiver (and also in his stomach, heart, and blood pressure)!

It is our contention that events do not in themselves produce stress reactions. Events in and of themselves are neutral . . . it is primarily our perceptions or appraisals of events that make them stressful. [4]

There is also a difference between *pressure, stressor,* and *stress.* [5]

Pressure refers to those elements in the environment that are problematic and require some sort of adaptation or response.

Stressors are those aspects of the environment that we consider grounds for becoming personally anxious.

Stress is in the person; the individual's attempt to make the physical and/or emotional adjustment required by the situation.

These distinctions are important, for they open up several possibilities for dealing with stress:

1. You can choose to remove yourself from a pressure situation;
2. You can re-engineer the situation to reduce or eliminate the pressure; or
3. You can teach yourself to react less intensely to many pressure situations.

Not all stress is bad, for good things can also trigger the stress response in our bodies. A new promotion, home, or marriage requires adaptation on our part . . . and therefore a certain amount of stress. Hans Selye, one of the foremost pioneers in the study of stress, clearly states "not all stress is distress. . . . Complete freedom from stress is death."[6] Put a bit more gently, Tubesing likens stress to "the tension on a violin string. If the string is too taut, it snaps; but if it's too slack, it won't make music."[7]

THE STRESS RESPONSE

This is the term coined by Selye to describe the third step of the stress model—how we react physically and emotionally to stress. It is most often referred to as the *fight-or-flight syndrome*. Some of the most common symptoms are: your heart begins to race; your hands grow cold and clammy and they tremble; you begin to perspire; and you become alert and ready for whatever action is required for your safety. Which action you decide on (fight or flight) is usually determined by whether the stressor creates anger or anxiety in you. *Anger triggers fight; anxiety suggests flight.*

Bonoma and Slevin illustrate it as follows:[8]

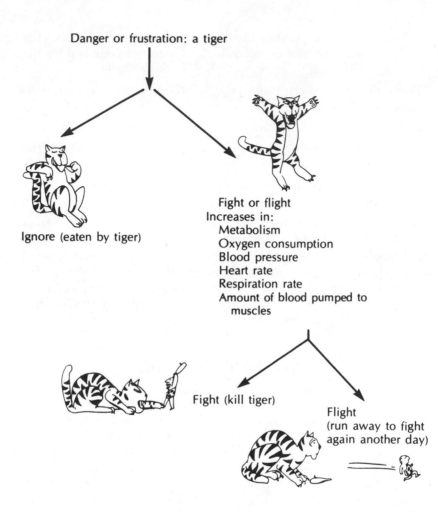

Danger or frustration: a tiger

Ignore (eaten by tiger)

Fight or flight
Increases in:
  Metabolism
  Oxygen consumption
  Blood pressure
  Heart rate
  Respiration rate
  Amount of blood pumped to
    muscles

Fight (kill tiger)

Flight
(run away to fight
again another day)

The cave man problem.

Karl Albrecht, *Executive Survival Manual, A Program for Managerial Effectiveness* by Thomas V. Bonoma and Dennis P. Slevin. ©1978 by Wadsworth Publishing Company, Inc., Belmont, California.

The "tigers" you face in your work are not the four-legged kind. Rather they are daily frustrations, missed deadlines, conflicts, unachieved goals, rushed meetings, and noncompliant subordinates. Still, they provoke the same kind of response.[9]

In the process of responding to stress, a whole series of reactions occur in the central nervous system.

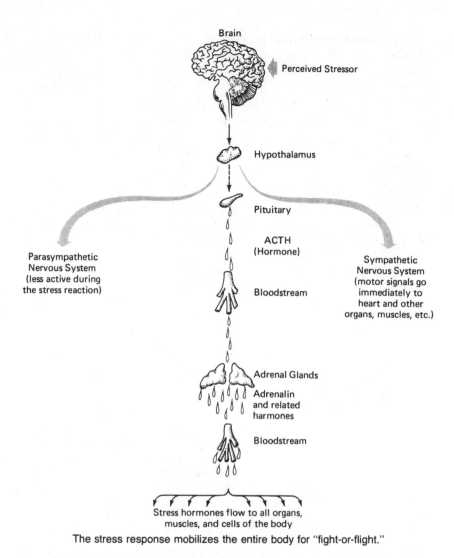

The stress response mobilizes the entire body for "fight-or-flight."

Note: From Albrecht, Karl A., *Stress and The Manager*, Prentice-Hall, Englewood Cliffs, N.J. 07632, 1979, p. 54

Clearly the stress reaction is a coordinated chemical mobilization of the entire human body to meet the requirements of life-and-death struggle or of rapid escape from the situation. . . . Of course the modern businessman [or businesswoman] or industrial worker as a social creature has a third possibility, namely, to stay within a stressful situation, neither fighting nor fleeing . . . this amounts to "stewing in our own juices," a process which, if long continued, can have very serious consequences to health and well being.[10]

195

In stress management, the goal is to reduce or eliminate the debilitating physical and emotional changes that occur during this third stage of stress, either by changing the environment (or one's perceptions of it) or by helping the body to handle stress more effectively.

I hesitate to get any further into the technical, physiological process related to stress for our purposes here. I would simply refer the more serious students of stress to the resources I found most useful:

> *Stress, Sanity, and Survival*, Robert L. Woolfolk, Ph.D. and Frank C. Richardson, Ph.D., New American Library, 1978.
>
> *Stress and the Manager*, Karl Albrecht, Ph.D., Prentice-Hall, 1979.
>
> *The Executive Survival Manual*, Thomas V. Bonoma and Dennis P. Slevin, Wadsworth Publishing Co., 1978.
>
> *The Stress of Life*, Hans Selye, M.D., McGraw-Hill, 1956.
>
> *Stress Without Distress*, Hans Selye, M.D., New American Library, 1974.

THE CAUSES OF STRESS

Albrecht has labeled the twentieth century as the age of anxiety. He states, "The great defining characteristics of this period—the first three-quarters of the twentieth century—have been *change, impermanence, disruption, newness and obsolescence, and a sense of acceleration in almost every perceptible aspect of American society.*"[11]

It is startling to realize the incredible number and variety of major technological breakthroughs that have occurred in the lifetime of a person who is seventy or eighty years old today. Here are just a few of them that have occurred since 1900:

—Airplanes, rockets, jet engines

—Electricity, automobiles

—Synthetic fabrics, plastics

—Radio, TV, LP records, and movies

—Mass production, mass transit

—Radar, atom and nuclear bombs, lasers

—Computers, transistors, calculators, word processors

—Food preservatives, frozen foods, supermarkets

—Antibiotics, tranquilizers, birth control pills

—Life support systems, organ transplants

—Space travel, moon landings

—Genetic engineering

At the same time all of these scientific miracles were taking place, significant changes were occurring in almost all of the other areas of American life. The most important life-style changes were:

1. *The change from rural to urban living*, which brought with it the stress-producing factors of crowding and an accelerated pace of life.

2. *The change from permanence and security to mobile, transient life situations.*

    The typical pattern for 1900 was to be born in a community, to grow up there, to work there, to marry and raise the family there, and to grow old there. The typical late-twentieth century style is to be born somewhere, to grow up in several different somewheres, to be educated somewhere else, to move from place to place as part of one's career, and to get married and divorced and remarried . . . the primary form of anxiety arising from the now mobicentric life style is the loss of a sense of permanence. [12]

3. *The change from self-sufficiency to dependence on others.* We became a nation of consumers as opposed to growers and makers. The aggressive and persuasive advertising industry successfully convinced each generation to become more avid consumers and acquirers of things than the last. An essential part of this mentality is that one not only gets things, but throws them away so you can get new things. This has created the general impression or mind-set that nothing lasts—or even should last. This undoubtedly generates a vague feeling of anxiety about the loss of permanence and stability in all aspects of life.

4. *The change from isolation to being world citizens.* Travel and communications now make us all citizens of the world and it is often a world in turmoil of some kind or another. We presently have the first generation raised from the cradle by the TV set (97 percent of all American homes have at least one). The A. C. Nielson Co. estimates that the average child or teen spends 22-25 hours per week in front of the tube and adult viewing

197

ranges from 24-30 hours. Much of the programming depicts life as violent, dangerous, and generally unsavory. This leads Albrecht to observe:

> *. . . the effect of heavy television viewing, in my opinion, is to create in the viewer a gradually accumulating feeling of anxiety and apprehension about the world in which we live . . . it overloads us with information about problems beyond our control, of alarming us about incidents far removed from our immediate experiences and of helping us to worry vaguely and without focus.* [13]

5. *The change from physically active occupations and lifestyles to relatively sedentary ones.* The work we now engage in (knowledge/service versus physical labor) encourages lack of physical exercise and the resulting deterioration of our bodies. The constant obsession with crash diets and pills does violence to our health, both physical and emotional. A much more hopeful trend is the increase in running, jogging, walking, biking, etc. It is important to note that a sedentary person seems to handle stress less effectively than a physically active person.

All of these technological and sociological changes have created what amounts to a stress epidemic in this country and yet until very recently, almost no serious attention was being given to this phenomenon by organizations in industry or human services.

Now the important task is to see how you personally are faring in this milieu. Each person not only lives as a part of this larger scenario, but we each have situations and events that impact us as individuals as well. These are unique for each of us and they, too, are constantly changing. The nature and extent of certain stress-producing events in your own life at any given time have a great deal to do with your ability to deal with this larger world of change and uncertainty. And more importantly, they affect your own physical and emotional well-being.

One of the most respected and widely used assessment tools regarding personal stress and its predictable effect on a person's health is the Holmes-Rahe inventory. After studying large numbers of actual case histories, they designed this instrument for use in predicting potential health breakdowns. The correlations have been remarkable. I suggest you take a moment to fill it out now. [14]

Instructions: Check off each of these life events that has happened to you during the previous year. Total the associated points.

THE SOCIAL READJUSTMENT RATING SCALE

LIFE EVENT	MEAN VALUE
1. Death of spouse	100
2. Divorce	73
3. Marital separation from mate	65
4. Detention in jail or other institution	63
5. Death of a close family member	63
6. Major personal injury or illness	53
7. Marriage	50
8. Being fired at work	47
9. Marital reconciliation with mate	45
10. Retirement from work	45
11. Major change in the health or behavior of a family member	44
12. Pregnancy	40
13. Sexual difficulties	39
14. Gaining a new family member (e.g., through birth, adoption, oldster moving in, etc.)	39
15. Major business readjustment (e.g., merger, reorganization, bankruptcy, etc.)	39
16. Major change in financial state (e.g., a lot worse off or a lot better off than usual)	38
17. Death of a close friend	37
18. Changing to a different line of work	36
19. Major change in the number of arguments with spouse (e.g., either a lot more or a lot less than usual regarding child-rearing, personal habits, etc.)	35
20. Taking on a mortgage greater than $10,000 (e.g., purchasing a home, business, etc.)	31
21. Foreclosure on a mortgage or loan	30
22. Major change in responsibilities at work (e.g., promotion, demotion, lateral transfer)	29
23. Son or daughter leaving home (e.g., marriage, attending college, etc.)	29
24. In-law troubles	29
25. Outstanding personal achievement	28
26. Wife beginning or ceasing work outside the home	26
27. Beginning or ceasing formal schooling	26
28. Major change in living conditions (e.g., building a new home, remodeling, deterioration of home or neighborhood)	25
29. Revision of personal habits (dress, manners, associations, etc.)	24
30. Troubles with the boss	23
31. Major change in working hours or conditions	20
32. Change in residence	20
33. Changing to a new school	20
34. Major change in usual type and/or amount of recreation	19
35. Major change in church activities (e.g., a lot more or a lot less than usual)	19
36. Major change in social activities (e.g., clubs, dancing, movies, visiting, etc.)	18
37. Taking on a mortgage or loan less than $10,000 (e.g., purchasing a car, TV, freezer, etc.)	17
38. Major change in sleeping habits (a lot more or a lot less sleep, or change in part of day when asleep)	16
39. Major change in number of family get-togethers (e.g., a lot more or a lot less than usual)	15
40. Major change in eating habits (a lot more or a lot less food intake, or very different meal hours or surroundings)	15
41. Vacation	13
42. Christmas	12
43. Minor violations of the law (e.g., traffic tickets, jaywalking, disturbing the peace, etc.)	11

There seems to be a well-documented and clear relationship between life change and physical disease. It is impossible to make accurate predictions on an individual basis, since

199

most of these findings are statistical. In our subjective judgment, we would estimate that you might be able to interpret your life change scores as follows:

LIFE CHANGE SCORE FOR PREVIOUS YEAR	PROBABILITY OF ILLNESS WITHIN NEXT 2 YEARS
Less than 150 (low stress)	Low
150-199 (mild stress)	30%
200-299 (moderate stress)	50%
300 or more (major stress)	80%

Note: From Holmes, Thomas H., and Rahe, Richard H., "Holmes-Rahe Social Readjustment Rating Scale," *Journal of Psychosomatic Research*, Vol. II, Pergamon Press, Ltd., 1967.

As a personal experiment, I completed this form based on my situation at the time I went on my retreat (described earlier in this chapter). My score was over 350 at that time. My body and emotions were definitely sounding all possible alarms and I finally stopped long enough to listen to them . . . and then act accordingly. My score at this moment is 205. The encouraging drop has come about due to a conscious and conscientious program of change including:

—Defining my goals and outlining actions based on a values clarification;

—Simplifying my business organization;

—Settling two stressful conflict situations;

—Engaging in a program of exercise (walking and aerobic dance);

—Modifying my eating habits;

—Beginning each day with meditation and devotion;

—Completing this book (a project of three years); and

—Spending more fun time with family and friends.

All of these have taken discipline, but I can assure you that the results have been well worth it. I have never felt better!

EMOTIONAL STRESSORS

Experts caution us to be aware of ways we continually stress ourselves emotionally in four general areas:

1. *Time stress:* We have vague and persistent anxiety over time running out; never having enough of it; having reams of "oughts and shoulds" that never get done. (Hopefully, the next chapter on Time Management will help you with this one.)

2. *Anticipatory stress:* We worry and have a sort of "free-floating fear" about events or catastrophes we anticipate but often can not name.

3. *Situational stress:* We are anxious about outcomes of situations, somehow fearing loss of status, significance, or acceptance by others. (Someone once observed that when we are young we spend a lot of time worrying what the world thinks of us; but by age 50, we realize the world really wasn't paying that much attention.)

4. *Encounter stress:* We are concerned over our interactions with with others, especially if there is a chance there will be conflict or unpredictable behavior. (That is why the chapter on Conflict Management is so important.)

Albrecht suggests the following tool to help you assess your present life style and suggest some changes that might create less stress in your everyday life.[15]

Stressful Life Style	Low-Stress Life Style
Individual experiences chronic, unrelieved stress.	Individual accepts "creative" stress for distinct periods of challenging activity.
Becomes trapped in one or more continuing stressful situations.	Has "escape routes" allowing occasional detachment and relaxation.
Struggles with stressful interpersonal relationships (family, spouse, lover, boss, co-workers, etc.).	Asserts own rights and needs; negotiates low-stress relationships of mutual respect; selects friends carefully and establishes relationships that are nourishing and non-toxic.
Engages in distasteful, dull, toxic, or otherwise unpleasant and unrewarding work.	Engages in challenging, satisfying, worthwhile work that offers intrinsic rewards for accomplishment.
Experiences continual time stress; too much to be done in available time.	Maintains a well-balanced and challenging workload; overloads and crises are balanced by "breather" periods.
Worries about potentially unpleasant upcoming events.	Balances threatening events with worthwhile goals and positive events to look forward to.
Has poor health habits (e.g., eating, smoking, liquor, lack of exercise, poor level of physical fitness).	Maintains high level of physical fitness, eats well, uses alcohol and tobacco not at all or sparingly.
Life activities are "lopsided" or unbalanced (e.g., preoccupied with one activity such as work, social activities, making money, solitude or physical activities).	Life activities are balanced; individual invests energies in a variety of activities, which in the aggregate bring feelings of satisfaction (e.g., work, social activities, recreation, solitude, cultural pursuits, family, and close relationships).

Finds it difficult to just "have a good time," relax, and enjoy momentary activities.	Finds pleasure in simple activities, without feeling a need to justify playful behavior.
Experiences sexual activities as unpleasant, unrewarding, or socially "programmed" (e.g., by manipulation, "one-upping.")	Enjoys a full and exuberant sex life, with honest expression of sexual appetite.
Sees life as a serious, difficult situation, little sense of humor.	Enjoys life on the whole; can laugh at himself; has a well-developed and well-exercised sense of humor.
Conforms to imprisoning, punishing social roles.	Lives a relatively role-free life; is able to express natural needs, desires, and feelings without apology.
Accepts high-pressure or stressful situations passively; suffers in silence.	Acts assertively to re-engineer pressure situations whenever possible; renegotiates impossible deadlines; avoids placing himself in unnecessary pressure situations; manages time effectively.

Karl Albrecht, Stress and the Manager: Making it Work for You, © 1979, p. 54. Reprinted by permission, Prentice-Hall, Inc., Englewood Cliffs, N.J.

Tubesing suggests a simple method to determine which changes may make sense *for you.* Simply complete the following statements:[16]

- Maybe I don't need to _____

  _____ anymore.

- Maybe I do need to _____

  _____ some more.

- Maybe I need to _____

  _____ sometime soon.

- Maybe I need to _____

  _____ once again.

- Maybe I need to _____

  _____ sometimes.

The first statement clarifies what you would like to change; the second what you want to hang on to. The third is a statement of future goals, while the fourth recalls a resource from the past. The fifth clarifies an area where you need more flexibility.

One of the most essential things to remember in any exercise like this is that its real purpose is *helping you clarify your own values.* So much stress is generated by the "oughts" and "shoulds" that we have inherited from others in the form of standards, demands, and expectations. We need to check those out for their relevancy from time to time. That is what values clarification is all about. For example, when I did mine, I simply:

1) listed the eight components or aspects of my life that were most important to me at that point in my life;

2) ranked them by order of importance; and

3) analyzed what percentage of my time and energy I was presently devoting to each.

A startling fact became immediately evident. Part of my stress was due to the fact that I had been devoting over 60 percent of my time to the last four items on my list. My values had somehow gotten overshadowed by the expectations and demands of others. So my work was then clearly cut out for me. I needed to turn the situation around so my time and energy commitments were more in line with my own personal values.

Mike Murray, a trainer and good friend, points out "a value is not a value until you have considered alternatives and chosen it." He also cautions: "People do not like to be should upon!"

When we seriously set out to more effectively manage ourselves, it is important to consider all aspects of our lives:

—Physical   —Intellectual

—Relational   —Emotional

—Vocational   —Imaginal

—Spiritual

The suggestions given throughout this book speak to all seven areas.

THE EFFECTS OF STRESS

One of the key determinants of the effects of stress on anyone's system is whether the stress is sporadic (episodic) or chronic. Most relatively healthy persons can deal with occasional episodes of stress and recover fairly quickly.

It is chronic stress that leads to serious health problems—that prolonged, unrelieved state of worry, anxiety, and arousal.

Selye identified three stages of the stress response in the body:[17]

1. *The alarm reaction:* the fight/flight syndrome; the initial mobilization of the organism to threat.

2. *The resistance stage:* the person resists the threat and battles for survival.

3. *The exhaustion stage:* the body runs out of adaptive energy if stress is too prolonged, resulting in serious illness and eventual death.

The more minor discomforts caused by stress, both physical and psychological, are well-known to each of us. Many of the complex and subtle chemical changes that take place in the overstressed body tend to disrupt the effectiveness of digestion, assimilation of nutrients, vitamin balances, sleep cycles, and even brain functions. We presently have only an inkling of the extent to which stress undermines the body's functioning, but the evidence is mounting rapidly as research proceeds.

What is relatively new is that almost all of the authors I read have identified stress as a major contributor to this "Who's Who" list of serious diseases:

—Ulcers	—Arteriosclerosis
—Heart disease	—Migraine headaches
—Cancer	—Colitis
—High blood pressure	—Spastic colon
—Strokes	—Asthma

The human body—your body—is capable of literally destroying itself when forced to maintain a high-stress, "alarm" state for long periods without relief. [18]

Another serious problem is the increase in secondary killers related to stress. That is simply those remedies we use to help us cope that are almost as destructive as the stress itself. Some of these "adaptive diseases" are:

—Alcoholism	—Tranquilizer addiction
—Drug addiction	—Overeating
—Smoking	—Suicide

To graphically illustrate the severity of this problem, may I quote from Barbara Gordon's moving autobiography, *I'm Dancing As Fast As I Can.* (Ms. Gordon is a world-renowned TV producer and reporter.)

You don't dash, I said to myself, you flee, as if moving quickly will somehow help you beat the terror. There it was, the old fear, back again, whenever I had to go someplace. And I was, at this point, afraid of my fear. My anxiety attacks had become so intense that I was often immobilized, paralyzed. So I hadn't dashed very far when the terror, greater than yesterday's, less than tomorrow's, swallowed me up like a vacuum cleaner . . . what are you frightened of? What was it? I was going to a shrink once a week and still the anxiety increased. Why didn't Dr. Allen help me? Dammit, I'd been seeing him religiously for ten years, ever since I left my husband. It was a routine, like brushing my teeth, a normal part of my life, as it was for most of the people I knew. He gave me Valium and I was taking it by the handful. So why was the terror growing? I must talk to him, must get more pills, must do something. [19]

What a poignant portrayal of anxiety and, unfortunately, the all-too-common remedy prescribed by the medical profession. At this point of the story, Ms. Gordon was taking thirty milligrams of Valium a day, *under a doctor's supervision.* She ended up in a mental institution when she finally decided to quit the pills "cold turkey." Yes indeed, these so-called cures for stress bear serious examination and hopefully reform. Later in this chapter we will explore some safe, more effective means of handling stress.

STRESS AND THE MANAGER

I recently saw this little quote on the desk of a friend:

How do I win the rat race . . . without becoming a rat?

Mark Twain said it a bit differently: "Let us so live that when we come to die even the undertaker will be sorry!"

Both of these adages point out the fact that management is much more than MBO, techniques, systems, and bottom lines. It is first and foremost *working with and through other people to get a job done.* And how those "others" feel about working with us has

→a tremendous impact on both the quality and quantity of work they will do . . . which has

→a tremendous impact on our own perceptions of our effectiveness as a manager . . . which has

→a tremendous impact on both our own stress level and that of our subordinates . . . which has

→ a tremendous impact on

our health and peace of mind.

205

Most of the effective managers I have known have been, first of all, effective as persons. By that I mean they are well-rounded, involved, enthusiastic life-long learners who always see themselves on a "journey of becoming."

Albrecht agrees. "A well-rounded, highly fulfilled individual will make a better manager than a lopsided one who has narrowed down his [her] life, interests, and thoughts to the routine of doing the job"[20] (A certifiable workaholic!). He urges managers to examine all of the various areas of their lives and to carefully add activities and interests *that bring rewards outside of work.*

Because nine out of ten workers in the United States now work in organizational structures, and since each of these workers brings with him both the generalized and personal stress discussed earlier in this chapter . . . stress management is very clearly a topic of importance for today's manager.

In the *Executive Survival Manual* by Bonoma and Slevin, we read,

> *As our technological society became more complex, our social organization expanded to manage the growing complexity. In the past few hundred years we have created a social environment characterized by huge hierarchical organizations, in which the individual's life is subject to many conflicting pressures and stresses. We have become the confused victims of the miracles we have wrought.*[21]

I believe they have identified one of the major stressors in the workplace today—the conflict between personal and organizational goals.

"Too often buying into the system is done at the expense of buying out of our uniqueness," according to Culbert.[22] That is precisely why I began this book with a serious look at creativity, problem solving, and power. In my estimation, we must become more skilled in all three of these areas if we are to survive as creative individuals in today's organizations. Wishful thinking and the game of "victim" will not change things.

> *Nothing is easier than fault-finding; no talent, no self-denial, no brains, no character are required to set up in the grumbling business.*
> . . . Robert West

The survival skills we are dealing with throughout this book require character and commitment but the dividends far outweigh the costs. After all, we spend over 2,000 hours of our lives each year at work. We cannot afford to squander them. Life is too short . . . and too precious.

Some of the stressors that are unique to the work place are:

—Unfulfilled career goals

—Unclear or ambiguous job definitions

—Unrealistic deadlines

—Conflicting personal and organizational goals

—Misunderstanding the reward system

—Inability to accomplish objectives

—Unhealthy work climate

—Unclear supervisory directives

—Conflicts between work groups

—Unsatisfactory pay, benefits or job security

—Competition versus collaboration

—Underutilization or overutilization of our abilities

—Lack of opportunity for growth and development

—Inhumane management philosophies that are task versus people oriented.

These stresses affect people at all levels of the organization: executives, managers and employees. Each person's ability to cope with them varies depending on their personality characteristics, emotional and physical health, and past experiences. It is important that each of us be aware of our optimal stress level and that we are aware of when we cross over into the danger zone, where our "stress meters" just keep ticking all the time and our time on that meter is running out. "Many times stress is not so much a product of inner conflict as of sheer grinding frustration."[23]

Organizations are beginning to realize that the cost of stress is staggering in terms of dollars and cents as well. (Albrecht and others estimate the annual cost of stress to organizations in the U.S. is $150 billion per year!) This is due to the side effects, i.e.:

—Absenteeism

—Low quality of performance

—Low productivity

—Health breakdowns

—Alcoholism and drug abuse

—Turnover

—Negativism

—Sick leave

—Accidents

—Anti-social acts (i.e., theft, waste).

Since so many of the job-related stressors pertain to either the work itself or to leadership, let's take a moment to examine each a bit more closely. Here is some wisdom from others:

ON WORK

- *What's not worth doing is not worth doing well.*

  . . . Abraham Maslow

- *My own code is based on the view that to achieve peace of mind and fulfillment through expression, most men [women] need a commitment to work in the service of some cause they can respect.*

  . . . Hans Selye

- *You can't sit on the lid of progress. If you do, you will be blown to pieces.*

  . . . Henry J. Kaiser

- *A sound labor philosophy for the eighties must rest on the basic need of human beings to be needed. People want to be responsible and efficient when they can perceive that their work serves a meaningful purpose. This latent individual need to serve is one of the pillars of ethics.*

  . . . Frederick Herzberg

- *We are committed to our jobs because of opportunities that they provide us to do something personally meaningful with our lives.*

  . . . Samuel Culbert

- *If you don't believe in life after death, just stand outside our company at 5:00.*

  . . . Anonymous

- *Isn't it funny, when the other fellow takes a long time to do something, he's slow. When I take a long time to do something, I'm thorough. When the other fellow doesn't do it, he's lazy. When I don't do it, I'm busy. When the other fellow does it without being told, he's overstepping his bounds. When I go ahead and do it without being told, that's initiative. When the other fellow states his opinion strongly, he's bull-headed. When I state my opionion strongly, I'm firm. When the other*

208

fellow overlooks a few rules of etiquette, he's rude. When I skip a few rules, I'm doing my own thing.

. . . Tom Knight

● *Wherefore I perceive that there is nothing better than that a man should rejoice in his own work, for that is his portion.*

. . . Ecclesiastes 3:22

● *Anything you like to do isn't tiresome.*

. . . Studs Terkel

● *There ain't no civilization where there ain't no satisfaction and that's what's the trouble now. Nobody is satisfied.*

. . . Will Rogers

● *Some people suffer in silence louder than others.*

. . . Anonymous

● *The spectre that haunts most working men and women today is this: the planned obsolescence of people that is of a piece with the planned obsolescence of the things they make. Or sell. It is perhaps this fear of no longer being needed in a world of needless things that most clearly spells out the unnaturalness, the surreality of much that is called work today.*

. . . Studs Terkel

ON LEADERSHIP

● *The traits for leadership success are humility, deep understanding of the nature of the business, deep respect for those on the firing line and those who can enjoy making the organization work, a demonstrated record of guts, industry, loyalty downward, judgement, fairness and honesty under pressure.*

. . . Robert Townsend

● *I came here to work, I didn't come here to crawl. There's a f------ difference!" (Quote from a steelworker)*

. . . Studs Terkel

● *Success is a journey, not a destination.*

. . . B. Sweetland

● *Our Age of Anxiety is, in great part, the result of trying to do today's job with yesterday's tools–with yesterday's concepts.*

. . . Marshall McLuhan

● *People take themselves too serious. They think if they don't break their necks from one place of business to another then the world will stop. Say, all they have to do is just watch some man die that is more prominent than they are, and in less than twenty-four hours the world has forgot he ever lived; so they ought to have imagination enough to know how long they will stop things if they left this old earth. People nowadays are traveling faster, but they are not getting further (in fact not as far) as our old dads [and mothers] did.*

. . . Will Rogers

● *He who talks about his inferiors hasn't any!*

. . . Anonymous

● *The common idea that success spoils people by making them vain, egotistical and self complacent is erroneous; on the contrary, true success makes them, for the most part, humble, tolerant and kind. Failure makes people bitter and cruel.*

. . . Somerset Maugham

● *Be kind. Remember everyone you meet is fighting a hard battle.*

. . . T. H. Thompson

● *I have yet to find a person, however exalted their position, who didn't do better work and put forth greater effort under a spirit of approval than under a spirit of criticism.*

. . . Charles Schwab

● *As leaders we need to be more like gardeners than manufacturers–we need to grow instead of make people. When you want tomatoes, you plant tomato seeds, carefully choose the right soil and place and take care of them. We don't* make *tomatoes—we allow them to* grow.

. . . Unknown

● *When I was growing up, there was a tea kettle in our house with a lid that did not fit tightly. When steam began to rise, that lid would shake and rattle and make a tremendous noise. Of course, the lid was doing no good. In fact, it was allowing the steam to escape, but it made quite a racket and impressed you as being very busy and important. I've always remembered that tea kettle and whenever I see a person who makes a lot of noise without accomplishing much, I say to myself, "That one has a loose lid!"*

. . . Morris Mandel

● *Power wielders respond to their subjects' needs and motivations only to the extent that they have to in order to fulfill their own power objectives, which remain their primary concern. True leaders, on the other hand, emerge from, and always return to, the wants and needs of the followers. They see their tasks as the recognition and mobilization of their followers' needs . . . the truly great or creative leaders do something more—they induce new, more activist tendencies in their followers; they arouse in them hopes and aspirations, and expectations.*

. . . James MacGregor Burns

● *The greatest good we can do for others is not just to share our riches with them—but to enable them to discover their own!*

. . . Sr. Corita

It is my firm conviction that if organizations took more seriously the importance of these two vital elements—job design and leadership—most work-related stress could be eliminated. My experience (and that of hundreds of others I have talked to during my training and consultations) is that there is a very real leadership crisis in this country. Far too many people in leadership positions are not leading anywhere . . . or leading anybody.

The frustration and resulting stress that comes from working in institutions led by either self-serving or inept leaders is enormous. It is what is killing the vital spark of creativity and innovation these very institutions must have if they are to survive. We simply *must* turn this around, both for the sake of the institutions and for the sake of the people who serve in them. That is exactly why "Quality of Work Life" is regarded by most experts as the number one issue before organizations of all kinds in this decade. I would certainly agree!

The resources I have found most useful in studying work-related stress are:

—*Stress and the Manager* by Karl Albrecht

—*Executive Survival Manual* by Thomas Bonoma and Dennis Slevin

—*The Feel of the Work Place* by Fritz Steele and Stephen Jenks

—*The Organization Trap* by Samuel Culbert.

MANAGING STRESS MORE EFFECTIVELY

Now that we know what stress is and the incredible effects it can have on our personal and professional well-being, it is important to move on to the logical question . . . what can we do about it?

In an article entitled "How to Master Stress," Selye advises that we should begin by being aware of the danger signs of too much stress:[24]

- General irritability; becoming either unusually aggressive or passive
- Pounding of the heart
- Accident-proneness
- "Floating anxiety"
- Trembling, nervous tics
- Tendency to be easily startled

- Stuttering and other speech difficulties
- Grinding the teeth
- Insomnia
- Frequent need to urinate
- Indigestion
- Headaches
- Premenstrual tension or missed periods
- Pain in the neck or lower back
- Either loss of appetite or excessive appetite
- Increased alcohol or drug use
- Nightmares

(I would also suggest you complete the instruments included at the end of this chapter in Appendix B.)

These are simply indicators that you may need to take action relating to one of the three stress-reducing options suggested earlier: 1) altering the environment that is causing stress; 2) changing your appraisal or evaluation of the stressors; or 3) reducing the detrimental physical or emotional reaction that occurs during prolonged stress.

The following 10 suggestions are a composite of the strategies proposed by most of the authoritites I researched. *Choose those that make sense to you.*

1. CLARIFY YOUR VALUES

It is essential to develop a keen self awareness regarding your own goals, needs, and expectations (instead of responding only to the "oughts and shoulds" of other people). Your personal value system should serve as the basis for all of the major life choices you make. It is important that your expenditure of time and energy be congruent with these values or stress is inevitable. It does not work for long to put first things last.

This may suggest that you will want to learn the art of "deobligation"—that is, saying no to low-value, high-stress commitments.

The *Executive Survival Manual* suggests the following exercises to help identify values:[25]

The Million-Dollar Exercise
Assume that you have just been given $1,000,000, tax free. List

seven things that you would do or buy in the next six months with this gift.

1. _____
2. _____
3. _____
4. _____
5. _____
6. _____
7. _____

The Lightning Exercise

Imagine you are going to be fatally struck by lightning in six months. All matters pertaining to your death have been attended to. List below seven things that you would accomplish in the next six months.

1. _____
2. _____
3. _____
4. _____
5. _____
6. _____
7. _____

Now go back and circle the items on each list that have nothing to do with money or time pressures. What goals can you accomplish now, even without the million dollars? What goals can you accomplish in the next six months even without the pressure of time?

You may be amazed to discover that many of these goals can be accomplished with some straightforward modifications of your current situation.

2. KEEP BEATHING . . . AND EXERCISE!

When you are tense, if you are like most people, you engage in very shallow breathing. This is unhealthy. Next time you experience stress, try the following:

1. Pretend you are about to have an X-ray taken—breathe in and then let it out completely without forcing; sigh. Your neck and shoulders will relax;
2. Breathe in fresh clean air—*fill your lungs*; let your breath lift your heart. Do this three or four times.

Or else try:

1. Deep breathe; sigh; make your mind blank;
2. Move and relax one or two key areas of your body (i.e., arms and legs; neck and shoulders);
3. Concentrate on a pleasant scene, thought, or feeling for a moment; and
4. Finish with another deep abdominal breath.

(We will discuss deep relaxation techniques later.)

More and more experts are also seriously suggesting a program of consistent, vigorous exercise as an excellent antidote for the ravages of stress on the body. They are particularly enthusiastic about aerobic exercises (those that elevate the heart rate to about 150 beats per minute for twenty minutes to an hour a day). Running, swimming, bicycling, and aerobic dance are some options. (I've tried an aerobic dance class this summer and can verify it works!) The physiological effect of this kind of exercise is to develop greater cardiovascular efficiency and remember—stress attacks that system particularly. It is best to check with your doctor before beginning such a program if you are over 30.

3. WATCH WHAT YOU EAT . . . AND DON'T EAT!

Remember the old adage, "An ounce of prevention is worth a pound of cure." Good nutrition is sound preventive medicine. It is important to watch not only what you eat, but how much. Excess weight is a serious physical stressor adding undue pressure to your body's vital organs. It is also a psychological stressor in a "thin is beautiful" culture.

4. CREATE AND USE PERSONAL SUPPORT SYSTEMS

Many people have a tendency to pull inward or withdraw from others when experiencing stressful situations. Like animals, we tend to retreat and lick our wounds. Research strongly suggests that this is exactly the opposite of what is most helpful. You need to have a sufficient number of "significant others" in your life to offer empathy, understanding, and support if you are to be successful at combating stress. In fact, some experts believe this is the most important factor of all. Besides family and friends, you also need those special others who respect and challenge you and serve as mentors and energizers. There is a tremendous difference between friends and acquaintances. In our society of strangers you need to work at having this small, but vital core of friends. (This somehow seems more difficult for men to do than women in our culture.)

It is also essential to acknowledge that giving needs to be a two-way proposition. When we invest ourselves in other people it helps eliminate an unhealthy obsession or preoccupation with self. *Self preoccupied people are rarely happy.*

Milton Mayeroff in his book *On Caring* states:

> *Man [woman] finds himself by finding his place, and he finds his place by finding appropriate others that need his care and that he needs to care for. Through caring and being cared for man experiences himself as part of nature; we are closest to a person or an idea when we help it grow.*[26]

If you, in the past, have had difficulty in making friends, Dale Carnegie has this practical advice: You can make more friends in two months by becoming really interested in other people than you can in two years by trying to get other people interested in you. (So take that first step!)

5. LEARN TO LET GO

One reason our personal loads seem so heavy is all of the extra baggage we carry along with us. (This is often referred to as "gunny sacking.") We drag along:

—Past hurts, resentments, and grudges;

  —Dead or toxic relationships;

    —Unhealthy attitudes; and

      —Bad health habits.

I love the motto shared with me by a quadriplegic friend:

NEVER STUMBLE ON ANYTHING BEHIND YOU

Philosophically almost everyone would agree with this. It is *how to let go* that is the problem. A growing number of stress authorities seem to be endorsing all or some of the following techniques to help you relax and let go:

- *Meditation*
- *Progressive or deep relaxation*
- *Deep breathing exercises*
- *Hypnosis*
- *Diary writing*
- *Prayer*
- *Exercise*
- *Biofeedback*

If you are interested in further reading in this area, besides the books already recommended, may I suggest:

—*The Relaxation Response* by Herbert Benson, M.D.

—*Search for Silence* by Elizabeth O'Connor

—*The Joy of Running* by Thaddeus Kostrubala

—*At a Journal Workshop* by Ira Progoff

—*Zen and the Art of Motorcycle Maintenance* by Robert Prisig

—*Gift of the Sea* by Anne Morrow Lindbergh.

(Also, check the example of a relaxation exercise at the end of this chapter, Appendix A.)

6. SEEK VARIETY

This is one of the antidotes to becoming a lopsided workaholic. It is what adds spice to an otherwise bland and uninteresting life. Someone once observed that all animals, except man, know that the principle business of life is to enjoy it.

Now that does not mean we must become lazy and self indulgent. Far from it! It means work should be a part of that business of life that we enjoy. We should plan carefully for changes of place and pace to help re-create us and revitalize our energies and take seriously the knowledge that growth and development are the most powerful personal motivators there are. New experiences are essential to keep us growing . . . and going.

Ruts, like old chairs,
Become too comfortable
To leave voluntarily
  Unless the house is on fire
  Or you become tired
  Of being tired
  And climb out
  Into the world again
In search of more
Exciting things to do.
                    . . . Lyman Randall

Check your calendar right now. Do you have personal time blocked out—vacation (a must!); holidays; a "goof-off" day now and then; time for friends, family, travel, cultural events, active sports, new restaurants, good books, quiet time? That calendar tells the story. If it is jammed only with business appointments—and oughts and shoulds—change it now. Gertrude Stein had some good advice for the driven professional: "When you get there, there isn't any there there."

7. SEEK TO MAKE YOUR WORKPLACE LESS STRESSFUL

John Adams is a consultant and trainer in the field of stress management. In an interesting article entitled "Improving Stress Management," he lists the following strategies or activities he has recommended to numerous organizations:[27]

  —*Stress management training or seminars for mixed employee groups on a continuing basis;*

  —*Stress assessment work done face-to-face with individuals or small groups to identify the stressors and make action plans to deal with them;*

  —*Revision (or development) of job descriptions and performance standards that will reduce the levels of role ambiguity and role conflict;*

  —*Stress management counseling provided;*

  —*Education of employees about the importance of exercise and dietary habits in maintaining good health;*

  —*Fresh fruits and juices offered as alternatives to coffee and jelly rolls in meetings and at coffee breaks;*

—*Exercise programs and facilities added and instruction in meditation/relaxation offered;*

—*Integration of stress management sessions with other appropriate training: i.e., MBO, time management;*

—*Physical examinations required annually with special counseling for those showing stress-related symptoms; and*

—*At least quarterly meetings between senior managers and supervisors to clarify and discuss issues, policies, and decisions. (Distortions of these items as they filter through the organization have been found to be major sources of work-related stress.)*

And finally, your own leadership philosophy and style are terribly important. Are you an enabler or disabler of those who work with you?

8. MAINTAIN OPTIMISM

Remember the self-fulfilling prophecy idea. If you expect to succeed (at stress management as well as anything else), you probably will. If you expend all of your energy on the "ain't it awfuls," and "poor me," you are trapped in a victim mentality and will probably succeed in staying there.

There is a vast difference between an optimist and a pessimist. Bernard Baruch had the right attitude. When asked how he felt about old age, he promptly replied, "Old age is always fifteen years older than I am."

(Someone else poignantly capsulized the attitude of a pessimist: "When they see the writing on the wall, they're sure it's a forgery.")

It is important to distinguish between a pie-in-the-sky, pollyannish attitude and a realistic, reasoned optimistic outlook. The first denies the existence of problems; the second acknowledges them, tries to analyze and understand them, and then acts to solve them,fully expecting to succeed.

One reason optimists so often succeed is that they learn the trick of setting smaller, achievable objectives (in other words, they tend to build "switch backs" into their trails). They take a problem one-step-at-a-time, one-day-at-a-time and have the good sense to know change comes slowly, so they do not get impatient or discouraged easily.

The characteristics of faith and trust, both in one's fellow human beings and in God, are common to many optimistic persons. They are not in this thing alone—and they know it.

9. DON'T BE HASSLED BY SMALL THINGS

It is a waste of time and precious energy to worry and fret over things that are either unimportant or over which you really have no control. Traffic jams; delayed doctors appointments; cancelled airplane flights; flat tires; inconsiderate bikers, joggers or drivers; rained out games; lost socks; busy signals; inflation and taxes all fit this criteria. You wish they would go away—but they won't. So learn to live with them.

William James once observed that *the art of being wise is knowing what to overlook.*

One absolutely essential prerequisite to this particular suggestion is a healthy sense of humor. Nothing breaks tension more quickly or effectively than a chuckle or good-natured smile. So, an invaluable tool in your arsenal to fight stress is the ability to laugh at yourself and to learn to see the funny side of things. (You may have to turn the "thing" over several times and examine it from all angles to find it, but it is almost always there.)

10. TAKE RESPONSIBILITY FOR YOURSELF!

It would be so comforting to be able to believe that stress . . . and time . . . and conflict are somehow the enemy; that they prey on innocent people; and that each of us ends up as unwitting and unwilling victims. That view is comforting because it makes all of those other things and people the problem, and that, in turn, removes the necessity (or even the possibility) of our doing anything about them. The reality is that we do not *really* believe that and therefore feelings of guilt, depression, and fear overtake us. If "they" are not the enemy, who is? As you struggle with the realization that all of these problems can only be solved by first of all acknowledging your own ownership of them, you can then move on to taking responsibility for dealing with them. It is challenging and exciting, for things are no longer out of your control. You can decide—and then act on those decisions.

A good motto might be this one, shared by a friend and taped on my refrigerator:

We all have to iron out our own wrinkles . . .
Or if we can't iron out our wrinkles
We either have to accept being wrinkled
Or accept how someone else irons.

In conclusion, I would like to return to the theme that I used to begin this chapter—that of simplifying one's life.

All truly deep people have at the core of their being the genius to be simple and to know how to seek simplicity. The inner and outer aspects of their lives match . . . they are so uncluttered by any self-importance within and so unthreatened from without that they have what one philosopher calls a certain "availability"; they are ready to be at the disposal of others . . . successful living is a journey towards simplicity and a triumph over confusion. [28]

. . . Martin Marty

REFERENCES

1. Albrecht, Karl A., *Stress and the Manager*, Prentice-Hall, 1979, p. 1, 35.

2. Woolfolk, Robert, and Richardson, Frank, *Stress, Sanity and Survival*, New American Library, 1978, p. 8.

3. Bolch, Jennifer, "How to Manage Stress," *Reader's Digest*, July 1980, p. 81.

4. Woolfolk and Richardson, p. 5.

5. Albrecht, pp. 47, 48.

6. Selye, Hans, *Stress Without Distress*, New American Library, 1974, p. 20.

7. Bolch, p. 82.

8. From *Executive Survival Manual, A Program for Managerial Effectiveness* by Thomas V. Bonoma and Dennis P. Slevin. © 1978 by Wadsworth Publishing Company, Inc., Belmont, California 94002. Reprinted by permission of publisher.

9. Ibid., p. 54.

10. Albrecht, pp. 55, 57.

11. Ibid., p. 2.

12. Ibid., pp. 11-13.

13. Ibid., pp. 21, 22.

14. Holmes, Thomas H. and Rahe, Richard H., "Holmes-Rahe Social Readjustment Rating Scale," *Journal of Psychosomatic Research*, Vol. II, Pergamon Press, Ltd., 1967.

15. Ibid., pp. 107, 108.

16. Bolch, p. 82.

17. Selye, p. 26 ff.

18. Albrecht, p. 71.

19. Gordon, Barbara, *I'm Dancing As Fast As I Can*, Harper and Row, Inc., 1979, pp. 15, 16.

20. Albrecht, p. 234.

21. Bonoma and Slevin, Foreword.

22. Culbert, Samuel A., *The Organization Trap and How to Get Out of It*, Basic Books, 1974, p. 15.

23. Woolfolk and Richardson, p. 12.

24. Selye, Hans, "How to Manage Stress," p. 34.

25. Bonoma and Slevin, p. 164.

26. Mayerhoff, Milton, *On Caring*.

27. Adams, John, "Improving Stress Management," *Social Change: Ideas and Applications*, Vol. 8, No. 4, 1978.

28. Marty, Martin, "Simplify Your Life," *Reader's Digest*, March, 1980, p. 79.

APPENDIX A

THE RELAXATION RESPONSE

1. Find a quiet place, preferably a semidark room.

2. Think just about your eyes. Try to feel all of the muscles around your eyes and in your eyelids which are tense. Try to relax them. Make no effort to close your eyes; they will close automatically as you master the relaxation response for just your eyes. Take all the time that you need. When you have succeeded, you will feel like there is a very tense area above your eyes and below your eyes, but no tenseness in your eyes or eyelids themselves, since they are now totally relaxed.

3. Now focus on your toes. Your goal is to make the muscles in your toes feel like the muscles in your eyes—totally relaxed.

4. Move successively through the muscles in your feet, your calves, your thighs, your groin, your chest, and finally, your neck and head.

5. Let your mind idle. Think of nothing special. If heavy distractions keep intruding on your thoughts, while you are trying to relax, concentrate on your breathing and letting your mind "float."

6. Practice this exercise for 20 minutes every day. *Don't* do it at bedtime, when partial success will be met by falling asleep. Very quickly, depending upon the intensity and rigor with which you practice, you will learn to be able to totally relax and experience a quite exhilarating feeling when you are done.

7. Do not worry about whether or not you are successful in totally relaxing. Just let relaxation occur at its own pace. What you need is quiet, a comfortable position like lying or sitting, and willingness to try. As you get more and more practiced at using the relaxation response, you will be able to elicit it very quickly, and even in noisy work environments.

From EXECUTIVE SURVIVAL MANUAL, A PROGRAM FOR MANAGERIAL EFFEC-TIVENESS by Thomas V. Bonoma and Dennis P. Slevin. © 1978 by Wadsworth Publishing Company, Inc., Belmont, California 94002. Reprinted by permission of the publisher.

APPENDIX B

JOB STRESSORS
(Developed by Tom Isgar, Ph.D.)

Please answer the following questions as they describe experiences in your current job in the past 12 months, by placing a number on the line preceding each question. The numbers correspond to the following descriptive terms:

6=Always   5=Frequently   4=Often   3=Occasionally   2=Seldom   1=Never

HOW OFTEN:

___ 1—do you feel overqualified/underqualified for the work you actually do?

___ 2—do you feel lack of identification with your profession?

___ 3—when you compare yourself with your co-workers and personal friends with respect to their accomplishments are you unhappy with your career?

___ 4—do you think that you will not be able to satisfy the conflicting demands of the various people around you?

___ 5—does your job interfere with your personal life?

___ 6—does your personal life interfere with your job?

___ 7—do you feel that you have to do things which are against your better judgement?

___ 8—are decisions or changes which affect you made without your knowledge or involvement?

___ 9—are you expected to accept others' ideas without being told the rationale?

___10—do you feel that you have too little authority to carry out your responsibilities?

___11—are you unclear about what is expected of you?

___12—do others you work with seem unclear about what you do?

___13—do you feel unclear about what the scope and responsibilities of your job are?

___14—does management expect you to interrupt your work for new priorities?

___15—must you attend meetings to get your job done?

___16—does your job require travel?

___17—do you have too much to do and too little time in which to do it?

___18—do you have too little to do?

___19—do you think that the amount of work you have to do may interfere with how well it gets done?

___20—do you have differences of opinion with your supervisor?

___21—do you lack confidence in management?

JOB STRESSORS . . . SCORING AND INTERPRETATION

To obtain your score add all of your answers and divide by 33. The higher your score the more job stress you are experiencing. In a study of 220 working adults the average score was 3.1, with a standard deviation of 1.3. Thus if your score is between 1.8 and 4.4 you fall within the normal population. Several studies have indicated that too little stress in the job can be as detrimental to your health as too much, so if your score is greater than 4.4. or less than 1.8 you might begin to look at the stressors or lack of stressors on your job. The questions measure different aspects of job stress as follows: 1-3=Fit w/job; 4-6=Role conflict; 7-10=Lack of authority; 11-13=Role ambiguity; 14-16=Interruptions; 17-19=Workload; 20-22=Supervision; 23-25=Peer relationships; 26-28=Relationships with other units; 29-30=Responsibility for others; 31-33=Evaluation. You might want to see if your high/low scores correspond to any set of questions. This will help determine specific sources of job stress for you.

In the study mentioned above job stress was positively correlated with social stress, type A behavior, lack of interpersonal support, and poor health. These relationships indicate that an individual experiencing job stress is probably also experiencing other stress. There has been a great deal of research done regarding job stress. When the researchers have asked workers about the stressors in their jobs the responses look like the list of questions above. Some jobs may have specific stressors because of the nature of the job; however, all jobs have the potential to cause the stressors listed here.

Since job stress is a result of the job or the way the worker is managed in the job, the first level of intervention to reduce job stress should be with the job itself, the supervision provided, or the environment of the job. If this fails or no changes are possible, then the individual should attempt to develop methods in which he can cope with the stress more effectively. This might be through an exercise program, better diet habits, or meditation. Too often the focus has been on helping people cope with stressful jobs rather than modifying the nature of the job. You might want to go back and look at any of the items you responded "1" or "6" to see if they are areas of change in your job. You might also use these scores to initiate a discussion with your supervisor or co-workers about the particular stress producing areas of your work.

INTERPERSONAL SUPPORT
(Developed by Tom Isgar, Ph.D.)

Please answer the following questions, as they describe your current situation or your experiences in the past 12 months, by placing a number on the line preceding each individual source of support. The number corresponds to the following descriptive terms:

5=Totally (total)   4=Very much   3=Some   2=A little   1=Very little   0=None

1—How much support do you receive from each of the following?
___1—Spouse or Lover
___2—Parent(s)
___3—Friend(s)
___4—Co-worker(s)
___5—Supervisor
___6—Children
___7—Other: _____

2—How much positive physical contact do you have with each of the following?
___1—Spouse or Lover
___2—Parent(s)
___3—Friend(s)
___4—Co-worker(s)
___5—Supervisor
___6—Children
___7—Other: _____

3—How willing are you to talk to each of the following about a problem?
___1—Spouse or Lover
___2—Parent(s)
___3—Friend(s)
___4—Co-worker(s)
___5—Supervisor
___6—Children
___7—Other: _____

4—How willing would each of the following be to listen to your personal problems?
___1—Spouse or Lover
___2—Parent(s)
___3—Friend(s)
___4—Co-worker(s)
___5—Supervisor
___6—Children
___7—Other: _____

5—How much personal time do you get with each of the following?
___1—Spouse or Lover
___2—Parent(s)
___3—Friend(s)
___4—Co-worker(s)
___5—Supervisor
___6—Children
___7—Other: _____

6—How much would you say your relationship with each of the following is mutually supportive?
___1—Spouse or Lover
___2—Parent(s)
___3—Friend(s)
___4—Co-worker(s)
___5—Supervisor
___6—Children
___7—Other: _____

7—To what extent would each of the following commit their resources to assist you if you needed them?
___1—Spouse or Lover
___2—Parent(s)
___3—Friend(s)
___4—Co-worker(s)
___5—Supervisor
___6—Children
___7—Other: _____

8—How much would you say each of the following like and trust you?
___1—Spouse or Lover
___2—Parent(s)
___3—Friend(s)
___4—Co-worker(s)
___5—Supervisor
___6—Children
___7—Other: _____

INTERPERSONAL SUPPORT . . . SCORING AND INTERPRETATION

To obtain your score (1) add your responses for each question, (2) add the eight totals for an overall score. In general the higher your score the more support you perceive. In a study of 220 working adults the average score was 170 and the standard deviation was 40.

In this study increased interpersonal support was related to decreased experience of job stress and social stress. Increased interpersonal support was also related to decreased reports of depression and physical health problems. Interpersonal support is positively related to ease of expressing emotions.

The literature, and the study mentioned above, indicate that as the amount of support increases your experience of stress decreases. In addition there is research which indicates that interpersonal support will mediate the impact of stressors in your environment. For example it has been shown that when there is interpersonal support for an expectant mother that the number of birth complications decreases and that the birth weight of the baby will increase. There is also evidence of fewer postoperative complications when the surgical staff is supportive both before and after the operation. Other research has shown that the support of the spouse was the primary predictor of changes in the health of workers who had lost their jobs. In one study with widows it was shown that when the widows had one individual who helped them through their grieving that they required less medication and experienced fewer sick days than when there was no one to help them during the mourning period. Finally one large study indicates that the presence of interpersonal support, particularly from family and friends, is related to increased life expectancy. All in all this research points out that interpersonal support is a very important factor in one's health. This is especially true in helping to prevent stress related problems.

In reviewing your score you might look at the following:

(1) Are your scores to Questions 3 and 5 lower than your scores to some of the other questions? If the answer is yes, then you may want to work on changing those answers.

(2) Do you receive most of your support from one or both sources? If the answer is yes you may want to a) be sure that the support is mutual (Question 6) and b) think about other individuals who could supply you with support.

(3) Do you receive the maximum amount of support from your spouse (lover) and from your supervisor? These two individuals have been shown to be the most critical sources of support for an individual. On the other hand when these two are antagonistic they become major stressors. Thus you may want to increase your efforts to insure maximum support from these two.

Finally you may wish to share these scores with the individuals in your support system and talk about how valuable you see their support. You might also have those individuals complete this questionnaire and then discuss their scores as well as your own.

HEALTH HABITS
(Adapted by Tom Isgar, Ph.D., from "Relationship of Physical Health Status and Health Practices" by Nedra B. Belloc and Lester Breslow.)

Circle the answers below which best describe your habits.
DO YOU:

1. EAT BREAKFAST

1. Always
2. Usually
3. Seldom
4. Never

2. SNACK BETWEEN MEALS

1. Always
2. Usually
3. Seldom
4. Never

3. SLEEP

1. 6 or fewer hours/night
2. 7 hours/night
3. 8 hours/night
4. 9 or more hours/night

4. EXERCISE VIGOROUSLY

1. Every day
2. Every other day
3. Once a week
4. Less than once a week

5. SMOKE

1. More than one pack/day
2. One pack/day
3. Less than one pack/day
4. Used to smoke
5. Never smoked

6. DRINK

1. 4 or more drinks/setting
2. 2 to 3 drinks/setting
3. 1 drink/setting
4. Don't drink

7. ARE YOU

1. 20% or more overweight
2. 10% overweight
3. 5% overweight or underweight
4. 10% or more underweight

HEALTH HABITS . . . SCORING AND INTERPRETATION

To obtain your score give yourself one point for each question if you answered it as follows. Only give a point if your answer matches one of the answers below:

Question Number	Correct Answer(s)
Question one	1
Question two	3,4
Question three	2,3
Question four	1,2
Question five	5
Question six	2,3
Question seven	3

In a study of 220 working adults the average score was 4.3 and the standard deviation was 1.3. Thus if your score falls between 3.0 and 5.6, you fall within the normal range. However, the higher your score the more likely you are to live a healthy and long life. One insurance company has calculated that as you raise your score from 4 to 6 that you will add an additional 12 years to your life expectancy. In the study mentioned above the more points individuals received on these questions the fewer health problems they tended to report.

This set of questions originated from a study of 6,928 people which lasted several years. The people in the study were asked to answer questions about their overall lifestyles. Seven years later the researchers looked at the relationship between personal habits and the individual's health levels. They concluded that the seven habits above all impacted health and that the more of the good health habits a person practiced the healthier the person reported being. In another study in 1977 of this same group, the researcher reconfirmed that the health habits impacted health and also were related to a person's life expectancy. Thus not only do the health habits seem to provide for a healthier life but also add years. The American Medical Association provides a pamphlet which lists these seven areas as aids to a healthier life. They also suggest regular check-ups.

BREAKFAST—There are two important reasons for breakfast. Your body has fasted for several hours and is ready for fuel for the coming day. Without breakfast you will spend most of the work day before having the necessary energy available to your body since lunch won't be converted to fuel until mid-afternoon. A second reason is that without breakfast the tendency will be greater to snack during the morning on junk food. Breakfast should consist of fruit or juice, protein, fiber, and a slow burning carbohydrate. You ought to consume 25-30 percent of your calories for breakfast.

SNACKS—If you snack between meals it often indicates poor diet habits and a lack of regular balanced meals. Frequently snacks lack food value and provide mostly sugar, fat, and calories. If on the other hand you snack on fruit or other healthy snacks and eat smaller meals, you can get one point for this question.

SLEEP—Sleep requirements will vary for individuals. However, in general 7 to 8 hours is related to good health. Sleeping more on the other hand is often an indicator of depression or of a generally poor physical condition. If you have regularly slept more or less than 7 to 8 hours and feel no ill effects you might get one point for this question.

EXERCISE—Current studies would indicate that you need to exercise vigorously for at least 20 minutes at least three times a week. The exercise could be running or it could be dancing but it has to raise your heartbeat to 65% of its maximum to count. Thus a long slow set of tennis could not count.

SMOKING—Some individuals who have stopped smoking want to know why they don't get a point. The brief answer is that the damage to the lungs and to the cardiovascular system has already been done and may not be reversible. However, if the recently stopped smoker is also involved in a vigorous exercise program and has a diet high in fiber and unprocessed food he might get a point for this question.

DRINKING—When these questions were developed in the original study, non-drinkers were given a point for this question. However, recent research indicates that there is a positive effect of moderate intake of alcohol, probably as a mediator of stressors and possibly as an agent for carrying away cholesterol.

WEIGHT—If you are not aware of the ideal weight for you, you can find out by calling your physician or your insurance company. One thing to be aware of, however, is that the figure you receive will be the average for your height. Since the population is overweight, knowing the average for that group may not be the ideal weight for you. Another more accurate method of determining your ideal weight is to have a skinfold test conducted which measures the percent of fat you carry. If you are 10% or more underweight and know that this is because you are a long distance runner, or equivalent, then you might get one point for this question.

These seven questions provide a quick, yet accurate, indication of your health habits and your probable level of health. Remember, if you are young and have poor health habits all of the results may not be currently noticeable. However, a great deal of research would indicate that for each question where you did not receive a point that you are harming your health.

CHAPTER VI

Time Management:
Organizing for Action

Beside the task of acquiring the ability to organize a day's work, all else you will ever learn about management is child's play.
. . . E. B. Osborn

*   *   *   *

Remember Alice in Wonderland when she came to a fork in the road and asked the cat which path she should take. The cat asked her where she wanted to go and when she replied she didn't care, the cat wisely observed "then any road will take you there."

Time is the common denominator in all of the topics we have dealt with thus far. It takes *time* to

—be more creative

    —utilize effective problem solving methods

        —understand power and strategize well

           —manage conflict productively

              —cope with stress

Have I then been suggesting the impossible to managers who are already far too busy? It would certainly seem so—if we did not deal with our present topic. I believe there is time available for each of us to do all of these things. We are just in the habit of using our time in much less productive ways.

Did you ever stop to realize that we each have

—24 hours per day

—168 hours per week

—720 hours per month

—8,760 hours per year

What a bank account! And it is up to each one of us how we choose to spend or waste it. Peter Drucker reminds us that effective executives manage their time, they do not let their time manage them. And Henry Ford observed, "People who have no time don't think. The more you think, the more time you have."

So our challenge is to seriously assess how we presently use or misuse time. Alec Mackenzie in his book *The Time Trap* states that "the term *time management* is actually a misnomer. In the strict sense one does not manage time, for the minute hand is beyond our control. It moves relentlessly on. Time passes at a predetermined rate no matter what we do. It is a question not of managing the clock but of *managing ourselves in respect to the clock . . . the heart of time management is management of self.*"[1]

Four resources I have found helpful in this area are:

How to Get Control of Your Time and Your Life, Alan Lakein, New America Library, 1973.

The Time of Your Life, an excellent training film starring James Whitmore, based on Lakein's book, Thompson-Mitchell and Associates, 3384 Peachtree Road, N.E., Atlanta, Ga. 30326.

The Time Trap: Managing Your Way Out, R. Alec Mackenzie, AMACOM, 1972.

Getting Things Done: The ABC's of Time Management, Edwin R. Bliss, Charles Scribner and Sons, 1976.

These resources have been particularly useful in helping me objectively examine my philosophy about time. One insight has been how frequently I have viewed time as the enemy. Deadlines, schedules, appointments, interruptions, unfinished projects, phones, paper, people . . . all compete for those same hours. Why can't there be more time to do it all! Often I have lived as though by some miracle I would be given 26 hours a day instead of 24 and that would solve my time crunch. I tried as long as possible to ignore the painful reality that the only way to manage time is to manage myself. I have too often shared the anguish in this poem:

NO TIME

If only I had more time,
I would stop and listen to you.
If only I had more time,
I might try something new.

If only I had more time,
I could rest my load awhile.
If only I had more time,
I might return your smile.

If the day had more hours,
I might get everything done.
And then I could take some time
To enjoy some hard-earned fun.

I hope I have some time
To spend before I die
To figure where my years went
And why I want to cry
   But no time now for tears
   Nor any time for prayers
   No time to calm my fears
     No time
       No time
         No time!
   . . . Lyman K. Randall

This business of viewing time as the enemy is often especially apparent during vacations and weekends. We usually begin with excitement and eagerness, looking forward to a welcome change of both pace and location. It feels so good not to be ruled by the clock. (I even refuse to wear a wristwatch on vacation.) This sense of "plenty" usually lasts until the vacation is about half over and then a subtle change occurs. Time the friend becomes the enemy. The countdown begins . . . only three days left, two days, one day. Somehow, when that process begins we are not psychologically on vacation anymore. And yet, how often have we been unaware it was happening?

After reading and reflecting on this topic of time, I am at last ready *and have found the time* to explore it with you. I now realize that how we spend our time is a statement of who we are and what we value. This is also true of how we spend our other resources— money, energy, and commitment. These all require personal value judgments regarding what is important and appropriate. Our choices reflect both who we are now and predict what we will become in the future. Therefore, time is not the enemy but one of our most precious assets. Let's learn how to appreciate and use it well.

A LOOK AT TIME WASTERS

One logical place to begin in trying to improve our management of self in regard to time is to thoroughly understand what we are presently doing with our time. That would suggest the importance of keeping a *time log* for a week or so—recording by 15 minute intervals exactly what we do and with whom.

Mackenzie makes a compelling case for this:

The time inventory, or log, is necessary because the painful task of changing our habits requires far more conviction than we can build from learning about the experience of others. We need the amazing revelation of the great portions of time we are wasting to provide the determination to manage ourselves more effectively in this respect . . . we think our time wasters are primarily external forces until we see a picture of ourselves . . . one surprise will be that time is generally wasted in the same way every day and another surprise is the small fraction of the day that is free and uncommitted. [2]

You can keep this log on your regular desk calendar or make up a simple worksheet like this:

Time	Activity	With Whom
7-7:15 a.m.		
7:15-7:30		
7:30-7:45		
7:45-8:00, etc.		

Do it faithfully, concisely, and honestly for a week or two and you will have an accurate picture of *your* time problems. Once you know what they are, you can go to work on them.

Another useful exercise is to take a few minutes and make a list of what you personally believe are your time wasters right now. Try to rank them in order of importance and then determine which are generated *internally*, by you, and which are caused *externally*, by other people or events. Then decide which of those caused by others you could possibly control or eliminate if you decided it was important to do so. Why don't you take time to make this list right now?

Fortune magazine once asked more than 50 chairmen, presidents, and vice-presidents of corporations to rank the ten worst wasters of their scarce and valuable time. The weighted order of finish, with a sampling of the comments received, was

How Others Waste My Time

1. Telephone: Answering all of those irrelevant questions with courtesy wears me down.
2. Mail: Monday is deluge day.
3. Meetings: Often an ego trip for the people who call them.
4. Public Relations: The company name ought to speak for itself.
5. Paperwork: The blizzard never ends.
6. Commuting: A big waste.
7. Business lunches: The conversations are often indigestible.
8. Civic duties: Long and boring.
9. Incompetents: The worst are those who violate company policy.
10. Family demands: No comment.

How I Waste My Time

1. Not shutting my phone off during conferences.
2. Not blocking out time for a major project and planning.
3. Not using the wisdom, time, and energy of co-workers.
4. Not delegating out part of my work.
5. Delegating out, then taking it back.
6. Letting others interrupt my planning time instead of saying "no."
7. Too many activities dilute the impact of all of it; need to operate with "systematic neglect" of less important items.
8. Not disciplining my mind to keep from shifting gears constantly.
9. Never concentrating on the task at hand.

10. Getting sidetracked into "browsing."

11. Getting too detailed and going beyond what is necessary.

12. Paper shuffling.

13. Personal chit-chat unrelated to work.

14. Inserting personal chores into the day's activity.

15. Not planning ahead.

How do these lists compare with yours?

What these exercises are intended to do is to help you put names to your habits regarding time and then to encourage you to decide which habits are positive (so you will be sure to preserve those) and which are negative (so you can set about changing them).

William James, the noted American psychologist, provided some valuable insight into good and bad habits over seventy-five years ago:

Habit is the flywheel of society, its most precious conserving agent. The great thing, then is to make our nervous system our ally instead of our enemy. We must make automatic and habitual, as early as possible, as many useful actions as we can, and guard against growing into ways that are disadvantageous as we guard against the plague. The more details of our daily life we can hand over to the effortless custody of our automatism, the more our higher powers of mind will be set free for their proper work. There is no more miserable person than one in whom nothing is habitual but indecision, and for whom the lighting of every cigar, the drinking of every cup, the time of rising and going to bed every day, and the beginning of every bit of work, are subjects of deliberation. Half the time of such a man [woman] goes to deciding or regretting matters which ought to be so ingrained in him as practically not to exist in his consciousness at all.[3]

This statement makes an eloquent case for the value of establishing good work habits and routinizing them so they become almost second nature. These kinds of habits can buy you the time you need for creativity and problem solving.

But how does one go about breaking old, unhealthy habits or establishing some new healthy ones? James suggests three crucial steps:[4]

1. *Launch your new practice as strongly and vigorously as you can.* It is also wise to tell others what you are doing. This both helps them understand your sudden change of behavior and also creates some healthy peer pressure for you to actually do it.

2. *Never backslide until the new habit is firmly rooted*, not even once if you can help it. "It is surprising how a desire will die if it is *never* fed."

3. *Act on your resolve to add or change a habit at the first possible chance.* The longer you wait to actually do what you have decided, the greater the chance is you will let your good intentions die by benign neglect. Decide and then act . . . the sooner the better!

Let's take a very common bad habit of many managers and follow it through James's three steps to see how we might change it. I would like to take *poor delegation* because curing that habit can free up time a manager needs for so many other things. The goal would be to stop being a poor delegator—or phrased positively—start being an effective delegator.

Step 1—Launch the new practice as strongly as possible.

a) Identify a *significant* project you are presently handling yourself, but which you feel is no longer a challenge to you since you have done it many times before; b) Carefully analyze your staff (paid and volunteer) and determine who possesses most of the qualifications to be able to handle that project if given the support, information, and orientation needed to succeed (your choice of person is *key*); c) Discuss the assignment with your staff person and if possible, get their commitment to assume the responsibility; d) Together agree on time lines, standards, and objectives of the project and write them out for both of you; e) Give the person the necessary authority that goes with the responsibility; f) Be available to provide the support they need; and g) *Turn them loose.*

It will be important for you to choose a project to delegate that has substance and importance. If you learn to delegate something significant, delegating lesser things will be easy (but the reverse is often not true).

Step 2—Never backslide.

You will have to practice self control almost immediately because your old habits will demand that you check in person or by phone constantly to see if the "delegatee" is really doing what he or she agreed to do, or if he is doing it like you would do it. *Do not allow yourself to do this* except at critical agreed upon checkpoints. It undermines the delegation and you really have not saved yourself any time or energy. The time you previously spent doing the job is now wasted in worrying about it. If your choice of people is sound and your support and training are effective, assume it will be done and done well until they prove you wrong. (I have found that when I delegate well, people usually exceed all my expectations regarding both time and quality. Have faith!)

One other absolutely forbidden urge is that of taking the project back once you have delegated it to someone else. It is so easy to convince yourself the person really would appreciate it or that you will rescue him at the critical stage just this once. If you do this, you have really not changed your bad habit at all. You can learn from the Alcoholics Anonymous' motto—"One day at a time" and practice delegation "One project at a time."

Step 3—Act on your resolve at the first possible chance.

Determine to delegate a project you are presently doing *right now*. If you wait for just the right one to come along, it will never happen. Review your time log and see if there is a significant portion of your time presently being consumed by certain projects. Ask —if I had all of the time I am presently spending on compiling the results of the employee attitude survey . . . or gathering the statistics for the sales analysis for last year . . . or setting up the interviews for new clerical staff, would I have the necessary time to do the long range planning I should do? (Remember—Choose something significant to delegate.)

Some critical questions you need to ask yourself are these:[5]

1) Do I have enough confidence in myself that I will not only accept, but actively seek out persons who may know as much as I do when I need help?

2) Am I willing to delegate *significant* parts of my program to qualified others . . . *and be glad*, not threatened, if they succeed?

3) Do the jobs I'm willing to delegate make a sensible, logical whole or are they bits and pieces of busy work that give the person little opportunity for growth or success?

4) Am I willing to shift from being a "doer" to being an "enabler"? In other words, can I become a good manager and find satisfaction in that?

Unless these questions can be answered affirmatively, your resolve to become a better delegator is really only wishful thinking. Habits can be changed but only with honest self-examination, dogged determination, and great self-discipline.

These same three steps should be followed in adding or changing any other habit relating to your use of time.

TEN TIPS TO HELP YOU MANAGE YOURSELF IN RESPECT TO TIME

In most of the literature relating to time management, these ten areas seem to be repeatedly stressed. Edwin Bliss, in his book *Getting Things Done: The ABC's of Time Management*, summarizes them as follows.[6]

1. Plan
2. Concentrate
3. Take breaks
4. Avoid clutter
5. Don't be a perfectionist
6. Don't be afraid to say *No*
7. Don't procrastinate
8. Apply radical surgery
9. Delegate
10. Don't be a workaholic

Let's examine each more closely.

PLAN

The idea of the necessity of planning is certainly not a new one to today's managers. Courses on management by objectives (MBO), reams of books, films, and management seminars have made the terms *goals, objectives, and action plans* bywords in almost every office. Of course, some managers are much better than others at actually implementing the planning process, and I suspect that most of us are much better at planning projects than at planning our use of time.

What we need to do is take what we already know about planning and apply it to time management. An overview of the planning process might be:

(1) *analyzing the present situation (where I am now),*

(2) *developing relevant assumptions (what conditions are likely to exist within the time span of the plan),*

(3) establishing objectives (what I want to achieve),

(4) developing alternatives (what different ways might attain these objectives),

(5) making and implementing decisions,

(6) establishing review and control procedures.[7]

We have already addressed items one and two by completing a time log, identifying time wasters, and determining some habits we want to add or change. This moves us on to steps 3-6, establishing objectives and developing alternatives, implementing and evaluating.

I believe it is at this stage that we often neglect to apply available knowledge about planning to our time problems. We all know it is essential to set goals and objectives for a program before action plans are implemented. It is the only way we can be sure our day-to-day actions will actually achieve our goals. But I suggest we reverse the process when it comes to time. Instead of setting our own personal life goals and then being sure the hours we spend each day move us toward those goals, we too often let the tide of present activities push us along towards an unknown and unexamined future. In fact, our present activities are helping to mold our future whether we realize it or not. May I illustrate this concept:

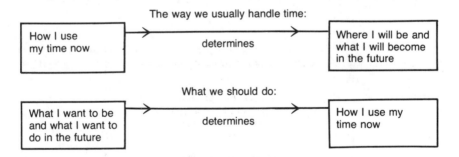

There is a subtle, yet critical difference in these two approaches. The primary difference is one of attitude. Instead of feeling out of control, you take charge of your own life. *You* decide what is important to you, both personally and professionally and then make your day-to-day priority choices based on those decisions. It helps you "select the best task to do from all the possibilities available" and then you go one step further and determine the best possible way of getting that task done.[8]

In an excellent article in the March 1980 *Personal Management Journal*, a British authority on time management, Chris Lane, discusses the importance of attitude:

> *If a particular task or goal is important enough, we will make sure it is achieved, irrespective of all obstacles and difficulties. "You can do almost anything you set your creative mind to do" would be a good motto for this treatment of the subject. One of the main justifications for taking an "attitude related" approach is to overcome one of the biggest problems managers face in looking at their management of time—the pressing feeling they have when they realize as a result of their time log how little of their time they are actually able to control themselves.* [9]

Lane goes on to suggest three essential points relating to one's attitude toward time management. [10]

1. Realize the problem is yours—*you* own it and can therefore influence the outcome.

2. Utilize your full mental capacity when dealing with problems—using the innovative, holistic, intuitive right brain as fully as your logical, analytical left brain. Approach new ideas and problems with the attitude of challenge instead of dismay.

3. Identify clearly the *value to you* of better time management, for otherwise there will be no real incentive to change.

Here is an outline of action that is both practical and simple:

Identify your goals—
both for your job and your private life

▼

Organize your goals into
key areas—and establish specific
objectives for each

▼

Organize your activities
into appropriate action plans

▼

Establish your priorities—
so you get the right things done

▼

Make a daily "To Do" list

Let's try out this method and see how it might look in practice:

GOALS: Job

Become a director of
a small human service
agency in 5 years

Be a free-lance management
consultant and author in
10 years

Private Life

Maintain a good marriage
and family life

Stay healthy physically,
emotionally, and
spiritually

Explore new avenues of
self development

KEY AREAS: Job

Management training
Varied job experiences
Writing/communications
skills

Private Life

Time as a family
Exercise
Hobbies
Church/spiritual growth
Friends/mentors

OBJECTIVES: Job

1. To attend 2 management
   seminars or workshops
   each year
2. To enroll in one appropriate
   course at a local college
   or night school each year
3. To read management literature
   and stay current with the "state
   of the art"
4. To be an active member of my
   professional associations
5. To take part in appropriate
   community affairs committees

Private Life

1. To spend 2-4 evenings
   a week at home
2. To go on 3 weekend
   outings every 6 months
   as a family or couple
3. To walk, jog, or swim
   3 times a week
4. To learn to play guitar
5. To attend church regu-
   larly, read inspirational
   books, and attend one
   retreat or growth
   session per year
6. To spend time with good
   friends at least twice
   a month and write to
   those out of the area
   every 3-4 months

Note: Objectives need to be *specific, measurable, achievable* and *compatible* with your
goals.

240

For each objective you must deal with the questions of *who, when, how, and cost,* i.e.,

Objective	Who	When	How	Cost
To attend two management seminars every year	I will be responsible	1st. month— get on pertinent mailing lists for information	Review options	$365.00
			Get supervisor's approval	$150.00
		1-6 months— Review brochures, journals, catalogs	Choose appropriate seminars	
			Send in reservations and fees	
		4-6 months— choose seminars	Attend	

This is where you will need to go back over your list of objectives and determine those that are most important to you, both at your work and in your personal life. That is the only way you can deal with Lakein's critical question, *"What is the best use of my time right now?"* He suggests the A-B-C method of prioritizing and strongly urges that a great deal of thought and attention be given to determining your A's. Those are the things that really matter to you and to your job—so do those first.

I have also found that it is extremely important when valuing both a career and family—to be sensitive to times when more time and energy can and should be given to one or the other. For example, when everything is running smoothly at home, more energy can be directed to my job. If a member of the family faces a crisis or needs more caring attention, then the balance needs to shift to provide that. Flexibility and being attuned to the needs of one's significant others is essential.

The way you ensure that you keep moving towards your goals and objectives and especially toward your "A" goals is to keep a daily "To Do" list.

Each day you have things that you are required to do and

things you would like to do. By making a list, you are more apt to get the important things in both categories accomplished and weed out the unimportant because you have given some thought to those decisions. An old adage is, "The thinking time you do before you start a job will shorten the time you have to spend working on it."

A typical "To Do" list might be:

To Do

1. Staff meeting re new hiring procedures
2. Mail
3. Phone calls
   —Return messages from last two days
   —Initiate calls to: Smith re deadline
                        Mom re birthday
                        Newspaper re ad
                        Husband re tennis
                        College re courses
4. Read *Management Review* Journals and others
5. Do budget projection for next three months
6. Jog
7. Meeting with church council
8. Plan staff retreat for next month
9. Give speech at Rotary
10. Stop by the laundry
11. See dentist
12. Clear out desk drawers

The mixture is the usual one of job required tasks, routine tasks, family oriented tasks, and long term goal-oriented tasks. You need to determine the priorities for the day. (Which will matter most if they go undone? Those are your "A's.") Start with those! Which tasks require your best thinking—do those during your "prime time"—when you are personally at your best (and it varies for each of us). Which tasks can be delegated? Which tasks can be grouped into logical time sequences. (Your mail may contain some information that affects your phone calls; your journal reading might best be done as you wait in the dentist's office, etc.) I have found my daily "To Do" list to be one of the most essential tools that keeps me moving toward my goals. I know where I am going, so I am encouraged to keep making those small, daily steps in that direction. Without it, I am convinced that interruptions, trivia, and the crisis of the immediate would take over. Also, I find that getting the tasks down on paper helps me to stop wasting time worrying about forgetting them.

I personally make a monthly or bi-weekly To Do list and then pull off the items to be tackled each day from that master list. That makes it unnecessary for me to keep transferring the more major projects on my To Do lists from day to day but they are always before me as I make my daily priority choices.

CONCENTRATE

Two of the biggest thieves of time are *distractions* and *interruptions*. Often we are responsible for the first and others seem to cause the second.

How often have you begun a task and found yourself distracted by a feeling of anxiety or lethargy—especially if it is a task you dislike or are unsure about? Somehow every sound, smell, and sight can be cause for distraction. And each time you go back to the task you have lost both momentum and time. The antidote for distraction is pure and simple self discipline. You must train yourself to concentrate fully on the task of the moment. It will help immeasurably in improving both the quantity and quality of your work. A critical question needs to be, "If I don't have time to do it right, when will I have time to do it over?"[11] And one way to do it right the first time is to give it your full attention.

This becomes much easier once the goal and priority setting process has been accomplished. So much of the anxiety and lethargy in the workplace today stem from people's feeling that what they are doing really does not matter anyhow. Someone once observed, *people's feelings about time spent and the people they spend it with are determined by the product*! When you realize that even the routine and mundane tasks are moving you towards goals important to you, the self discipline to concentrate is more easily attained.

Interruptions are more comfortable to talk about because they seem to be so clearly someone else's fault. Yet are they? Once again,

243

much of the responsibility rests with you, for you allow them to happen.

Sune Carlson, who studied Swedish managing directors, drew this startling conclusion:

> Up to now I imagined the boss as a bandmaster leading an orchestra. Now I know that this comparison is wrong, and I rather imagine the boss as a puppet whose strings are drawn by a crowd of unknown and unorganized people. [12]

What a vivid image that is. Instead of the active verb "leading" we see the passive verb "drawn" and when he describes the people pulling the strings as unknown and unorganized, we must ask, "who's in charge here?"

Leaders have a responsibility to concentrate on those situations and issues that really matter to the organization. When critical planning and thinking time is repeatedly wasted on trivia, it is a violation of the trust of leadership. Concentrate your energies and time on those things you uniquely can and should be doing by virtue of your position and expertise. The future of the organization deserves no less. "One simply cannot achieve excellence of performance without concentrating effort on critical areas." [13]

But how does one know which areas are critical? There is a theory called the Pareto time principle which may help. It illustrates the concept of the "vital few" and "trivial many." Both Lakein and Mackenzie stress this principle. [14]

Lakein states,

> If all items are arranged in order of value, 80 percent of the value would come from only 20 percent of the items, while the remaining 20 percent of the value would come from 80 percent of the items. . . . The 80/20 rule suggests that in a list of ten items [your "to do" list], doing two of them will yield most (80 percent) of the value. Find these two, label them A, get them done. . . . It's important to remind yourself again and again not to get bogged down on low-value activities but to concentrate on the 20 percent where the high value is. [15]

The Pareto time principle.

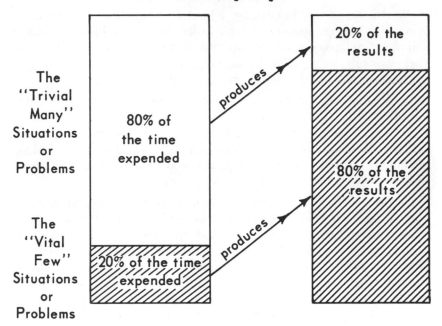

I have also found it helpful to give my full attention to one thing at a time, and whenever possible see it through to completion before moving on to something else. I call this "compartmentalizing my mind." When the mind's door is open to one person or project, I close the doors to others to ensure full concentration. When this is possible, a very productive interview can be accomplished in half an hour that would take twice that long with phones ringing or people interrupting and the quality of the encounter is also doubled. The same is true for meetings, planning, writing, counseling, family interactions, and so on. This is the only way I have found it possible to juggle the many and varied responsibilities of my multiple roles of wife, mother, lecturer, author, friend, trainer, board member, etc.

The next logical question is—*How* do you control the interruptions to allow for this kind of concentration? In the appendix of this chapter there are close to fifty suggestions from Mackenzie on how to "spring the time trap." Many of these deal with the interruptions of phones, visitors, and meetings. These suggestions are practical and workable—try them!

TAKE BREAKS

We discussed this in Chapter I in connection with the creative process and utilizing the right brain more effectively. Your left brain will often make a compelling case that it is more *efficient* for you to keep working over coffee breaks and lunch hours, but all of the evidence indicates it is not more *effective.*

Your physical, mental, and emotional natures have very real limits of endurance and breaks allow for revitalization of all three. This applies to breaks in your daily schedule, weekends without bringing work home, and vacations. They are all essential! The question is—do you care enough about yourself and the value of what you do to insist on being at your best?

Dorothy Sayers suggests that "work is not the thing one does to live but rather the thing one lives to do."[16] Mackenzie adds, "When work assumes a worthwhile meaning of its own—when it is what one lives to do and to find fulfillment in—leisure acquires a purposefulness of its own. It becomes a means of self-renewal, of revitalization of our energies and talents for the joyful pursuit of what we are best suited to do."[17]

On the other hand, if you have a job you hate, breaks are essential to merely survive. My advice is to get out of that job at the first possible opportunity.

AVOID CLUTTER

As I sit in my office looking at the stacks of paper and books surrounding me as I write this . . . I can only say, good luck! I know that whenever I have been able to achieve this goal, whether at home or at my office, it makes a tremendous difference in my attitude. The feeling of slaying the "paper dragon" is a great one, so I keep trying.

Lakein has some very useful advice.[18] It has to do with your "To Do" list. He suggests that as each letter or memo comes to your desk, *try to handle it only once.* Determine at that time if it is of A, B, or C importance. Whenever possible take immediate action on C or B items (jot your reply on the bottom of the memo or letter; make the necessary decision). Keep only A's on your desk. He claims it is often the C's that create the clutter because we keep shoving them from one stack to another, never having the time or incentive to deal with them. He urges two courses of action:

1) Ask with every C—"What can I *not* do?" Ask this as you first

handle a piece of paper and also as you prioritize your "To Do" list each day. What would happen if this goes undone?

2) Dispense with C's by taking the necessary action immediately, or by relegating them to an indispensable area called your "C-drawer." Lakein describes the "C-drawer" as the place unimportant items can be put safely out of the way when you don't dare throw them in the wastebasket immediately. If you have not had any inquiry or follow up request on an item in the drawer for several weeks, you then know it didn't matter if you did it in the first place. You then periodically transfer your "C drawer" to the wastebasket.

The essential concept here is not letting the avalanche of C's physically obscure the fewer critical A's. (However, I have a friend who insists it is helpful to keep a few "C's" around to do when he needs to "prime the pump" of his energy. They are usually quick and they help to get his mental juices flowing.)

I remember one supervisor I had early in my career in Personnel who actually had stacks of papers, journals, and memos on the floor of his office. On weekends he would bring in a box and load several stacks into it to take home. Somehow he never seemed to eliminate them; he just kept rearranging them. It was an absolute nightmare to try to find information in that office.

So for both your own peace of mind and the sanity of those who work with you . . . avoid clutter.

DON'T BE A PERFECTIONIST

This is an especially difficult rule for those who value excellence. The problem with perfectionists is that they demand excellence of themselves and others not only in the vital 20% of the tasks (which they should)—but also in the 80% of trivial or routine matters. That is where the problem lies. If they could only realize that by lowering their sights a bit on the unimportant, everyone (including themselves) would have the needed time and energy to do the important things well.

This is especially essential for today's working woman who is also a wife and mother or a single head of a household. Standards that were reasonable regarding housework, ironing, and meals when you were a full-time homemaker must be altered when you have two careers. Your health and peace of mind demand it. Yet, it is so easy to fall into the trap of being Superwoman both at home and at work.

247

If standards of perfection in the routine 80% are not lowered, "burn out" is almost assured and the unfortunate result is all too often not enjoying either work or home. I have found that learning to delegate more effectively at home has been a critical factor in helping me survive and in allowing our teenagers to grow in their own abilities and self-confidence. Usually the key has been for me to clearly admit that I *need* their help and then to be open to negotiating with them as to details. After all, they have their own To Do lists and priorities to consider also.

This trait of perfectionism is also one of the major blocks keeping executives from delegating to subordinates. The fear that "the job won't be done like I would do it" is the clue to watch. If the person is already experienced, he very likely will not do it just like you would, but the results are what count and the outcome might be as good or even better than yours.

Another unfortunate aspect of an obsession with perfection on the part of managers is that it severely inhibits the freedom to risk, both for yourself and your subordinates. And without the freedom to risk and even fail, innovation and creativity die. The need for success in everything dictates a norm of only attempting the tried and true. This limits the potential of everyone involved, including the perfectionist.

DON'T BE AFRAID TO SAY NO

There are so many reasons it is difficult to say "no":

    —we do not like to admit we cannot be all things to all people

    —we know what needs to be done

    —we care about that person, project, or goal

    —we do not like to let people down

    —we like to keep our fingers in the pie

    —we do not really trust others as we should

    —we like to be known as someone who gets a job done

    —we see the request as a crisis

For all of these reasons, we find ourselves running day after day to cover all the commitments we have said "yes" to. Once again, *how many of these things are in the trivial 80% category?* It is terribly important to make that determination, because those commitments may be what are keeping you from the critical 20%. Once again, your personal and work goals will help you determine which category each item fits into.

The tyranny of the urgent lies in its distortion of priorities—its subtle cloaking of minor projects with major status, often under the guise of "crisis". One of the measures of a manager is his ability to distinguish the important from the urgent, to refuse to be tyrannized by the urgent, to refuse to manage by crisis . . . they must learn to forget the unnecessary and to ignore the irrelevant. [19]

Many management experts suggest the intriguing notion that *the true measure of a leader is what he or she decides to leave undone.* What a hopeful encouragement to chronic "doers" who want to reform!

After you have ruled out those commitments that are unimportant, irrelevant, or unnecessary—take those still on your 20% critical list and ask yourself—"Is it simply important that this be done, or is it important that I do it?" This will help you explore some delegation opportunities.

DON'T PROCRASTINATE

It is important to learn to distinguish between tolerating ambiguity in order to allow the creative process the necessary time it needs to come to fruition . . . and delaying decisions or actions simply because you want to avoid or ignore them. The latter is what is called procrastination. You hope if you ignore the task long enough it will somehow go away (and if it is a C, it probably will).

But how about an A task or project—one you know is important, but you keep putting off either because it seems either overwhelming or distasteful. For "overwhelming A's", Lakein suggests the "Swiss Cheese" approach. Break the overall project down into a series of objectives and smaller activities and every time you get a few extra minutes or hours, poke a hole in the large project by doing one or more of the essential smaller tasks. Eventually you will see enough progress that you will not feel so overwhelmed by the entire project.

An example of this might be:

Overwhelming A Goal: Reorganize the Public Relations Department during the next six months due to impending budget cuts.

Some "Swiss cheese" action steps:

—Call the Personnel Department and get records of all employees in the PR Department.

—Call the Finance Department and get payroll statistics

—Set up a meeting of PR staff to discuss present and projected projects

—Arrange interviews with three local advertising agencies to see about contracting for services

—Review products of the PR Department: newsletter, news articles, slide presentations

Each phone call, meeting, and review of data brings you closer to achieving the goal, if you plan well and keep at it every chance you get. But you do not have to wipe out all of your time and energy still needed for other A's.

The worst thing about procrastination is that it so often entails "deciding by not deciding." The result of being immobilized by indecision is demoralizing for both the manager and the staff. How many others are kept from completing their assignments when you put off doing your part?

This is especially frustrating in meetings. So often, necessary actions and decisions must be delayed and still another meeting called because someone failed to complete an assignment crucial to the pending next steps. A very useful "norm" for any group is that there is a fully understood commitment on the part of every member to deliver whatever they agree to do on time for the sake of the whole. And nobody is allowed to violate this norm. Peer pressure can help a procrastinator change his or her ways faster than anything else.

For those A tasks that are delayed because they are unpleasant, try to be creative in ways to "sweeten the job" by incentives you value. Work steadily on it for three hours and then go to your favorite restaurant for lunch; read that 75 page statistical report at the park or in the quiet of your own patio; do the three months' ironing while watching your favorite TV shows; have your difficult staff meeting in a retreat setting. Just be sure you tackle it, for it will be preying on your mind and using up time and energy unproductively until you do. Just "bite the bullet" and do it!

Lakein suggests there are some common escape routes most of us have developed to help us procrastinate:[20]

1) *Indulging ourselves—before, not after or during, tackling a dreaded or overwhelming job.*

We take the rest of the day off, go on a shopping binge, take a long leisurely bath, play tennis, go to a movie—anything to fill the time we should be spending on the task. (We rationalize that it will help us get in the mood.)

2) *Socializing.*

We welcome an open door policy that lets any stray person into our office to use up time. We linger over phone calls, coffee breaks, and lunch.

3) *Reading.*

We decide to tackle reading that huge backlog of journals, periodicals, and junk mail we have accumulated.

4) *Doing it ourselves.*

Doing routine and time consuming details we could and should delegate; writing letters and memos in long hand rather than jotting notes and letting the secretary compose the text or using the dictaphone; helping solve everyone else's problems.

5) *Overdoing it.*

"Being so diligent in giving the boss progress reports that there is little time to make progress." Reorganizing our desks and files; following up constantly on subordinates.

6) *Running away.*

Doing in person things that could and should be done by phone, memo, or mail; organizing unnecessary and time consuming visits to the home office or the field office; taking long coffee breaks, lunch hours, and excessive sick leave; setting up and attending unnecessary meetings.

7) *Daydreaming.*

Unproductively worrying about things not done at work or home; reliving past conversations and actions; dreaming about next year's vacation or the hoped-for bonus.

I'm not saying there is anything wrong with indulging yourself, reading, socializing, daydreaming. Quite the contrary; much of the fun in life comes from such things. Indeed, that is precisely why they are so appealing. The problem is you're trained to these escapes when you should be doing the A-1."[21]

And that is called procrastination.

APPLY RADICAL SURGERY

Robert Townsend, in his delightful book *Up the Organization* suggests every organization ought to have a *Vice President in Charge of Killing Things.* His point is that so many activities, customs, norms, and procedures that once were appropriate and needed are still done long after the need is passed, simply out of habit or tradition. Changing circumstances require that you not only examine and add new ways of doing things but that you be willing to drop old ways when necessary. However, tradition and habit die hard.

Earlier in this chapter we explored the necessity of saying "No". This most often applies to requests to add inappropriate things to your schedule. Applying radical surgery refers to those things you have already said "yes" to that you may need to drop. And that is even more difficult. Take a moment to look over your time log again and see if you can spot some potential candidates to eliminate. Now review your "To Do" lists for the last few days and see if any surgery is indicated there—especially in line of the critical question "What is the best use of my time right now?"

This poem poignantly portrays the problem:

IF I COULD JUST GET ORGANIZED

There may be nothing wrong with you,
    The way you live, the work you do,
But I can very plainly see
    Exactly what is wrong with me.
It isn't that I'm indolent
    Or dodging duty by intent;
I work as hard as anyone,
    And yet I get so little done,
The morning goes, the noon is here,
    Before I know, the night is near,
And all around me, I regret,
    Are things I haven't finished yet.

I do the things that don't amount
    To very much, of no account,
That really seem important though
    And let a lot of matters go.
I nibble this, I nibble that,
    But never finish what I'm at.
I work as hard as anyone,

And yet, I get so little done.
I'd do so much you'd be surprised,
If I could just get organized!
                    . . . Douglas Malloch

The decision regarding what to cut back will be easier once you identify those items that do not contribute to either your own work or personal goals. That would indicate that even though it may be important that this task be done, you may not be the right one to be doing it. It all has to do with priorities again.

One thing that has a tremendous influence on priorities and thus on what activities you might want to keep, add, or drop is where you are on Maslow's hierarchy of needs at any given time. This classic theory is taught in almost every psychology and behavioral science class, but often the profound implications it has on day-to-day choices about our lives are overlooked.

Abraham Maslow, a former President of the American Psychological Association, got the unique idea that we could learn as much about people by studying healthy, well-adjusted people as we could by studying those with problems, so that is what he did. His conclusion was that each of us has various levels of need and as we satisfy one need level, we move up to the next. [22]

These need levels he categorized as follows:[23]

Physiological—the basic needs for food, water, air, sex, etc.

Safety—the need to be safe from harm, to have security.

Social—the need for affiliation or closeness with others; to be liked.

Esteem—the need to be recognized as a person of value; to be rewarded.

Self-Actualization—the highest need, which Maslow calls life's peak experience. This means a person will not be ultimately happy unless he is doing what he is fitted for . . . what a person can be, he must be.

It seems logical that our priorities, as well as energy to pursue different types of activities would vary a great deal depending on where we are on this scale.

For example:

Physiological and Safety Levels: Time is money and basic survival needs require most of a person's time and energy.

Social Level: Time becomes a commodity to spend with others. Time spent in meeting together, even for extended periods, is not considered wasted as it helps meet the need to socialize.

Esteem and Self-Actualization: Time is more available for planning, futuring, and innovation since there are fewer distractions due to personal crisis and emergencies. There is more freedom to risk new and untried ventures because there is more time and more self assurance.

To illustrate how we move up and down on Maslow's scale and therefore need to keep reevaluating our priorities, may I share this true story. One of the participants in a training session I conducted covering this theory related the following experience. She was a secretary and program assistant for a church. For the first two years she was busy learning, growing, and beginning to introduce innovation from time to time. She thoroughly loved her job and stated she would think about her ideas and challenges while doing the dishes, laundry, and housework at home on evenings and weekends. Then she experienced a difficult divorce and was dismayed to find that she no longer had time, energy, or motivation to spend her spare time thinking about enriching her job. Instead, basic survival issues emerged, i.e., Who's going to get the children? Can I even afford to stay in the job because it's so low-paying? Will we have to move out of this house and neighborhood we've lived in for ten years? Time and energy priorities changed drastically and she said Maslow's scale helped her understand what was happening and gave her hope that she would someday return to her esteem and self-actualization priorities.

When you find you have moved either up or down on this needs scale, it would indicate some "radical surgery" might be in order.

DELEGATE

There's that word again! It seems to be a factor in almost every aspect of this book and every other one that you will read relating to management. We all know we should do it, but most of us do not do it well.

One of the critical times to deal with this issue is after you have received a promotion to a higher management position. It is so tempting to take up the ladder with you most of what you did in your past assignment, especially if you liked it and were good at it. A difficult but essential axiom to remember is "the higher one goes on the management ladder, the less time he [she] should spend operating and the more managing." Mackenzie illustrates this principle as follows:[24]

Proportions of managing and operating work at various management levels.

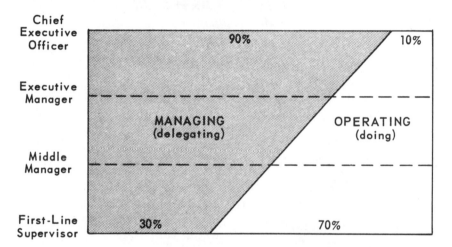

This is a good time to reflect on your personal management style. I would like to suggest we each have a choice as to how we see our job of manager. The choice we make regarding style has major implications regarding both our ability to accomplish program goals and objectives, and how others feel working with and for us.

Some of the choices of management styles are:

Boss—The maker of all *significant* decisions; also called an autocrat.

Expert—The knower of all *significant* things.

Doer—The doer of all *significant* things.

Abdicrat—The manager who decides by not deciding; retires without leaving.

or

Enabler—The manager who sees his/her job as helping subordinates and others do their jobs well. This may require using each of the other styles at certain times—when the person, situation, or time suggests it is appropriate. The enabler serves as a mentor in order that subordinates can keep growing.

(The enabler is the only style that really allows for—actually demands—truly effective delegation.)

DON'T BE A WORKAHOLIC
Life is too short!

May I share another Randall poem that illustrates this so well:

EXECUTIVE SUITE

Men at the top
Sit solemnly behind wooden slabs
Separating them
From others,
And the world,
While puzzling their loneliness.

These men who have it made
Toss at night
With dreams turned sour
From fear of facades
Crumbling with time
And unkept promises.

Men at the top
Search their in-box
For the prize,
They worked so hard to win,
And secretly want
To exchange their purchase
For twenty lost years paid.

. . . Lyman K. Randall

256

I would like to end with some important words from Voltaire, in his book *Zadig, A Mystery of Fate*:

What, of all things in the world, is the longest and the shortest, the swiftest and the slowest, the most divisible and the most extended, the most neglected and the most regretted, without which nothing can be done, which devours all that is little, and enlivens all that is great?

Time.

Nothing is longer, since it is the measure of eternity,
Nothing is shorter, since it is insufficient for the
accomplishment of your projects.
Nothing is more slow to him that expects, nothing
more rapid to him that enjoys.
In greatness it extends to infinity,
in smallness it is infinitely divisible.
All men neglect it; all regret the loss of it;
nothing can be done without it,
It consigns to oblivion whatever is unworthy of
being transmitted to posterity,
and it immortalizes such actions as are truly
great,
Time is man's most precious asset. [25]

CONCLUSION

And so we come to the end of our journey together. Throughout these pages we have explored the complex maze that constitutes today's organizations. Hopefully I have also helped you chart a realistic and achievable course through the maze so that you can survive as a creative, productive, and healthy manager in the decade ahead. It is essential for you as a person and for your organization.

When I was younger, I often found myself wishing impatiently that "they" would take care of the obvious problems and injustices of this world. The older I get, the more clearly I recognize that there is no magical "they" . . . *we* are they! If wrongs are to be righted, if dreams are to be realized, it is the responsibility of each one of us to do whatever we can, wherever we are, with whatever we have. Organizations can be more creative and humane . . . let's you and I see to it!

REFERENCES

1. Mackenzie, Alec R., *The Time Trap: Managing Your Way Out* (New York: AMACOM, a division of American Management Associations), p., 3, 7.

2. Ibid., p. 20 ff.

3. James, William, "Making Habits Work for You," *Reader's Digest*, August, 1976.

4. Ibid.

5. Wilson, Marlene, *The Effective Management of Volunteer Programs*, Volunteer Management Associates, 279 S. Cedar Brook Road, Boulder, CO 80302, pp. 31, 32.

6. Bliss, Edwin R., *Getting Things Done: The ABC's of Time Management*, Charles Scribner and Sons, 1976.

7. Mackenzie, pp. 44, 45.

8. Lakein, Alan, *How to Get Control of Your Time and Your Life*, New America Library, 1973, p. 11.

9. Lane, Chris, "Beating Time to Meet Objectives," *Personnel Management*, March, 1980.

10. Ibid.

11. Mackenzie, p. 49.

12. Carlson, Sune, *Executive Behavior: A Study of the Work Load and the Working Methods of Managing Directors*, Strombert (Stockholm), 1951.

13. Mackenzie, p. 56.

14. Ibid, p. 52.

15. Lakein, p. 71.

16. Sayers, Dorothy, *Creed or Chaos*, Methune, 1954.

17. Mackenzie, p. 13, 14.

18. Lakein, pp. 73-75.

19. Mackenzie, pp, 42, 43, and 55.

20. Lakein, p. 143 ff.

21. Ibid, p. 144.

22. Wilson, p. 43..

23. Hersey, Paul, and Blanchard, Kenneth H., *Management of Organizational Behavior*, Prentice-Hall, Inc., 1972, pp. 23-26.

24. R. Alec Mackenzie, *Managing Time at the Top* (New York: The Presidents Association, 1970). Copyright ©1970 by the Presidents Association. Reprinted by permission.

25. Quoted in *The Public Speaker's Treasure Chest*, Prochanow, Herbert V., Harper and Row, 1964, p. 296.

APPENDIX A

HOW TO SPRING THE TIME TRAP*
R. Alec Mackenzie

Below are listed the time wasters I have most commonly encountered in eight years of consulting on time management with senior executives in a dozen countries. . To assist the reader in analyzing his own time wasters, possible causes and solutions are suggested for each. These are not intended to be exhaustive but merely to serve as guidelines for further diagnosis. Causes and solutions tend to be personal, while the time wasters themselves are universal in nature.

Time Waster	Possible Causes	Solutions
Lack of Planning	Failure to see the benefit	Recognize that planning takes time but saves time in the end.
	Action orientation	Emphasize results, not activity.
	Success without it	Recognize that success is often in spite of, not because of methods.
Lack of priorities	Lack of goals and objectives	Write down goals and objectives. Discuss priorities with subordinates.
Overcommitment	Broad interests	Say no.
	Confusion in priorities	Put first things first.
	Failure to set priorities	Develop a personal philosophy of time. Relate priorities to a schedule of events.
Management by crisis	Lack of planning	Apply the same solutions as for lack of planning.
	Unrealistic time estimates	Allow more time. Allow for interruptions.
	Problem orientation	Be opportunity-oriented.
	Reluctance of subordinates to break bad news	Encourage fast transmission of information as essential for timely corrective action.
Haste	Impatience with detail	Take time to get it right. Save the time of doing it over.
	Responding to the urgent	Distinguish between the urgent and the important.
	Lack of planning ahead	Take time to plan. It repays itself many times over.
	Attempting too much in too little time	Attempt less. Delegate more.

259

Paperwork and reading	Knowledge explosion	Read selectively. Learn speed reading.
	Computeritis	Manage computer data by exception.
	Failure to screen	Remember the Pareto principle. Delegate reading to subordinates.
Routine and trivia	Lack of priorities	Set and concentrate on goals. Delegate non-essentials
	Oversurveillance of subordinates	Delegate; then give subordinates their head. Look to results, not details or methods.
	Refusal to delegate; feeling of greater security dealing with operating detail	Recognize that without delegation it is impossible to get anything done through others.
Visitors	Enjoyment of socializing	Do it elsewhere. Meet visitors outside. Suggest lunch if necessary. Hold stand-up conferences.
	Inability to say no	Screen. Say no. Be unavailable. Modify the open-door policy.
Telephone	Lack of self-discipline	Screen and group calls. Be brief.
	Desire to be informed and involved	Stay uninvolved with all but essentials. Manage by exception.
Meetings	Fear of responsibility for decisons	Make decisions without meetings.
	Indecision	Make decisions even when some facts are missing.
	Overcommunication	Discourage unnecessary meetings. Convene only those needed.
	Poor leadership	Use agendas. Stick to the subject. Prepare concise minutes as soon as possible.
Indecision	Lack of confidence in the facts	Improve fact-finding and validating procedures.
	Insistence on all the facts—paralysis of analysis	Accept risks as inevitable. Decide without all facts.
	Fear of the consequences of a mistake	Delegate the right to be wrong. Use mistakes as a learning process.
	Lack of rational decison-making process	Get facts, set goals, investigate alternatives and negative consequences, make the decision, and implement it.

Lack of delegation	Fear of subordinates' inadequacy	Train. Allow mistakes. Replace if necessary.
	Fear of subordinates' competence	Delegate fully. Give credit. Insure corporate growth to maintain challenge.
	Work overload on subordinates	Balance the workload. Staff up. Reorder priorities.

*This list is adapted from "Troubleshooting Chart for Time-Wasters," in R. Alec Mackenzie, MANAGING TIME AT THE TOP (New York: The President's Association, 1970).

APPENDIX B

PARADOXES IN TIME MANAGEMENT*

Open-door paradox—By leaving a door open in hope of improving communication, managers tend to increase the wrong kind of communication, that of a trivial or socializing nature. This multiplies interruptions and distracts them from more important tasks. The "open door" was originally intended to mean "accessible," not physically open.

Planning paradox—Managers often fail to plan because of the time required, thus failing to recognize that effective planning saves time in the end and achieves better results.

Tyranny-of-the-urgent paradox—Managers tend to respond to the urgent rather than the important matters. Thus long-range priorities are neglected, thereby ensuring future crises.

Crisis paradox—Managers tend to over-respond to crises, thereby making them worse.

Meeting paradox—By waiting for latecomers before starting a meeting, we penalize those who came on time and reward those who came late. So next time those who were on time will come late, and those who were late will come later.

Delegation paradox—A manager tends not to delegate to inexperienced subordinates due to lack of confidence. Yet subordinates can win the manager's confidence only by gaining the experience that only comes through delegated authority.

Cluttered-desk paradox—Managers leave things on their desks so they won't forget them. Then they either get lost or, as intended, attract attention every time they are seen, thus providing continual distractions from whatever the manager should be doing.

Telephone paradox—By insisting on talking to the boss instead of his secretary, a caller may delay getting information he urgently needs.

Long-hours paradox—The longer hours a manager works, the more fatigued he becomes and the longer he assumes he has to complete tasks. For both reasons he slows down, necessitating still longer hours.

Activity-vs.-results paradox—Managers tend to confuse activity with results, motion with accomplishment. Thus, as they gradually lose sight of their real objectives, they concentrate increasingly on staying busy. Finally, their objective becomes to stay busy, and they have become confirmed "workaholics."

Efficiency vs. effectiveness—Managers tend to confuse efficiency with effectiveness. They will be more concerned about doing the job right than about doing the right job. No matter how efficiently a job is done, if it is the wrong job, it will not be effective..

Paradox of time—No one has enough, yet everyone has all there is.

*from "Time Management Strategies for Women," Schwartz and Mackenzie, 1977.

PERSONAL PLAN OF ACTION WORKSHEET

1. I want to achieve the following goals: _____

_____

2. What are some of the positive things that might happen if I reach this goal?

_____

_____

3. What are my chances for success?

_____Very Good   Why do I feel this way?

_____Good   _____

_____Fair   _____

_____Poor   _____

_____Very Poor   _____

4. What are some of the negative things that might happen if I reach this goal?

_____

_____

5. What could keep me from reaching this goal?

_____I don't really have the skills, ability, and/or knowledge needed.

_____I don't want it badly enough to really work for it.

_____I'm afraid that I might fail.

_____I'm afraid of what others might think.

_____Others don't want me to reach this goal.

_____The goal is really too difficult to ever accomplish.

Some other reasons might be: _____

_____

6. What are some things I could do so the above things don't prevent me from reaching my goal?

_____

_____

7. Do I still want to try to reach this goal?

_____Yes

_____No

_____Undecided

8. Who can help me?

_____   _____

_____   _____

9. What are some first steps I could take to reach this goal?

_____

10. What else must I do if I am really to succeed?

_____

_____

11. Am I going to take the above steps?

_____Yes

_____No

_____Still Undecided

102747

12. If my answer to No. 11 is Yes, I make the following self-conract

----

SELF CONTRACT

I, _____, have decided to try to achieve the

goal of _____. The first step I will take to reach

this goal will be to _____ by _____.

My target date for reaching this goal is _____.

Date _____   SIGNED _____

                         WITNESSED BY _____

(Developed by Dr. Violet Malone, University of Illinois, Urbana, IL)